COMPOSITION IN THE AGE
OF AUSTERITY

COMPOSITION IN THE AGE OF AUSTERITY

Edited by
NANCY WELCH
TONY SCOTT

UTAH STATE UNIVERSITY PRESS
Logan

Published by Utah State University Press
An imprint of University Press of Colorado
5589 Arapahoe Avenue, Suite 206C
Boulder, Colorado 80303

 The University Press of Colorado is a proud member of
The Association of American University Presses.

The University Press of Colorado is a cooperative publishing enterprise supported, in part, by Adams State University, Colorado State University, Fort Lewis College, Metropolitan State University of Denver, Regis University, University of Colorado, University of Northern Colorado, Utah State University, and Western State Colorado University.

The paper used in this publication meets the minimum requirements of the American National Standard for Information Sciences—Permanence of Paper for Printed Library Materials. ANSI Z39.48-1992

ISBN: 978-1-60732-444-7 (paperback)
ISBN: 978-1-60732-445-4 (ebook)

Library of Congress Cataloging-in-Publication Data

Names: Welch, Nancy, 1963– editor. | Scott, Tony, 1968– editor.
Title: Composition in the age of austerity / edited by Nancy Welch, Tony Scott.
Description: Logan : Utah State University Press, [2016] | Includes bibliographical references.
Identifiers: LCCN 2016003040 | ISBN 9781607324447 (pbk.) | ISBN 9781607324454 (ebook)
Subjects: LCSH: English language—Rhetoric—Study and teaching (Higher)—Political aspects—United States. | English language—Rhetoric—Study and teaching (Higher)—Economic aspects—United States.
Classification: LCC PE1405.U6 C59 2016 | DDC 808/.042071173—dc23
LC record available at http://lccn.loc.gov/2016003040

Cover illustration © Ricardo Reitmeyer / Shutterstock

CONTENTS

COMPOSITION IN THE AGE OF AUSTERITY

Introduction
COMPOSITION IN THE
AGE OF AUSTERITY

Tony Scott and Nancy Welch

AFTER SYRACUSE

In August 2013 President Barack Obama brought to Syracuse, New York, his plan for the future of US higher education. The choice of Syracuse was strategic: a once bustling economic hub, Syracuse has yet to recover from its loss of manufacturing jobs; close to half its children and teens live below the poverty line. The venue—a public city high school—was a smart choice, too: the hot auditorium was packed with children, parents, and teachers in a city whose schools have struggled as the city's tax base has declined. After recognizing that the country—and this audience—had seen tough times, Obama described a recovery that is now fully underway thanks to the "resilience of the American people" and the ability of his administration to "clear away the rubble from the financial crisis and start laying the foundation for a better economy" (Obama 2013). He also understood that for this Syracuse audience, "We've still got more work to do," and he openly acknowledged that over the past decade "we've seen growing inequality in our society and less upward mobility in our society." He even asserted, "[W]e've got to reverse these trends" and return to a time when "we put these ladders of opportunity [up] for people." But then, rather than announce a twenty-first-century version of the opportunity programs of generations past—such as the GI Bill or the Higher Education Act of 1965—President Obama moved from the metaphor of *ladders* to *pathways*: proposing the solution of "more pathways" for "people to succeed as long as they're willing to work hard" with government stepping in to assist not with stepped-up funding but with new measures of accountability.

Enter the College Scorecard—what one might think of as No Child Left Behind for higher education, except that instead of measuring and valuing math and reading to the near exclusion of all other subjects, the

DOI: 10.7330/9781607324454.c000

scorecard uses metrics like speed to degree completion, loan default rates, and post-graduation earnings. For an audience largely priced out of higher education, left behind not only by the most recent economic recovery but all the proclaimed recoveries of the past twenty years, and further ravaged by racism in an ostensible post-racial era, such a speech touted *access, opportunity,* and *hope.* It did so, however, through *austerity.* Through rhetorics of austerity, institutions of higher education are admonished to make themselves more efficient and affordable amid deep funding cuts, and would-be students are counseled to be wise consumers and keep their personal debt levels down by seeking the cheapest, fastest route to a degree. Acknowledging that his Syracuse audience had been devastated by the neoliberal leave-it-to-the-market policies of the past forty years, Obama unveiled as the solution to this crisis the accelerated marketization of higher education. The speech he delivered provided a textbook example of how the neoliberal economic and social policies that have driven what is now a multi-generational trend toward ever-increasing inequality can be packaged and applauded as common-sense populism.

We start the introduction to this volume with President Obama's Syracuse speech because we imagine an audience for *Composition in the Age of Austerity* that shares the sense of urgency and (increasingly dashed) expectation that brought teens, teachers, and parents to that high school gym on a sweltering August day. Composition as a contemporary discipline has been sponsored by the ladders of opportunity of earlier eras, fostering access to and support in higher education for working-class, minority, and international students; connecting campuses and communities in public rhetorical works programs; and promoting critical and creative literacy education K through college with the National Writing Project. Even as the always tenuous rungs of these ladders are gradually removed—the rungs of long-term and secure faculty positions, of funding for writing programs, and of access and affordability for students— the expectation of opportunity and service provided by the field remains. Many of us—including adjunct faculty teaching without healthcare coverage and without assurance of continuing work beyond the next sixteen weeks, including directors charged with meeting new mandates on a downsized or eliminated budget—are also struggling to figure out where we can find a toehold and for how long. This collection responds to a felt sense of crisis among those who teach and do research in postsecondary writing education that is wrought by the intensifying sway of neoliberal logics in US higher education, compounded by stepped-up austerity measures in the wake of the 2008–2009 economic crisis.

Of course, austerity and a low-frequency sense of crisis are nothing new to this field. The professional lives of compositionists—whether as contingent teachers or administrators in chronically underfunded introductory writing programs, as faculty on the margins of English departments, or as staff for extra-departmental entities—have long been characterized by making do in institutional borderlands. Professional work in composition means arguing for more resources, continually recalibrating to make do with less, and pursuing a scholarly legitimacy that perpetually seems just over the next hill. Yet this new felt sense of crisis is different—in part because of the scale and pace of the changes and in part because it has become clear that these changes are not temporary but permanent, composition having served as canary in the coalmine for a wide-scale restructuring of higher education as a whole. *Academic Capitalism and the New Economy* (Slaughter and Rhoades 2004), *Wannabe U: Inside the Corporate University* (Tuchman 2009), *University, Inc.* (Washburn 2005), *How the University Works* (Bousquet 2008), *The Unmaking of the Public University* (Newfield 2008): such are the titles of just a handful of academic bestsellers chronicling the shifting sands beneath the feet of *all* academic workers as state legislatures cut funding and impose curricular and accountability mandates; as tenure and professional agency erode with power and resources shifting to administrators and governing boards; and as an increasingly part-time and precarious faculty are saddled with new efficiency imperatives and admonishments to make up for depleted budgets through entrepreneurial schemes, industry partnerships, and the repackaging of programs as revenue-generating streams. The task of coming to terms with the broad scope of these changes, what they mean for the present and future of composition, and how writing educators and researchers might respond to them can easily seem overwhelming.

Those of us who work in composition struggled with these issues long before many of our institutional colleagues in other fields. The large-scale operation of composition teaching has historically been delivered by mostly marginalized and exploited teachers. This is a condition to which composition studies has been normed, if sometimes with objections and unease, the field's scholars finding ways not institutionally granted to carry on research and advance discussions about rhetoric, literacy, pedagogy, public writing, service-learning, research methods, and more. Some of these scholars have contributed to a long-running conversation about the problem of "adjunctification" that defined composition long before departments of history, political science, and geography woke up to the news that more than 75 percent of US college and university instructional faculty do not have access to tenure (Curtis and Thornton 2013, 8). Yet such important work as Schell and Lambert Stock's (2001) *Moving a Mountain: Transforming the Role of Contingent Faculty in Composition and Higher Education* and Marc Bousquet et al.'s (2004) *Tenured Bosses and Disposable Teachers,* along with *College Composition and Communication*'s occasional stand-alone section devoted to contingent faculty issues, sits alongside—distinct from and largely unremarked upon by—work that celebrates composition's public and service-learning initiatives, explores new media ecologies, and chronicles the pragmatic negotiations of writing program administrators. As the neoliberal reordering of higher education deepens and widens, composition still lacks a developed understanding of how labor conditions shape pedagogy, scholarship, and the production of literacy and students' writing.

In the age of corporatization and austerity, we now face the consequences of a field that has never established a scholarly habit of positioning composition scholarship in relation to the powerful political economic factors and trends that shape composition work. Lacking such a critical purchase, the field—long prone to proceeding from what Donna Strickland (2011) terms a "managerial unconscious"—is poised to celebrate the pedagogical "innovations" that come under the gun of cost-cutting and to embrace neoliberalism's privatizing and commodifying market pursuits as somehow compatible with the field's public ethos and mission. Our concern is not that composition is trying out new instructional configurations; it is that, with scant discussion, both the Margaret Thatcher mantra of "There is no alternative" and the opportunism that characterizes "Shock Doctrine" disaster capitalism are becoming the taken-for-granted center of what we are—of how we think and act as writing professionals.

Through the chapters collected here and the discussion we hope this collection will initiate, *Composition in the Age of Austerity* seeks to create space and impetus for coming to terms with and critiquing the impact of neoliberal economics and austerity regimes on composition scholarship and practices. The collection is informed by the broader critique of, and calls for resistance to, higher-education restructuring, but we keep our focus on composition programs, which have been on the leading edge of both democratizing and corporatizing trends in US higher education and whose instructors have served as the advance guard of professorial labor casualization. Uniting the essays in this collection are two goals:

- To document the full and far-reaching implications of higher education defunding and restructuring of the work and mission of

composition through understanding composition work within political economic frames.

• To examine how our cherished rhetorical ideals—favoring bridge-build-
ing, mediation, and problem-solving by the wily, can-do WPA—and
increasingly disembodied and dematerialized critical theories leave
the field insufficiently prepared to respond to austerity measures and
vulnerable to new entrepreneurial schemes that threaten to dissolve
existing connections between scholarly research and pedagogy.

Although this collection does not offer quick fixes or guarantees, we
also have in mind a third goal: to explore rhetorics and strategies of
resistance. Especially by offering critical frames for understanding the
terms and direction of our work, *Composition in the Age of Austerity* aims
to provide points of departure from which we may develop reflexive, collective strategies for response.

CRITICAL VOCABULARY BUILDING: NEOLIBERALISM

Neoliberalization is a way to describe the changes we are seeing in
higher education that have had their analogues in virtually every
sector of society, especially in the public and governmental sector.
From schools to garbage pickup to prisons, we have seen over the
past forty years a sea change toward privatization and the economiza-
tion of public services, and this change is often called neoliberalism.
Neoliberalism, Welch writes in *Living Room: Teaching Public Writing in
a Privatized World*, "is, in part, a reassertion of classical economic liber-
alism's central tenet that major political and social decisions are best
decided by the market" (Welch 2008, 7). But obscured by this "leave-
it-to-the-market" rhetoric is the powerful role neoliberalism assigns to
the state in assisting in the conversion of public resources and institutions—including institutions of education—into private hands. While
neoliberalism was devised as a solution to the economic crises that
spelled the end of the long post–World War II boom, "it has proceeded
since the mid-1970s, with accelerating speed and whether in moments
of economic boom or bust, to roll back a century's worth of public
programs and social rights" (8). Similarly, David Harvey chronicles
the changing role of the state under neoliberalism from underwrit-
ing and supporting social welfare programs to creating and maintaining "a good business climate" (Harvey 2006, 25). Neoliberalism is rife
with paradoxes, but among them is the perpetuation of the theory that
government best achieves the greater public good by serving private
interests and privatizing government functions. "Neoliberalism," writes

sociologist William Davies, "might therefore be defined as the elevation of market-based principles and techniques of evaluation to the level of state-endorsed norms" (Davies 2013, 37).

Davies calls the neoliberal transformation of liberal democracies "the pursuit of disenchantment of politics by economics" because the neoliberal state assumes that when human relations are marketized, the best ideas and courses of action become self-evident (Davies 2014, 4). Indeed, by feigning to represent a non-ideological pragmatism—a politics that is apolitical—and promising to resolve the challenges of public life through the indifferent application of market-based principles rather than through messy democratic processes, neoliberalism gains its authority (21). This claim to authority is therefore operational rather than moral or philosophical; techniques once reserved for economic analysis appear to be a common sense that can be spread across all sectors of societies. Even when areas of public life such as public education are not placed entirely under the control of private entities, they are managed according to market logics that assume that "rational" methods can be fruitfully applied to any area of society and desirable outcomes can be quantified and compared. Disagreements concerning methods and goals, along with the existence of qualitative factors that aren't subject to quantification, are ignored or dismissed as irrelevant.

The disenchantment of politics by economics explains much that has happened in the scene of composition studies that chapters in this collection will chronicle: the managerialism that insists upon quantification while ignoring or denying the qualitative consequences for learning and the profession; the use of assessment to create more scalable curriculums or bypass the need for direct writing instruction altogether; and scholarship claiming to be "post-hegemonic" and even "post-critical" that cedes composition teaching to the realm of market algorithms and efficiency imperatives as it imagines a scholarly future for rhetoric blissfully detached from responsibility for and ideological struggle over writing education.

CRITICAL VOCABULARY BUILDING: AUSTERITY

An important aspect of neoliberalism is its reliance on crisis as a catalyst for its transformations. In *The Shock Doctrine*, Naomi Klein (2007) describes how crises have presented a strategic opportunity—termed "shock therapy"—for the neoliberalization of governments and economies throughout the world. As Nobel Prize-winning economist Milton Friedman (1962) explained in his classic blueprint for neoliberal

economics, *Capitalism and Freedom*, "[O]nly a crisis—actual or perceived—produces real change" as ideas that had been "politically impossible" (think here of the dismantling of welfare, cuts to Social Security,
the elimination of collective bargaining rights, the privatization of urban
public schools) become "politically inevitable" (Friedman qtd. in Klein
2007, 7). In the wake of a shock, austerity programs are rapidly imposed
on populations, even when it means widespread hardship and requires
a radical restructuring of political frameworks. The point is to move
quickly and with great force to minimize organized resistance or even
full public consciousness of what is happening at the broad level of strategy and structure.

From this angle, then, we can understand austerity as the following:

- a set of policies enacted by governments and institutions, including
  institutions of higher education, to reduce budget deficits and cut
  programs, especially social programs, during the shock of especially
  bad economic times
- an opportunistic ideological strategy
- the initiation of funding cuts in the public sector that then becomes the
  new normal in policy over time

In the perennial declarations of financial crisis on US college and
university campuses, and in the repeated calls for faculty and staff to join
in "shared sacrifice," we can see how austerity measures—wage freezes,
staff cuts, program retrenchment, class size increases—are at once an
opportunistic response to specific instances of declared crisis and part
of a widespread, long-term national (and, though this is beyond our
book's scope, global) agenda to fundamentally restructure postsecondary education.

Although austerity represents a long-term policy, it also describes the
shock-therapy intensification taking hold with the global economic crisis
that reached its zenith in late 2008. Coming on the heels of more than
a decade in higher education funding cuts, that crisis led—or created
the opportunity for—near-catastrophic reductions in state budgets for
public colleges and universities at the same time that sources for federal grant support were drying up. Austerity is not only about defunding, however. It is also about cost-shifting: in this case the intensifying
cost-shift from public to private, with student debt by 2014 surpassing
the $1 trillion mark. The financial press's heralds of economic recovery
notwithstanding, higher education has not returned to pre-crisis levels
of funding. Funding declines in some states even accelerated after the
stimulus money from the American Recovery and Reinvestment Act ran
out in 2012 (State Higher Education Executive Officers 2013, 7). In

constant dollars, state appropriations per FTE were lower in 2012 than in any year since 1980 (19).

CRITICAL VOCABULARY BUILDING: ACCOUNTABILITY

Accelerating too is the zeal for accountability "reforms"—the economic crisis having provided a political opportunity for furthering the reach of the market into education, a political opportunity seized by the Obama Department of Education. In other words, the global economic crisis of 2008–2009 has not only provided states with the opportunity to further divest themselves of financial responsibility for public education; from Washington the crisis has also presented the opportunity to insist on reforming institutions of higher education. In a single breath US colleges and universities are cast rhetorically as both a means of fostering economic mobility and as antiquated, wasteful, and unresponsive to the needs of students or the public more broadly. Through reforms promoted by a combination of government officials, quasi-nonprofit foundations, policy think tanks, and corporations seeking to cash in on the growing education market, US colleges and universities are also being reoriented and retooled to be responsive to private (including and especially private-profit) interests and needs (see, for example, Newfield 2008; Tuchman 2009; Slaughter and Rhoades 2004).

How do the stepped-up calls for accountability serve this project to bring higher education to market? Consider: the neoliberal state's calls for stepped-up accountability represent a remarkable sleight of hand, one masking how neoliberalism always presents *more defunding* as the solution to the problems of defunding. Stumping for his College Scorecard, for instance, President Barack Obama presented the problem (students priced out of college) and a key contributing factor (state funding cuts) but then swapped out the evident solution (restore public funding) for *accountability*. Here, the solution to the *economic* gap is not *economic* restructuring (i.e., restored funding) but instead *educational* restructuring through accountability and efficiency mandates that push foundational changes in curriculum, pedagogy, and—by tying the "value" of a college degree to the speed of its completion and the earnings of its recipient—what a college degree signifies.

A closer look at the College Scorecard and other reforms reveals the handmaiden role accountability plays in the corporate restructuring of US higher education. Along with window-dressing proposals that purport to compel colleges to admit and support students with less advantaged backgrounds, the initiative proposes changes in funding, delivery, and requirements for degrees. Recommendations include the following:

- Developing a Department of Education–maintained system to rate colleges according to their value. What constitutes "value" remains frighteningly undefined, but among the factors to be considered are the earnings of graduates and the number of years students take to finish their degrees. The goal is to tie federal funding, including Pell Grants and college loans, to the rating system by 2018. Those institutions that don't hit the prescribed benchmarks will receive less federal funding for their students' tuition. The College Scorecard is thus No Child Left Behind for higher education. (Though most recently the Obama administration has backed down from its plan to tie funding to the rating system, many colleges and universities have already embraced the rating system itself, internalizing and policing its narrow and market-minded ideas of "value.")

- Changing the standards by which degrees are conferred from credit hours to what is being called "competency-based learning" (CBE)—or learning that is verified primarily by assessments rather than classes successfully completed. The initiative calls this a system of credentialing based on "learning, not seat time." Touted as a positive example is Western Governors University, which claims to offer its online competency-based degree with "an average time to a bachelor's degree of only 30 months" (The White House 2013).

- Promoting online learning, championed as a means to improve efficiency and help students to achieve learning outcomes more cheaply and in less time.

Essentially, for working-class and many middle-class students across the country and the public colleges and universities that have served them, this is access and hope through austerity.

The College Scorecard, like No Child Left Behind and Race to the Top, does not promote itself as downsizing and outsourcing education, of course. Rather it is promoted through the common-sense appeal of such a neoliberal phrase as "learning, not seat time" and bolstered by pseudo-scientific measures that conflate learning "outcomes" with cost "reductions" and replace a word like "teachers" with "technology." Take this passage from the Obama administration:

The National Center for Academic Transformation has shown the effectiveness of the thoughtful use of technology across a wide range of academic disciplines, improving learning outcomes for students while reducing costs by nearly 40 percent on average . . . Arizona State University's interactive algebra lessons helped students perform 10 percent better, despite meeting half as often, and at a lower cost. The University of Maryland redesigned an introductory psychology course, reducing costs by 70 percent while raising pass rates. (The White House 2013)

Such rhetoric, and the on-the-ground realities it helps create and naturalize, has plenty of discontents—most visible in waves of student protest against "Corporate U" and being "sentenced to debt" as well as in teacher and faculty strikes, the massive Quebec student strikes since 2012, and the More than a Score and United Opt-Out movements. Davies points to the soft spot of neoliberalism's credibility that these movements and mobilization target when they expose the incompatibility of market valuation with democratic values: "The rendering of economy, state and society as explicit and as quantified as possible is an implicitly moral agenda, which makes certain presuppositions about *how and why and what to value* . . . Hence, efforts to replace politics with economics, judgment with measurement, confront a limit beyond which they themselves collapse" (Davies 2014, 8; emphasis in original).

But even as Davies theorizes and sporadic movements try to bring us to the limits of neoliberalism's transformation of higher education, we are faced here and now with the escalation of corporate audit culture. That audit culture—where everything must be assessed against institutional benchmarks and comparator/competitor schools and measured for its value added—not only adds to administrative bloat (the class of managers to do the weighing, measuring. It also threatens to transform our consciousness—our available vocabulary and our available ideas for talking together about the work that we do. The chapters in this book thus focus on and chronicle how neoliberal political economy shapes not only writing assessments, curricula, and funding but teacher's agency and philosophies of program administration. Chapters focus too on how neoliberal political economy is dictating the direction of scholarship. Here is another core argument of this collection: that the economic and political agenda shaping the terms of work, the methods of delivery, and the ways of valuing and assessing writing *also* shapes the primary concerns and directions of scholarship. If, as Marx held, consciousness does not determine being but rather, being—the conditions we find ourselves laboring and schooled within—determines consciousness, composition as a field needs to grapple with how the material conditions and mandates of neoliberalism and austerity are shaping our scholarly assumptions, commitments, and horizons.

CONSCIOUSNESS RAISING

Part 1, Neoliberal De-Forms

Chris Gallagher's "Our Trojan Horse: Outcomes Assessment and the Resurrection of Competency-based Education" starts off this section on neoliberalism's reform movements with a glimpse of the endgame. Composition's embrace of outcomes assessment, he argues, has opened the door to competency-based education, which reduces writing to a "discreet, commodified vocational skill," writing students to "workers-in-training," and writing teachers to as-needed "success coaches." Compositionists are, nevertheless, hard-pressed to abstain from participating in campus assessment movements, writes Deborah Mutnick in "Confessions of an Assessment Fellow," especially when abstention would result in the work shifting to another colleague and under the threat of lost accreditation. Her chapter is a call for understanding the political economic forces creating assessment and accountability regimes—forces that call for *collective* resistance.

A challenge in coming to terms with and mounting collective response against neoliberal de-formations is recognizing the corporate reform movement's rhetorical sleights of hand. For instance, the push for hybrid or redesigned writing classrooms, observes Emily Isaacs in "First-Year Composition Course Redesigns: Pedagogical Innovation or Solution to the 'Cost Disease'?," appeals to our field's best impulses toward pedagogical and scholarly advancement but with the aim of delivering cost savings through increased adjunctification and even outsourcing writing instruction beyond faculty ranks. Reminding us of the progressive critical and creative literacy pedagogies that reform movements and mandates are pushing aside is Marcelle Haddix and Brandi Williams' "Who's Coming to the Composition Classroom? K–12 Writing in and outside Common Core State Standards." In this chapter Haddix and Williams return us to Syracuse, a site of President Obama's unveiling of his College Scorecard, and the impact of another Obama Department of Education-backed program: the Common Core State Standards (CCSS). CCSS, with its limited aim to judge writers as "competent or incompetent according to the standardized and timed testing measure," displaces diverse, expansive, and fully preparatory literacy practices to the extracurriculum.

Part 2, Composition in an Austere World

As Haddix and Williams describe, programs promoting copious and commodious literacy practices and perspectives are increasingly shifted to the realm of extracurricular, service, or volunteer labor. In "The National Writing Project in the Age of Austerity," Tom Fox and Elyse Eidman-Aadahl chronicle how in an instant this national project serving K–12 teachers lost its $25 million budget; while project sites continue

through the resilience and hard work of faculty and teachers in a de-
centralized and largely grant-funded network to "be at the side of teachers, especially in the most desperate of situations," Fox and Eidman-
Aadahl also warn of the challenges of maintaining the National Writing
Project's core identity and principles, particularly in a "federal climate
promoting competition over equity." The struggle to carry forward the
radical history of basic writing is likewise at the heart of Susan Naomi
Bernstein's "Occupy Basic Writing: Pedagogy in the Wake of Austerity."
In this chapter she revisits a series of devastating blows, beginning with
the decimation of City University of New York's basic writing program
and the suicide of a dear friend and colleague, that also propel her to
Occupy Wall Street's Zuccotti Park, Occupy Sandy, and beyond—to joining and cultivating spaces in which writing helps writing teachers and
students bear witness to dispossession, fostering mutual aid.

Basic Writing and the National Writing Project, as these contributors
suggest, have been early casualties of the neoliberal assault on higher
education. But perhaps the earliest victim (along with the replacement
of welfare-to-college programs with low-wage workfare requirements)
is the prison writing program. As Tobi Jacobi points out in "Austerity
Behind Bars: The 'Cost' of Prison Writing Programs," President Bill
Clinton's 1994 elimination of Pell grant support for prisoners resulted
in the free-fall of programs from 350 at the start of the 1990s to fewer
than a dozen today. Yet, she argues, even as compositionists struggle to
meet writing program obligations on their campuses, the field has a
continuing political and ethical responsibility to the men and women
behind bars, especially if composition wants to claim a social justice
ethos in a nation that leads the world in mass incarceration.

Implicit in this section's chapters is the importance of historical
understanding: the political and social commitments upon which and
the material conditions in which the National Writing Project, CUNY's
SEEK and basic writing program, and prison educational rights movements and offerings were founded. Mary Ann Cain in "Buskerfest: The
Struggle for Space in Public Rhetorical Education" foregrounds the
importance of historical memory through parallel stories. One story is
of doors opening with the founding of Chicago's South Side Community
Arts Center in a period of rising labor and Civil Rights struggle and
expanded federal funding. The other is of doors closing with the loss
of steady funding and a physical space for the Three Rivers Institute of
Afrikan Art and Culture, the long-time partner for Cain's community-
focused writing class. In an historical period marked by the rollback of
Civil Rights gains and the eradication of spaces in which people can

pursue emancipatory visions, Cain concludes, "telling (and writing) these stories to whoever will listen" is crucial lest the memory of what public education and public institutions provide is also erased.

The section ends with an austerity tale from first-year composition: a first-year writing program that was defunded even before it was launched and yet still charged with implementing and assessing a campus-wide foundational writing requirement. In "First-Year Writing and the Angels of Austerity: A Re-Domesticated Drama," Nancy Welch asks us to consider that neoliberalism has brought two forms of privatization to higher education: corporate privatization that moves to the market all commodifiable aspects of university work *and* domestic re-privatization that moves to the realm of unwaged and volunteer labor those social reproductive activities—including the activities of mass literacy instruction—that capitalism requires but cannot make profitable.

Part 3, Composition at the Crossroads

What to do? What to do? As the chapters leading up to this final section suggest, this is an appropriate moment—an *urgent* moment—in which to reprise June Jordan's (1986) question for members of the National Council of Teachers of English, a question which also provided the conclusion to J. Elsbeth Stuckey's (1990) *The Violence of Literacy*. Four decades into the neoliberal reordering that Jordan and Stuckey gave early warning of, Jeanne Gunner examines composition's "collective collaboration with austerity measures" including growing social inequality within writing faculty ranks. In "What Happens When Ideological Narratives Lose Their Force?" Gunner further probes the possibility that such collaboration is not borne of "false consciousness or inevitable interpellation" but fatigue, especially as our usual forms for critique and resistance appear to be no match against powerful and "mega-monied" corporate forces. What to do? Gunner concludes her chapter with a survey and assessment of digital media and posthuman rhetorical theories that (at least in the research universities that austerity's reworking of the higher education landscape seems likely to leave intact) may create a hybrid space between complicity and disruption.

If ideological critique from the halls of composition has thus far proven ineffective, suggests Ann Larson in "Composition's Dead," that may be owed to the field's resistance to shining critical light on its own claims (to being, for instance, higher education's "beacon of democracy") and pursuits (of professional respect and institutional rewards that fall only to a small elite). What to do? A "principled disengagement" from the field as it is, Larson suggests, "may be the only morally defensible choice"—a choice that frees the "bottom ranks of the education factory" to forge coalitions with low-wage workers across and beyond the academy.

A challenge to mentoring a new generation of teachers for relationships of solidarity and collective action, Shari Stenberg points out, is that students and teachers enter the academy "already fluent in neoliberal values" and already steeped in the belief that there is no alternative to the "'standard' neoliberal subject: one who is rational, competitive, autonomous, neutral, and productive." What to do? "Beyond Marketability: Locating Teacher Agency in the Neoliberal University" details the work of Stenberg and her students in a graduate seminar for new teaching assistants that turns to feminist models for expansive ideas of agency and relationship that counter neoliberalism's restrictive conception of who belongs and how to belong in the university. Paralleling Stenberg's critique of the normative neoliberalism into which our students, and future professoriate, have been inculcated, Tony Scott argues that entrepreneurialism has become "the dominant idiom of higher education" as the austerity-driven "fragmentation and dissolution of composition" clears the way for entrepreneurs to create even more efficiencies through technocratized, scalable pedagogies and teacherless, brand-able writing education. Entrepreneurialism does not promise to revive composition studies but instead "decomposes" it, supplanting a coherent and principled professional culture, field of scholarly praxis, and set of public, democratic commitments with a zombie's "urgent, itchy desire" that is guided by "no memory or distinguishing identity."

Yet Scott also points out in "Animated by the Entrepreneurial Spirit: Austerity, Dispossession and Composition's Last Living Act" that the death of composition and its reanimation in servitude to the market is not inevitable. In the gap between neoliberalism's rhetoric of abundance for all and the visible reality of a growing precariousness and eroded democratic voice, we can find—as Lil Brannon also underscores in her afterword to this collection—many others among the dispossessed who want to reclaim and *write* education's next chapter.

References

Bousquet, Marc. 2008. *How the University Works: Higher Education and the Low-Wage Nation.* New York: New York University Press.

Bousquet, Marc, Tony Scott, and Leo Parascondola. 2004. *Tenured Bosses and Disposable Teachers: Writing Instruction in the Managed University.* Carbondale: Southern Illinois University Press.

Curtis, John W., and Susanna Thornton. 2013. "Here's the News: The Annual Report on the Economic Status of the Profession." *Academe* (March–April): 4–19.

Davies, William. 2013. "When is a Market not a Market? 'Exemption,' 'Externality' and 'Exception' in the Case of European State Aid Rules." *Theory, Culture & Society* 30 (2): 32–59. http://dx.doi.org/10.1177/0263276412456567.

Davies, William. 2014. *The Limits of Neoliberalism: Authority, Sovereignty and the Logic of Competition.* Thousand Oaks, CA: Sage Publications.

Friedman, Milton. 1962. *Capitalism and Freedom.* Chicago: University of Chicago Press.

Harvey, David. 2006. *Spaces of Global Capitalism: Towards a Theory of Uneven Development.* New York: Verso.

Jordan, June. 1986. "Problems of Language in a Democratic State: 1982." In *On Call: Political Essays*, 27–36. Cambridge, MA: South End Press.

Klein, Naomi. 2007. *The Shock Doctrine: the Rise of Disaster Capitalism.* New York: Metropolitan Books/Henry Holt.

Newfield, Christopher. 2008. *Unmaking the Public University: The Forty-Year Assault on the Middle Class.* Cambridge: Harvard University Press.

Obama, Barack. 2013. "A Transcript of President Obama's Speech in Syracuse." August 22, 2013. Syracuse.com. http://www.syracuse.com/news/index.ssf/2013/08/a_transcript_of_president_obamas_speech_in_syracuse.html.

Schell, Eileen, and Patricia Lambert Stock, eds. 2001. *Moving a Mountain: Transforming the Role of Contingent Faculty in Composition and Higher Education.* Urbana, IL: NCTE.

Slaughter, Sheila, and Gary Rhoades. 2004. *Academic Capitalism and the New Economy: Markets, State, and Higher Education.* Baltimore, MD: Johns Hopkins University Press.

State Higher Education Executive Officers. 2013. "State Higher Education Finance, FY 2012." http://www.sheeo.org/sites/default/files/publications/SHEF-FY12.pdf

Strickland, Donna. 2011. *The Managerial Unconscious in the History of Composition Studies.* Carbondale: Southern Illinois University Press.

Stuckey, J. Elsbeth. 1990. *The Violence of Literacy.* Portsmouth, NH: Heinemann.

Tuchman, Gaye. 2009. *Wannabe U: Inside the Corporate University.* Chicago: University of Chicago Press. http://dx.doi.org/10.7208/chicago/9780226815282.001.0001.

Washburn, Jennifer. 2005. *University, Inc.: The Corporate Corruption of Higher Education.* Cambridge, MA: Basic Books.

Welch, Nancy. 2008. *Living Room: Teaching Public Writing in a Privatized World.* Portsmouth, NH: Heinemann.

The White House. 2013. "FACT SHEET on the President's Plan to Make College More Affordable: A Better Bargain for the Middle Class." The White House Office of the Press Secretary. http://www.whitehouse.gov/the-press-office/2013/08/22/fact-sheet-president-s-plan-make-college-more-affordable-better-bargain-.

PART I

Neoliberal Deformations

1
OUR TROJAN HORSE
Outcomes Assessment and the Resurrection
of Competency-Based Education

Chris W. Gallagher

September 2012, electronic portfolio research coalition meeting. A high-ranking official of a regional accrediting agency joins the group, led and largely populated by compositionists, to discuss how eportfolios might be used for accreditation purposes.

It's going well. Our guest talks about reflective, integrative learning and performance-based, authentic assessment. She talks about surveys in which employers favor eportfolios over standardized tests. She talks about "throwing away the bell curve" and providing all students opportunities to learn and to demonstrate their learning. In short, she speaks our language.

We happily nod along as she homes in on how eportfolios provide rich evidence of the kind of learning we all value. We are pleased to learn that accrediting agencies and the federal government are looking into eportfolios. Yes, we are told, eportfolios fit nicely into the Obama administration's renewed emphasis on quality assurance—on accountability. They will help with standard-setting and comparability. With rigorous documentation of bottom-line results. Transparency. Benchmarking. Outcomes.

Her seamless shift in language now has *us* shifting in our seats. When she informs us that the US Department of Education "is interested in breaking up the little monopoly campuses have right now," we realize what she's done: drawn us into another discursive orbit, aligning us with the Spellings Commission report, which had used the same monopoly metaphor six years earlier. Somehow we have moved, in the space of a few moments, from champions of learning for all students to perpetrators of an insidious plot to maintain market dominance by edging out suppliers of alternative goods or services. Our guest chides us for being

DOI: 10.7330/9781607324454.c001

selfish and out of touch, unaware that as the twenty-first century progresses, "less and less learning will happen in a traditional classroom." People learn all the time in all kinds of contexts, she reminds us: on the job, online, even while watching television. We must recognize that the future of faculty work is formulating and validating competencies, running diagnostics, evaluating student work, and coaching—in short, "more assessment, less teaching."

We are less happy now. We express a range of objections and worries—about the dismissal of classroom experiences, the stubborn digital divide, the fact that we got into this profession to *teach,* not merely to evaluate—each of which our guest deftly deflects with the kind of patient, patronizing smile usually reserved for the senile or otherwise infirm.

We coalition members have been drawn together by our shared commitment to exploring the teaching and learning affordances of eportfolios. We see eportfolios as technologies that allow us to deepen students' learning experiences. We also see them as social tools, allowing students to compose digital spaces in which they interact with a range of interlocutors and audiences. But it is now dawning on us that eportfolios are being conscripted into an outcomes-based agenda in which the learning experiences students have with us and with each other are quite beside the point: the game is for individuals to amass credentials based on learning that happens, as the saying now goes, "anytime, anywhere, in any way."[1]

We have been bamboozled.

**

I have come to see the moment described above as emblematic of a larger reality in which composition finds itself in the age of austerity. While we continue to regard writing as a complex practice through which people make sense of and construct the personal and social worlds they inhabit, we are increasingly conscripted into a neoliberal agenda whose endgame, I have come to believe, is competency-based education (CBE). CBE is a highly individualized educational approach in which students amass credentials through demonstrated competencies, usually in a self-paced manner, rather than through "seat time" (i.e., courses and curricula). As I will show in this chapter, CBE has disastrous implications for composition. In this model, *writing* is understood as a discrete, commodified, vocational skill; *writing students* are understood as individual workers-in-training who need to "pick up" this skill for purely instrumental purposes; *writing teachers* are understood as success coaches to, or evaluators of, those individuals; and *writing classrooms* are quaint relics of a bygone era when we naively thought the best way to learn to write was to study and practice it with other writers under the guidance of a teacher who facilitated a set of coordinated learning activities. But before I describe CBE in more detail, and suggest how compositionists might respond to it, I examine compositionists' complicity in clearing the conceptual ground for CBE through our participation in outcomes assessment.

OUTCOMES ASSESSMENT: OUR TROJAN HORSE

In a *College English* article called "The Trouble with Outcomes," I argued that outcomes assessment operates within institutional and ideological logics—technical rationality, instrumentalism—that serve the interests of the managed university (Gallagher 2012). I suggested that outcomes assessment tends to "limit and compromise the educational experiences of teachers and students" through its insistence on the primacy of (predetermined) "outputs" (43). Here I want to take that argument a step further to suggest that our participation in this practice—our tacit acknowledgment that results are all that really matter in education—has opened the door to CBE, which, in its worst forms, disregards the educational experiences of teachers and students altogether. Outcomes assessment has functioned as our Trojan horse: through our acceptance of it, we've unknowingly invited CBE.

CBE is an "outcomes-based approach to education where the emphasis is on what comes out of postsecondary education—what graduates know and can do—rather than what goes into the curriculum" (Soares 2012). This definition comes from the putatively "progressive" Center for American Progress, and it bears a striking resemblance to the way compositionist Michael Carter (2003) frames outcomes assessment for our field:

> We're used to thinking about education primarily in terms of inputs: we designate a particular set of courses for students to take and when the course is completed we declare them educated and send them on their way. We assume that the inputs we provide for students will lead to certain outcomes, the knowledge, skills, and other attributes we believe graduates should possess. However, an outcomes-based approach to education does not rely on this assumption. By that method, faculty identify the educational outcomes for a program and then evaluate the program according to its effectiveness in enabling students to achieve those outcomes. (4–5)

This sounds like common sense, and I am aware from responses to my *College English* article that many compositionists believe outcomes are "merely" neutral tools. But again, my argument was that outcomes assessment is embedded in instrumentalist and managerial logics that produce certain *tendencies,* including—and here I drew on language from John Dewey—fixity and rigidity in the formulation of ends; diversion of attention away from the existing conditions for teaching and learning; narrow fixation on singular results rather than openness to emergent consequences; and imposition on students and teachers (Gallagher 2012, 45–46). Now I see that in aligning ourselves with an institutional practice and logic in which "outputs" are all that matter, we opened the door to those who argue that where and how and under what circumstances one learns are irrelevant. As we turned to outcomes assessment, we failed to insist that we were offering particular kinds of *experiences* that could not be attained elsewhere. We might have thought we were being good citizens. We might have thought outcomes were just a neutral tool. We might have thought we could have it all. If so, we were wrong.

Consider how outcomes assessment functions even in highly regarded programs run by well-known compositionists. In his contribution to the collection *Writing Assessment in the 21st Century,* Irv Peckham (2012) describes how his writing program at Louisiana State University used an online, end-of-semester, outcomes-based test to exempt some students from a second semester of composition. The test asked students to read 8–10 articles on an issue and write an essay "to explain what the issue was about" (174). Teachers were encouraged to use the test scores as a guide to grading (175). That the course grades of students who participated in writing classes were determined by a test on which they were asked to "explain" an "issue" shows clearly that a narrow set of outcomes are what really matter here.

Peckham also points out that the outcomes assessment saves money: "approximately $46,000 a year by exempting students from required writing classes; this was equivalent to the cost of 1.3 teachers at an average annual salary of $36,000" (176). He reproduces a letter he sent to his dean explaining how much money he saved. His letter doesn't explain that the outcomes assessment also had resulted in redefining the purpose of the first-year writing course as helping students pass a test and a consequent narrowing of the curriculum (176); a competitive environment in which instructors "gloat" about their students' performance relative to those of other instructors; less writing instruction for students; and less work for already poorly paid teachers. Instead of arguing that first-year writing is a valuable *experience* for all students and therefore worth paying for, Peckham accedes to a managerial logic in which his job is to save money by "identifying students who have shown that they clearly do not need another writing course to succeed in their other undergraduate courses" (177). Outcomes assessment functions to diminish the value and purpose of writing program, while burnishing its image in the eyes of efficiency-minded administrators.

THE ENDGAME: COMPETENCY-BASED EDUCATION

Follow outcomes assessment to its logical conclusion and you will find competency-based education (CBE). Several versions of CBE are emerging. Some, like those at Alverno and DePaul, retain courses and curricula but replace grades with competencies that students must demonstrate through performance assessments; others eschew these "outmoded" structures and rely only on competencies. Some programs offer students online modules through which they must work and others rely on "prior learning assessment," in which students are given college credit for life and work experience. In this chapter, I have in mind what proponents of CBE generally mean when they talk about this "game-changer": so-called "self-paced," mostly or fully online programs, typically offered on an "all you can learn" subscription model and organized not around courses or credits but around a set of competencies that students earn.

A number of CBE models are emerging, from programs and institutions that replace course grades with competencies but retain the basic course-and-curriculum structure to full-on competency programs with no curricula or courses. In any case, CBE is enjoying enormous momentum as a result of an increasingly supportive policy context; the forced competitiveness of cash-strapped institutions of higher education in the age of austerity; the emergence of a workable business model that often features collaboration with corporate partners and the capturing of customer bases previously thought out of range (working adults, those without sufficient funds for traditional education); the ever-growing availability of free online educational resources; and, not least, the deep pockets of predatory philanthropists.

The Obama Administration has made CBE a key strategy in the president's higher education plan, dubbed "A Better Bargain for the Middle Class." The plan extends the Race to the Top competition to higher education, with "special focus on promoting paying for value as opposed to enrollment of just seat time." It emphasizes hastening time-to-degree, encouraging states to "provide accelerated learning opportunities." To this end, the plan touts innovative use of new technologies such as Massive Open Online Courses (MOOCs); credit for "prior learning"; and competency-based programs (White House Office of the Press Secretary 2012).

Early in 2013, the US Department of Education issued a letter to colleges and universities informing them that they may apply for federal aid for students enrolled in competency-based programs rather than programs based on credit hours. Although the letter was offered as a "clarification," it is widely viewed as auguring a radical shift away from traditional academic metrics—credit hours, seat time—and toward "direct assessment" (in fact, the letter seeks to address the "direct assessment" provision of the Higher Education Act; see Field 2013). A month after the release of the letter, the USDoE approved Southern New Hampshire University, a private institution, to receive federal funding for students enrolled in its fully online, self-paced College for America program.

Designed in collaboration with corporate partners, the College for America offers associates and bachelors programs and is billed as a low-cost alternative to traditional credit-hour-based programs ($2500/year for "all you can learn"). There is no curriculum and there are no traditional (i.e., classroom) teachers. The program assesses 120 competencies based on Lumina's Degree Qualifications Profile and the US Department of Labor's competency pyramids. Students access free, online resources to help them perform a task, which they submit for evaluation against the competencies after accessing free online resources. They are also assigned "coaches" and required to identify an "accountability partner." The tasks are evaluated by part-time adjuncts (Parry 2013). The assessments, some of which are automated, are overseen by an assessment expert from the Educational Testing Service, now College for America's chief academic officer (Fain 2013).

College for America is partially funded by the Bill and Melinda Gates Foundation, one of two leading private foundations pushing CBE (the other is the Lumina Foundation, though other foundations, like Nellie Mae, also fund CBE initiatives). Between 2008 and July 2013, Gates has spent $472 million on higher education and Lumina has spent a little more than half that amount (Parry, Field, and Supiano 2013). Gates and Lumina promote "college completion" (read: anti-remediation), CBE, "value-added measures" for teacher evaluation, and workplace readiness. In other words, quick, efficient, low-cost education defined by the needs of business.

As public dollars have been drastically reduced, these private players have gained enormous influence, including impacting where the small number of public dollars go.[2] States have been forced by austerity to buy into Race to the Top; in higher education, Gates has paid millions for the successful lobbying of the federal government to provide financial aid to CBE programs. The foundation also has established a range of media partnerships, donating to various outlets and sponsoring ventures such as *Waiting for Superman*. And Gates grants are so valuable in this age of austerity that many in higher education are loath to criticize Gates publicly. (On the enormous impact of Gates on education policy K–16, see Barkan 2011; Mangan 2013; Parry, Field, and Supiano 2013.)

Many of the claims the federal government now makes about CBE and the value of "personalized learning" (see http://www.ed.gov/oii-news /competency-based-learning-or-personalized-learning) can be found in the Gates- and Lumina-funded New America Foundation/Education Sector report *Cracking the Credit Hour*. This 2012 report, which showcases competency-based programs at Western Governors University and Southern New Hampshire University, encourages the US Department of Education to consider financial aid plans that cover prior learning assessment as well as learning "outside of traditional faculty and institutional boundaries" (Laitinen 2012, 19).[3]

Despite market-driven reformers' purported commitment to data and bottom-line results, CBE is enjoying significant momentum without any evidence that it results in improved learning for students. This is doubly ironic, as CBE *is not new*. We could go as far back here as the "acceleration movement" of the late nineteenth century, when, according to Collins (1979), "utility-minded administrators attacked the 4-year curriculum as a useless tradition inherited from the medieval universities, and they introduced reforms to allow students to move through college at their own pace, acquiring training on an individual basis" (125; see also Rudolph 1962). But a more recent version of CBE emerged— with a vengeance—in the 1970s.

This historical context is important, for many of the related developments we find in the 1970s are familiar today: a "crisis" in public confidence in colleges, faculty, and graduates; concerns about the costs of college; fear that US higher education is "falling behind"; changing student demographics ("new" students then were working class; today, they tend to be multilingual and international students); business interests clamoring for more "competent" workers; considerable funding by the federal government and business leaders for initiatives meant to promote productivity and efficiency.

Despite the clear historical parallels, and while there is much to learn from this earlier CBE movement, including its dissolution in the United States,[4] we should not assume that 1970s CBE was identical to today's CBE. Indeed, the conversation around CBE in the 1970s was not solely about efficiency, economy, and vocational education, as it tends to be today; CBE was also promoted by advocates of civil rights and women's liberation in the name of social empowerment (Neumann 1979; Oleson 1979; Riesman 1979). For some CBE promoters, this alternative approach to education provided an opportunity to expand civic and professional opportunities and outcomes, not just for individuals but also for traditionally excluded groups. David Riesman (1979) suggested that CBE afforded the nation an opportunity to confront the common American "dialectic" between individual liberty and achievement and equitable outcomes for "entire, previously disadvantaged groups" (40). Alas, CBE is sponsoring no such conversation in the United States today; while the movement is promoted as an "access" initiative for older, working individuals, the group-empowerment agenda has fallen away entirely. In fact, contemporary CBE proponents tend to emphasize the least successful features of CBE programs of the 1970s: hyper-individualization, excessive specification, narrow workplace prerogatives, top-down implementation, and placelessness.

Despite their often noble goals, CBE programs in the 1970s were riddled with problems, including but not limited to high drop-out rates; poor student self-monitoring; lack of institutional preparation; inadequate institutional leadership; excessive bureaucratization; lack of opportunities for socialization into academic life and thinking; higher than expected costs; and the routinization, atomization, and codification of competencies (Grant and Associates 1979). While a three-year, FIPSE-funded team of researchers declared itself ambivalent about CBE, its leader, Gerald Grant, acknowledged in 1979 that CBE programs had a poor track record—and a "high mortality rate" (14). This was largely because the program had not "proved particularly attractive to students" and had not won "the loyalty of faculty" (14).

In the 1970s, CBE took root almost exclusively in colleges and programs in which tenure was not awarded. As today, its supporters touted the "unbundling" of roles, with some faculty formulating and validating competencies, others coaching students, and still others evaluating student work. Team member Peter Elbow (1979), while praising the clarity gained by disaggregated roles, observed a significant increase in "the use of such adjunct persons as undergraduate tutors and nonprofessional counselors, helpers, and mentors" (100). In light of the ensuing erosion of the tenure system and the concomitant rise of the use of contingent workers, we can see that CBE has contributed to—and today is accelerating—the casualization of academic labor.

Whatever led to CBE's dissolution in US education by the early 1980s, one thing is clear: no one ever showed that it worked—that it had better results than much-derided "traditional education." (Not that this is a disqualifying deficiency in American educational reform—see charter schools and test-based accountability.) Grant (1979) was quick to note that there were no reliable data to support the contention that students in CBE programs were "in fact more competent or employable than similar students from traditional programs" (12; see also Ewens 1979; Oleson 1979). To this day, no reliable data of this sort have been proffered by advocates of CBE, despite their claims that students "learn better" in their model.

Nor has anyone shown that CBE addresses the important social justice issues it purports to solve. Again, CBE is often touted today as an access initiative, lowering barriers to adult learners already in the workforce as well as young people without the deep pockets necessary to afford "traditional" higher education. What these claims fail to acknowledge, however, is that only students with some degree of cultural capital, access to digital technology, and the confidence and savvy necessary to engage in largely self-sponsored learning will benefit from CBE. Indeed, one of the Grant team's findings in the 1970s was that CBE might not be well-suited for those who needed it most. Elbow (1979) observed that disadvantaged students were often the first to drop out, leading him to suggest that "the competence approach fits elite students best, that is, it fits confident, well-prepared students who can say, 'Just tell me what I need to know and don't bother me with your classes and lecturers. I'll tell you when I'm ready. Now get out of my way, I'm in a hurry'" (121). Traditionally marginalized students, meanwhile, are likely to find themselves even more flummoxed and excluded than they had been before the advent of CBE. In these ways, CBE threatens to exacerbate, rather than ameliorate, social inequities that currently plague higher education.

Moreover, CBE today imagines writing not as a means of participating in social and civic contexts, but rather as a means of producing material to be evaluated. Students are not provided the experience of writing, or the experience of being read, outside of a strictly utilitarian, strictly evaluative context. They may receive just-in-time feedback from mentors or success coaches as they work with lesson materials or prepare for assessments, but they do not participate in communities of writers or form the kinds of relationships with peers or teachers that nurture writing development over time.

The limited, utilitarian conception of writing in these programs was made evident to me at a recent eportfolio conference, where I attended a two-person panel presentation by a self-described writing instructor and an instructional technology expert. The topic was prior learning assessment, a linchpin of CBE. At the presenters' institution, a largely online college catering to working adults, students were required to write a 10–15 page "experiential learning narrative" that made the case for the acceptance of prior learning for academic credit. The problem, according to the panelists, was that students struggled mightily with writing the narrative: they didn't know how to interpret and represent their experiences in ways evaluators expected; they were intimidated by the length and complexity of the text required of them; and they found revising multiple drafts—they were rarely awarded credit on first try—to be discouraging. The writing instructor described spending "countless hours" coaching these students, only to be met with student frustration and resistance. Many students dropped out.

Here is where the "eportfolio" came in. Using the form capability of a major blog vendor, the instructional technology expert designed an interface that broke the task down. Instead of writing one long narrative, students now uploaded and annotated various artifacts. The electronic templates kept the students on task, not allowing them to "go off on narrative tangents." This freed up time for the writing coaches, who now received only occasional and mostly logistical questions. Once they uploaded and annotated their artifacts, students pressed a button and a compiled version of their "experiential learning narrative" was generated. This is what writing looks like under CBE: a highly instrumentalist means of conveying information for the purpose of evaluation. Instructors don't so much *teach* writing as they facilitate the completion of tasks that happen to require writing.

WHAT TO DO?

Drawing on John Dewey (1916), who in his magisterial *Democracy and Education* defined education as "the continuous reconstruction of experience," Maja Wilson (2013) reminds us that "if we are interested in the education of *writers* . . . we're interested in the ways in which writers learn to use language to shape and express and create experiences—their own, and those of their readers" (219). But CBE evacuates the educational transaction of experience by fetishizing outcomes. Any present activity is important only insofar as it allows students to check another box on their way to a credential. CBE refuses the very conception of education as a social process through which learners engage in the continuous reconstruction of experience.

Experience is the ground on which faculty must make our stand. We are not just another set of content providers; we are expert shapers of educative experiences for individuals and groups. We offer a kind and quality of experience—in *courses* and *curricula*, and in and through writing—that cannot be replicated or by-passed by vendors. We know our subject matter, to be sure, but we also know how to build environments and experiences that promote students' learning of it. And we know our students—not as bundles of competencies, but as human beings in the midst of richly social and contextual learning experiences. These kinds of experiences help shape discernment and judgment, and these capacities help our students learn not only how to make a living, but also how to make a life and how to live well with others in a participatory democracy. We must couple critiques of "reforms" such as CBE and refusal to participate in outcomes assessment when it makes us complicit in our own obsolescence with persuasive accounts of the kinds of educative experiences our writing courses and curricula offer.

Just as important, for the sake of that democracy, we need a movement dedicated to getting Big Money out of education reform. Fortunately, there are signs that just such a movement is underway:

- A recent article in *The Atlantic* critiques "market-based educational reforms," pointing out that education policies rooted in standardization and distrust of teachers tend to fail and that many people have come to be suspicious of the corporate reformers themselves; the article predicts a "coming revolution" to that will reclaim public education from corporate reformers (Tierney 2013).
- *Dissent* recently ran a well-researched expose called "Got Dough? Billionaires Rule Our Schools" (Barkan 2011). The piece pulls no punches in describing the hubris of corporate reformers, and it concludes, "Private foundations should not be setting policy for [public schools]. Private money should not be producing what amount to false advertising for a faulty product. The imperious overreaching of [the foundations] undermines democracy just as surely as it damages public education."
- Former proponent of market-based reforms Diane Ravitch has begun a campaign to renounce the quick-fix mentality of corporate reformers and recommit to a robust conception of public education. (See Ravitch 2013.)
- A coalition of Chicago K–college teachers, citing the failures of No Child Left Behind, urged US Education Secretary Arne Duncan to "put your faith in teachers rather than corporate interests . . . Do not allow corporations to control American education." (http://www .commondreams.org/views/2013/02/16/get-corporations-out -education-open-letter-arne-duncan)
- Postsecondary educators have responded to President Obama's "New Bargain for the Middle Class" with a range of trenchant critiques, pointing out for instance that the plan "focuses on certain

measureable student outcomes—such as graduate rates—but would
do little to ensure actual student learning" (Flaherty 2013).

- *The Chronicle of Higher Education* has run a series of articles detailing the
  inordinate power wielded by foundations such as Gates and Lumina
  and companies such as Pearson, as well as growing resistance to this
  power (see, for instance, Mangan 2013; Parry, Field, and Supiano 2013).
- In a discussion of "tech mania" in higher education, David Kirp (2013)
  argues in in pages of *The Nation* that "there's no cheap solution to higher
  education's woes, no alternative to making a serious public investment,
  no substitute for the professor who provokes students into confronting
  their most cherished beliefs, changing their lives in the process."

These are just a few of the voices rising up against corporate reformers and arguing for public education, K–college, as a public good worthy of public investment. Perhaps they represent the beginning of a
movement to get Big Money out of education reform and to get public
money back into K–12 and higher education. Perhaps, too, they represent a shift away from the idea that institutions of higher education are
credential factories and back toward the notion that colleges and universities are places where people gather to learn together. As compositionists who teach one of the core arts of engagement, and whose very
profession and discipline hang in the balance, we should not only be
participating in these developments, but leading them.

Notes

1. See Henry (2006) and Plater (2006) on the use of eportfolios in competency-based
   programs.
2. Education reform has become big business. Individuals like charter school entrepreneur Van Gureghian, oil billionaire Philip Anschutz, and former New York mayor
   Michael Bloomberg; foundations like the Bill and Melinda Gates Foundation, the
   Walton Family Foundation, and the Eli and Edythe Broad Foundation; "Astroturf"
   (fake grassroots) groups such as Michelle Rhee's Students First and parent "trigger-
   law" supporters Parent Revolution; and a range of testing, test prep, and educational services corporations pour billions into, and reap billions from, neoliberal
   corporate education reform (see Ramey 2013).
3. Prior Learning Assessment is the institutional practice of awarding credit for experiences and achievements accomplished before enrollment in academic programs.
   It, too, is becoming big business, as online education providers like StraighterLine
   offer courses on subscription pricing plans ($99/month plus $49/course) and
   organizations like Council for Adult and Experiential Learning and American
   Council on Education work with institutions to offer credit for such courses. See
   Center for American Progress and the Council for Adult and Experiential Learning
   2011; Mandell and Travers 2012.
4. CBE never fully died out; while it waned in the United States as the 1970s wore on,
   it was taken up with fervor in Great Britain and elsewhere in Europe in the 1990s
   and eventually morphed into the various national, outcomes-based vocational

qualifications initiatives in Europe and Australia and, later, the pan-European qualifications framework designed by the Bologna Process. See Gaston 2010; Jessup 1991; Reinalda and Kulesza 2005; Wolf 1996.

References

Barkan, Joanne. 2011. "Got Dough? How Billionaires Rule Our Schools." *Dissent* (Winter). Accessed May 28, 2014. http://www.dissentmagazine.org/article/got -dough-how-billionaires-rule-our-schools.

Carter, Michael. 2003. "A Process for Establishing Outcomes-Based Assessment Plans for Writing and Speaking in the Disciplines." *Language and Learning Across the Disciplines* 6 (1): 4–29.

Center for American Progress and the Council for Adult and Experiential Learning. 2011. "Prior Learning Assessments: Tools to Help 21st Century Students Achieve Their Postsecondary Education Goals and Keep America Competitive." Accessed May 28, 2014. http://www.americanprogress.org/issues/2011/09/pdf/pla_brief.pdf.

Collins, Randall. 1979. *The Credential Society: A Historical Sociology of Education and Stratification.* New York: Academic Press.

Dewey, John. 1916. *Democracy and Education.* Project Gutenberg. Accessed May 28, 2014. http://www.gutenberg.org/files/852/852-h/852-h.htm.

Elbow, Peter. 1979. "Trying to Teach While Thinking about the End." In *On Competence,* ed. Gerald Grant, and Associates., 95–137. San Francisco: Jossey-Bass.

Ewens, Thomas. 1979. "Analyzing the Impact of Competence-based Approaches on Liberal Education." In *On Competence,* ed. Gerald Grant, and Associates., 160–98. San Francisco: Jossey-Bass.

Fain, Paul. 2013. "Credit Without Teaching." *Inside Higher Ed,* April 22. Accessed May 28, 2014. http://www.insidehighered.com/news/2013/04/22/competency-based -educations-newest-form-creates-promise-and-questions.

Field, Kelly. 2013. "Student Aid Can Be Awarded for 'Competencies,' Not Just Credit, U.S. Says." *Chronicle of Higher Education,* March 19. http://chronicle.com/article /Student-Aid-Can-Be-Awarded-for/137991/ Accessed May 28, 2014.

Flaherty, Colleen. 2013. "Disappointed, Not Surprised." *Inside Higher Ed,* August 23. Accessed May 28, 2014. http://www.insidehighered.com/news/2013/08/23/faculty -advocates-react-obamas-plan-higher-ed#sthash.wijjs37q.dpbs.

Gallagher, Chris W. 2012. "The Trouble with Outcomes." *College English* 75 (1): 42–60.

Gaston, Paul. 2010. *The Challenge of Bologna: What United States Higher Education Has to Learn from Europe, and Why it Matters That We Learn It.* Sterling, VA: Stylus.

Grant, Gerald. 1979. "Prologue: Implications of Competence-based Education." In *On Competence,* ed. Gerald Grant, and Associates., 1–17. San Francisco: Jossey-Bass.

Grant, Gerald, and Associates. 1979. *On Competence.* San Francisco: Jossey-Bass.

Henry, Ronald J. 2006. "ePortfolio Thinking: A Provost Perspective." In *The Handbook of Electronic Portfolio Research,* ed. Ali Jafari and Catherine Kaufman, 54–61. Hershey, PA: IDEA Group. http://dx.doi.org/10.4018/978-1-59140-890-1.ch006.

Jessup, Gilbert. 1991. *Outcomes: NVQs and the Emerging Model of Education and Training.* NY: Routledge.

Kirp, David. 2013. "Tech Mania Goes to College." *Nation (New York, N.Y.),* September 4. Accessed May 28, 2014. http://www.thenation.com/article/tech-mania-goes-college/.

Laitinen, Amy. 2012. *Cracking the Credit Hour.* New York: New America Foundation and Education Sector.

Mandell, Alan, and Nan Travers. 2012. "The Power of Experience Inside Out " *Prior Learning Assessment: Inside Out* 1 (1). Accessed May 28, 2014. http://www.plaio.org /index.php/home/article/view/23/32.

Mangan, Katherine. 2013. "How Gates Shapes State Policy." *Chronicle of Higher Education*, July 14. Accessed May 28, 2014. http://chronicle.com/article/How-Gates-Shapes-State/140303/.

Neumann, William. 1979. "Educational Responses to the Concern for Proficiency." In *On Competence*, ed. Gerald Grant, and Associates., 66–94. San Francisco: Jossey-Bass.

Oleson, Virginia. 1979. "Employing Competence-based Education for the Reform of Professional Practice." In *On Competence*, ed. Gerald Grant, and Associates., 199–223. San Francisco: Jossey-Bass.

Parry, Marc. 2013. "U.S. Education Department Gives a Boost to Competency-Based Education." *Chronicle of Higher Education*, April 18. Accessed November 25, 2015. http://chronicle.com.ezproxy.neu.edu/blogs/wiredcampus/u-s-education-department-gives-a-boost-to-competency-based-education/43439.

Parry, Marc, Kelly Field, and Becky Supiano. 2013. "The Gates Effect." *Chronicle of Higher Education*, July 14. Accessed May 28, 2014. http://chronicle.com/article/The-Gates-Effect/140323/.

Plater, William M. 2006. "The Promise of the Student Electronic Portfolio: A Provost's Perspective." In *The Handbook of Electronic Portfolio Research*, ed. Ali Jafari and Catherine Kaufman, 62–73. Hershey, PA: IDEA Group. http://dx.doi.org/10.4018/978-1-59140-890-1.ch007.

Peckham, Irvin. 2012. "Assessment and Curriculum in Dialogue." In *Writing Assessment in the 21st Century: Essays in Honor of Edward M. White*, ed. Norbert Elliot and Les Perelman, 169–85. NY: Hampton Press.

Ramey, Jessie B. 2013. "A Handy Reference Guide on Who Is Donating to Corporate-Style Education Reform." Alternet, May 15. Accessed May 28, 2014. http://www.alternet.org/education/handy-reference-guide-who-donating-corporate-style-education-reform.

Ravitch, Diane. 2013. *Reign of Error: The Hoax of the Privatization Movement and the Danger to America's Public Schools*. New York: Knopf.

Reinalda, Bob, and Ewa Kulesza. 2005. *The Bologna Process: Harmonizing Europe's Higher Education*. Leverkusen, Germany: Barbara Budrich.

Riesman, David. 1979. "Society's Demand for Competence." In *On Competence*, ed. Gerald Grant, and Associates., 18–65. San Francisco: Jossey-Bass.

Rudolph, Frederick. 1962. *The American College and University: A History*. New York: Knopf.

Soares, Louis. 2012. "A 'Disruptive' Look at Competency-based Education." Center for American Progress, June 7. Accessed May 28, 2014. http://www.americanprogress.org/issues/higher-education/report/2012/06/07/11680/a-disruptive-look-at-competency-based-education/.

Tierney, John. 2013. "The Coming Revolution in Public Education." *Atlantic (Boston, Mass.)*, April 25. Accessed May 28, 2014. http://www.theatlantic.com/national/archive/2013/04/the-coming-revolution-in-public-education/275163/.

White House Office of the Press Secretary. 2012. "Fact Sheet on the President's Plan to Make Higher Education More Affordable: A Better Bargain for the Middle Class." White House website, August 22. Accessed May 28, 2014. http://www.whitehouse.gov/the-press-office/2013/08/22/fact-sheet-president-s-plan-make-college-more-affordable-better-bargain-.

Wilson, Maja Joiwind. 2013. "Writing Assessment's 'Debilitating Inheritance': Behaviorism's Dismissal of Experience." PhD diss., University of New Hampshire, Durham.

Wolf, Alison. 1996. *Competence-Based Assessment*. London: Open University Press.

2
CONFESSIONS OF AN
ASSESSMENT FELLOW

Deborah Mutnick

What we measure affects what we do; and if our measurements are
flawed, decisions may be distorted . . .
            Joseph E. Stiglitz, Amartya Sen, Jean-Paul Fitoussi (2008)

Soaring tuition, student debt topping $1 trillion, and a national gradua-
tion rate of 59 percent at four-year institutions raise troubling questions
about the value of a college education (US Department of Education,
National Center for Education Statistics 2013). At the same time,
according to a 2014 study by the Pew Research Center, graduates with
a four-year degree earn 98 percent more an hour than dropouts or people who never attended college (Pew Research Center 2014). Yet access
is in jeopardy, increasingly tied to completion, grades, test scores, and
ability to pay, thus rolling back the debate about who goes to college
nearly half a century. Meanwhile, teachers at all levels are struggling
to cope with budget cuts and externally set policies from the Common
Core State Standards in K–12 to outcomes assessment in colleges and
universities that are commodifying education and eroding autonomy
and resilience in a neoliberal era of privatization, deregulation, financialization, and austerity.

   My aim here is to situate outcomes assessment in the larger context
of the neoliberal university, a topic about which I write from the perspective of an "assessment fellow"—one of several hats I wear at Long
Island University-Brooklyn (LIU), the private, multi-campus university
where I have taught writing and rhetoric since the late 1980s. As is true
for the majority of college writing teachers across the United States in
the wake of open admissions, I teach at an urban campus that serves a
predominantly lower middle- and working-class, first-generation student
population. Several years ago, as the university approached its decennial

DOI: 10.7330/9781607324454.c002

evaluation by the Middle States Commission of Higher Education (MSCHE), a director of assessment was hired to ensure compliance with Standard 14, the assessment of student learning—noncompliance having put increasingly more institutions on warning, probation, or worse. After a year of meetings of a university-wide committee that I participated in as a faculty representative, a structure emerged in which programs were mandated to develop goals, objectives, and measures of student learning in order to use data effectively to improve outcomes. Faculty fellows rather than administrators—my idea, as I recall it—were appointed to engage with other faculty as we navigated the tension between assessment for internal *improvement* of student learning and external *accountability* to accrediting agencies and policymakers. But many professors, at LIU and elsewhere, view outcomes assessment as "an ideological smokescreen" (Bennett and Brady 2012, 2), dependent on a "reductive logic" that appeals to a "generic general public" (Emery and Graff 2008, 256). That critique, with which I sympathize, and my often uncomfortable participation in my own institution's assessment program have provoked these reflections.

To those conversant with the discourse of neoliberal capitalism, two familiar starting points for my analysis of the role of outcomes assessment in higher education are:

1. the problem is not scarcity but rather distribution of resources; and

2. academic underpreparedness and the so-called "achievement gap"— which drive the assessment industry—are primarily the result of underlying social problems of poverty, racism, and economic inequality that are neither inevitable nor natural but rather result from policies created and enacted by human beings.[1]

While in some circles it may be second nature to criticize former British Prime Minister Margaret Thatcher's slogan "There Is No Alternative" [to capitalism], otherwise known as TINA, this outlook predominates in a culture in which many people simply feel buffeted by political economic forces without understanding their origins or designs. Reinforcing such obedience to the status quo is the difficulty of decoupling what seem like reasonable demands, such as improving learning outcomes—the smokescreen—from the ideological networks through which they are more and more aggressively circulated.

Popular support for charter schools, for example, attests to deep yearnings for solutions to complex problems and susceptibility to the promises of powerful corporate and literacy sponsors. The privatization of education is part of a capitalist offensive to concentrate wealth in what is now famously known as the 1 percent, an assault waged with increasing indifference to human suffering, at times vicious but more often subtly coercive, enforcing what Gramsci called cultural hegemony. In higher education, this more subtle coercion takes multiple forms. These forms include a shift in focus from access to completion rates, increased faculty exploitation and proletarianization, ideological attacks on faculty, fierce competition for resources, and rising tuition and student debt. In addition, regional accrediting agencies have mandated outcomes assessment as a self-regulatory tool to ward off government intervention and assure the "value" of a college education in a transnational capitalist economy marked by job insecurity, flexible employment, and wealth inequality.

THE ROAD TO PRIVATIZATION: FROM INPUTS TO OUTPUTS

The primary driver of educational reform in the twenty-first century is the 2001 No Child Left Behind (NCLB) Act, a reauthorization of the 1965 Elementary and Secondary Education Act. Unlike this earlier legislation, which poured funding into education in response to national and political concerns—including the civil rights movement at home and anti-colonial struggles abroad—and prohibited federal intervention in curricular matters, NCLB ushered in a new era of federal control over K–12 public education and, indirectly, colleges and universities. Although K–12 was its main focus, NCLB fomented calls for increased accountability for public and private dollars spent on higher education to be measured, among other metrics, by outcomes assessment of student learning. Since then, NCLB and Obama's competitive funding program Race to the Top have increasingly pitted students and parents against teachers in the name of educational equality and blamed underfunded, high poverty schools, particularly teachers, for academic failure.[2]

A quick summary of this transformation of American education helps explain the pivotal role played by outcomes assessment. In 2006, the Commission on the Future of Higher Education, appointed by US Secretary of Education Margaret Spellings, reinforced NCLB's emphasis on accountability, pressuring regional accrediting bodies to enforce systematic, data-driven assessment in higher education or else face some form of standardized testing similar to that mandated by NCLB. As former MSCHE vice president Linda Suskie (2009) put it: "To be blunt, the American higher education community is now on borrowed time. If American colleges and universities assemble compelling evidence of student learning now, demonstrating through assessment that their students graduate with important skills such as writing, critical thinking, and analysis, they have a much better chance of warding off inappropriate mandates and are far more likely to receive the support they need. If they do not do so, the risk of an external mandate dictating what and how to assess—and in a useless, burdensome fashion—is very real" (62). This logic of complying with the mandate to defend against more egregious government intervention drove the regional accrediting bodies to adopt new standards based on outcomes and drove colleges to create and implement systematic, evidence-based assessment of student learning.

Despite considerable resistance, the admonition "If we don't do it ourselves, they'll do it for us" has persuaded a critical mass of faculty to develop outcomes assessment programs. I confess that I was among the faculty at my university who became involved in building an institution-wide approach to program-level assessment because I believed that faculty needed to participate in order to ward off administrative as well as governmental interference. I was convinced that if the university was to remain accredited and solvent, we needed to develop an outcomes assessment infrastructure to prepare for our decennial review for reaccreditation, then just a few years away. I was not then—nor am I now—hostile to the idea that better assessment could improve teaching and learning, especially given composition's leading role in developing critical evaluation theories and practices (see, e.g., O'Neill et al. 2009; Scott and Brannon 2013). However, upon hearing the mantra "if we don't do it ourselves" repeated yet again at the 2012 MSCHE conference, I could not help but mutter that we had simply "done it" for them.

Outcomes assessment not only disciplines college teachers to participate in costly, system-wide assessment programs, burdening them with what often amounts to busy work and diverting them from more meaningful activities, but also embodies the shift from "inputs" to "outputs" in order to rationalize cutbacks. Where once regional accrediting bodies sought to ensure the academic quality of higher education through "inputs," such as tenure-track appointments, a sufficient range and number of relevant course offerings, ample classrooms and labs, and good libraries, they are now measuring "outputs"—learning outcomes—to demonstrate that, as the Middle States Commission decrees, "at graduation . . . the institution's students have knowledge, skills, and competencies consistent with institutional and appropriate higher education goals." Such tellingly nebulous, tautological statements have created a lucrative industry of assessment administrators, textbooks, standardized tests, rubrics, and scoring systems that rarely if at all correlate with what and how students learn.

At LIU Brooklyn, the initial form of university-wide mandated outcomes assessment in the 1990s was based on inputs—for example, hiring writing faculty in the English Department—and bore no resemblance to the system that began to evolve in 2009. We started then in earnest, ahead of a few and catching up to many institutions already doing outcomes assessment, to implement systematic assessment of outputs—student learning outcomes. Professional programs with their own accrediting bodies were generally more amenable to the new regime than liberal arts and sciences faculty with the exception perhaps of the Writing Program, which had pioneered portfolio evaluation on campus based on composition's leading role in assessment. The new outcomes assessment system required every program to complete biannual reports in prescribed tables indicating goals and objectives to be assessed, direct measures to perform the assessment (for instance, an essay evaluated by a rubric), interpretations of data, and plans for improving student learning. While this mechanistic, abstract system is no doubt partially responsible for our reaccreditation in 2013, it squeezes the life out of education, fetishizing data through a discourse of assessment presumed to proclaim educational "value" that in fact commoditizes, reifies, and obscures the dynamic, messy, material, socially useful, inescapably values-driven labor of teaching and learning. To give an example of what LIU's currently required assessment model looks like, I have excerpted a page from the English Department's 2013 phase II report (Table 2.1).

Multiply this report by hundreds of programs university-wide, all uploaded to a password-protected website, and imagine the experience a reviewer would have of trying to comprehend the academic goals, objectives, and outcomes of any genuine learning. The quantification of performance, the atomization of written composition into discrete skills, the relatively small number of students assessed (due in part to increasingly few humanities majors), and the predictable claims of "a strong level of proficiency" all make painfully clear the limitations of this type of assessment. In addition to the significant resources and time expended on outcomes assessment across the university, participation in most programs is minimal with a small number of faculty accepting the responsibility for marshaling the majority of grateful, even if critical, colleagues through a pretense of meaningful evaluation of student work or improvement in teaching. What this type of outcomes assessment achieves is the appearance of dutiful compliance with the external standards set by accreditors, driven by federal K–12 policies and empty calls for accountability. Before

Table 2.1 2013–2014 Academic Year Table: For data to be *collected* in phase II current academic year, please report the following for each objective assessed:

PHASE I		PHASE II
Student Learning Goals and Objectives. Students will . . .	Measurement Tool (e.g., research paper scored with a rubric in EDU 690, Spring 2013)	Data Findings (report results that indicate a need for action, e.g., 60% of students need improvement in a dimension of a rubric)
GOAL: 4. DEMONSTRATE PROFICIENCY IN RESEARCH SKILLS AND INFORMATION LITERACY.		
Objective: 4d. "BE"Evaluate and use primary and secondary sources in a variety of formats (written, visual, aural, etc.)	Direct Measure 1:A rubric applied to students' coursework in mid-program courses (ENG 129, 137, and 159).	Students perform well on this measure. The three classes recorded the following percentages for "proficient" and "advanced" combined, respectively: 92%; 91%; 66% • Average proficient/advanced for all three classes: 83% • "Advanced" alone received the following percentages, respectively: 45%, 50%, 11% • Average for "advanced" for all three classes: 35%. While there is some variation between different classes, students in all three classes demonstrated a strong level of proficiency or better in evaluating and using secondary sources, overall.
Objective: 4d.1 "DD"Suitability of sources	Direct Measure 2:A rubric applied to students' coursework in mid-program courses (ENG 129, 137, and 159).	Students performed well on this measure: • Proficient/advanced: 91%; 83%; 78% • Average for proficient/advanced: 82% • "Advanced" alone: 45%; 50%; 33% • Average of "advanced": 43%

proposing how we might reclaim assessment and perform it on our own terms, I turn to the question of how outcomes assessment fits into the political economy of early twenty-first century education.

FINANCIALIZATION AND PRIVATIZATION: RACING TO THE TOP FOR "BEST VALUE" EDUCATION

It was not until George W. Bush enacted NCLB in 2001 that the concerns raised by the 1983 "Nation at Risk" report resulted in any major educational reforms on a national scale. Since then, billions of dollars have been spent on enforcing standardized testing and all the accouterments of NCLB. Obama's Race to the Top, passed in 2009 as part of the American Recovery and Reinvestment Act, similarly allocates funding on a competitive basis of compliance with the goal of raising and achieving standards tied to standardized testing, teacher evaluation, charter school development, and other externally imposed reforms. Since the turn of the century, policymakers, corporations, and neoliberal think tanks have aggressively and transparently pushed an agenda to transform US education by creating a "crisis" in order to provide and profit from solutions to it. As Common Core architect and College Board president David Coleman (2012) put it: "The Common Core State Standards aim to change everything—and for innovators and entrepreneurs, they may. With the simultaneous implementation of the Common Core State Standards in 46 states and D.C., there is the potential for a truly national market." This agenda blames teachers, mandates testing, and "scripts" curricula in order to monetize education; it pours billions of dollars into education reform and markets traceable to corporate sponsors like Boeing and State Farm—both members of the American Legislative Exchange Council (ALEC)—while forcing educators at all levels to take increasingly defensive positions in order to survive.

The backstory of assessment in K–12 and higher education reveals a fascinating web of relations among private donors, lobbyists, political offices, and transnational publishing companies, especially Pearson,[3] with deep roots in ALEC, the McKinsey Company, and the American Enterprise Institute.[4] Even though higher education has so far eluded the threat of a standardized national test, it must grapple with the influence of these powerful forces not only on assessment but also on the alignment of the Common Core with AP courses, SAT tests, dual enrollment, college and career readiness programs, educational technology, curriculum development, and textbooks as well as their successes in cutting or eliminating post-secondary remediation and thereby restricting access to college. These K–12 initiatives are both outside the purview of higher education and intimately connected to it, stimulating the accountability movement with various instruments and rating systems, including data-driven learning outcomes presumed to guarantee comparable standards of academic rigor and "excellence."

Less well understood than its role as a talisman warding off government intervention is how outcomes assessment in higher education validates the rhetoric of excellence, the sort of rhetorical maneuver that Nancy Welch (2011) refers to as *"la langue de coton"*—the use of such language to manipulate an audience—in her description of her own university's road to "academic capitalism." As Bill Readings (1996) pointed out two decades ago, the term "excellence" begins to appear in university mission statements as Western political discourse shifts from cultural conflict to economic development and management, and higher education's historical role of transmitting "national culture" gives way to

its new identity as a "transnational corporation" (13).[5] Readings argues
that the globalization of capital undermines the very premise of the
university as a repository for the production and reproduction of culture because "the nation state is no longer the major site at which capital reproduces itself"; hence, "what goes on in the University, and as a
result, what exactly gets taught or produced as knowledge matters less
and less" (13).

Outcomes assessment enacts this logic by reducing the complex process of teaching and learning to a packaged product used to satisfy the
promise of excellence, a floating signifier untied to any concrete, tangible content, whose meaning we think we know but can never name.
Instead, each university is branded as unique, stamped with "excellence"
and explicit marketing slogans like "best value" and "return on investment," and defined by graduation rate, tuition, discounts, loan default
rate, employment, and potential earnings, all of which prospective
students and their parents can now review on the College Scorecard.
Although these hallmarks of neoliberalism were evident in universities
before 2008, the crash and ensuing recession accelerated the process of
corporatization and state defunding of education, deepening the divide
between elite and non-elite institutions and leaving the latter strapped
for funds, their students ever more deeply in debt. Obama's Race to the
Top for Higher Education meanwhile rewards innovations like Massive
Open Online Courses (MOOCs) and "flipped" classrooms for "driving
down costs while preserving quality" and encouraging innovators "by
stripping away unnecessary regulations" ("Fact Sheet" 2013).

As higher education grapples with the implications of corporatization, jettisoning unprofitable programs, slashing budgets, and competing for government dollars, composition and rhetoric stands at a
crossroads, defined both by an increased desire to professionalize the
discipline through the establishment of upper division and graduate
writing programs and its historic commitment to expanding educational
access and thereby participatory democracy. Arising from the rebirth of
modern rhetorical studies in the mid-twentieth century and the radical
student movements of the 1960s, including the struggle for open admissions led by working class black, Mexican-American, Native American,
and Puerto Rican students, professionalization in composition was
underwritten by the reaffirmation of the first-year writing requirement
and the birth of a whole new subfield of basic writing. Ironically, just
as composition gained a toehold, contributing however inadvertently
with its largely contingent workforce of adjuncts and graduate students
to the institutionalization of post-Fordist working conditions (e.g., see

Bousquet 2008; Schell 1998; Scott 2004), the professoriate—tenure track as well as adjunct faculty—started to undergo the same process of proletarianization as the rest of the professional managerial class (Ehrenreich and Ehrenreich 2013). This "hollow prize"—a term used to describe suburban cities devastated by racial tensions in the 1960s now governed by politicians of color—was also won by students who fought for open admissions only to enter universities that were being defunded and corporatized.

Less obvious perhaps than the effects of its exploitative working conditions is how composition's democratic aspirations, especially its advocacy for educational access, contribute to maintaining structural inequalities. As Richard Ohmann (2000) observes, "[E]qual opportunity and universal access to education are compatible with great inequality, and, because they make it seem the result of unequal merit and effort, they also make it seem both inevitable and just" (37). Ohmann calls this logic "inescapable" insofar as bourgeois civil liberties are a prerequisite for capitalist growth, permitting individuals to enter freely into market activities whether as laborers or capitalists. For the field of composition, especially basic writing, the struggle for access has been both decisive and, like the fight for equality in public schools, unwinnable (e.g., see "Sense of the House Motion, CCCC 2011" indicating the perception of basic writing's invisibility even at the Conference on College Composition and Communication). Just as "excellence" circulates as an empty term obscuring the deep inequalities and failures not of the educational system per se but of our highly stratified society, the rhetoric of civil rights deployed by the education reform movement, epitomized by the attack on teacher seniority and tenure in *Vergara v. California*, is confusing to many people who understandably support ostensible efforts to improve schools and colleges. As higher education continues to corporatize, eliminating remedial courses and rebranding to recruit more academically and financially qualified students, access for working-class students, particularly those of color, will constrict and the programs and institutions that serve them will become extinct.

Just as the more egalitarian economy of the New Deal era turns out to have been a blip on the screen of history, the country having reverted by the end of the twentieth century to an extreme polarization of wealth, the promise of open admissions extracted through political struggle in the 1960s had already been broken by the late 1990s, with public universities like City University of New York (CUNY) closing the doors they had once opened to students from "New York's ethnic or racial enclaves" (Shaughnessy 1977, 2–3). Today, while low-income students with exceptional academic records may benefit from Obama's plan, the majority of working and poor people will be subject to increasingly unequal, racially segregated public education and enter college—if at all—not only unprepared for academic rigor but also bearing multiple responsibilities of family, work, and study. They are part of the growing number of the dispossessed, subject to the transfer of wealth that Marxist geographer David Harvey (2007, 34) calls "accumulation by dispossession."

THE DISPOSSESSED: FACULTY AND STUDENTS IN THE AGE OF AUSTERITY

Like the crash of 2008, the implosion of higher education, though a slower-moving process, is intensifying economic inequalities for students and faculty. The ranks of tenure-track faculty are increasingly threatened by the backlash against academia while those of poorly compensated, itinerant, contingent faculty and graduate students are multiplying everywhere, making it difficult to respond effectively to corporate forces reshaping higher education.[6] Minority and low-income students—despite the liberal-sounding rhetoric of foundations like Lumina, closely tied to ALEC—are less likely to attend four-year colleges and more likely to drop out even as the Economic Policy Institute reports a record high pay gap between Americans with and without a college degree. In addition to numerous court rulings against affirmative action that have impeded efforts to diversify campuses, administrators, donors, and policymakers have pressured colleges and universities to eliminate both need-blind admissions policies and remedial courses, policies that disproportionately affect poor and working class students of color, including those who are highly academically qualified.

For those who need academic support, some pre-college programs have been successful. CUNY Start, for example, is designed to support students who fail one or more of the University's entrance exams through an intensive $75 immersion course that claims a 70 percent exam pass rate for students who fail in one subject area. However, the fact remains that nationwide only one quarter of low-income students receives a bachelor's degree by age twenty-four in contrast to 90 percent of their higher income counterparts. Similarly, while early college programs and accelerated learning in remedial college courses have had some good results (Adams et al. 2009), they only affect a small percentage of students and cannot overcome the adverse effects for most people living in or at the edge of poverty and attending under-resourced, segregated public schools for most of their lives. As Stephen Krashen (2011), who has long named poverty as the problem, proclaimed at a lecture at Fordham University, "There's nothing wrong, seriously wrong, with our schools. There is no crisis. The crisis is 100 percent manufactured. The whole thing is a hoax."

Pious bipartisan concern for data-driven learning outcomes, the achievement gap, rising tuition costs, and mounting student debt masks the effect of initiatives like NCLB and the Common Core Standards, which is to track students by class—and therefore race, in our highly segregated society—into low-end service and vocational jobs or colleges. The worldwide economic divide within and among nations can be seen at all levels of US education. While K–12 public education continues to suffer from what Jonathan Kozol (1991) more than twenty years ago called "savage inequalities," federal and state budget cuts at public universities and colleges have decreased admission rates for low-income students of color. Since 2008, their enrollment in California's public four-year colleges dropped by one-fifth. A report published by the Community Service Society of New York (Treschan and Mehrotra 2012), found that the rate of blacks and Latin@s attending four-year CUNY colleges also dropped precipitously, noting that although 72 percent of New York City's high school students are students of color, they constituted only 48 percent of CUNY's entering class and only 29 percent at the top five campuses in 2010.

Concrete, material conditions—racial resegregation, poverty, and cuts in federal and state educational spending—explain gaps in educational performance between upper- and lower-income children, with race continuing to play a role in determining class status and social opportunities. These gaps, which persist to college, became glaringly apparent in the late 1960s and resulted—through mass struggle—in open admissions. Now, instead of addressing fundamental social problems of racism and poverty that result in academic underperformance, governmental and private interests backing educational reform blame schools and teachers for failing to meet standards, impose rigid student and teacher evaluation systems on them, and allocate competitive funding to those that comply with federal reforms such as the expansion of charter schools. New measures such as Obama's College Scorecard, purportedly intended to make college more affordable and attainable, likewise put the onus on higher education to increase graduation rates and lower costs in the face of persistent state budget cuts and underlying social problems. Such pressures for institutions like LIU Brooklyn are more likely to result in jettisoning access than expanding opportunity as universities raise the bar of admission in an effort to recruit students whose SAT scores and median family income fit the profile of "success"—a strategy that might backfire given other institutional realities such as physical plant, size, and demographics.

The transformation of higher education into a marketplace that Readings brilliantly described in the mid-1990s is well underway as colleges and universities struggle to cope with multiple frontal assaults from budget cuts and skyrocketing tuition to student debt, swelling ranks of contingent labor, and pressure from regional accrediting bodies. Yet, even if outcomes assessment in its current form is primarily a tool to manage the professoriate and comply with external accrediting and legislative bodies, simply refusing to participate within one's own institution strikes me as pointless if the result is to shift the burden of responsibility to other colleagues or jeopardize accreditation. As one colleague put it, "A gun to the head is no way to negotiate." Rather, we need to understand the political economic forces that explain our predicament and find ways of resisting politically as a collective body across institutions and pedagogically within our own places of employment. Like Readings' "university in ruins," the professional-managerial class (PMC), which Barbara Ehrenreich and John Ehrenreich saw as coextensive with the new left in the 1960s, including the professoriate, is fast disappearing, the degree of autonomy it gained after World War II attenuated by the same neoliberal market forces redefining the function of education. As Ehrenreich and Ehrenreich (2013, 10) observe, "The center has not held. Conceived as the 'middle class' and as the supposed repository of civic virtue and occupational dedication, the PMC lies in ruins."

If, indeed, we are all workers now, we need to figure out how best to fight for the right to an education that is neither nostalgic for a mythical past nor complicit with the marketplace values that increasingly define the twenty-first century university. I would suggest three types of response to neoliberalism's assault on education:

- The first is to join growing resistance to the underlying structural transformation of higher education through radical formations like the MLA Subconference, which held its first meeting in January 2014 and titled its second meeting in 2015 "Non-Negotiable Sites of Struggle."
- The second is to form and join coalitions across institutions and disciplines in higher education and with K–12 teachers, such as United Opt-Out: The Movement to End Corporate Education Reform,[7] and eventually cross-sectorial alliances like Occupy Wall Street or the "casserole movement" in Quebec that emerged in response to official attempts to quell student protests against tuition increases.
- The third, as Readings suggests, is to "keep the question of value open in relation to pedagogy . . . [to] provide a notion of educational

responsibility, of accountability, that is markedly at odds with the logic of accounting that runs the University of Excellence" (151).

Concretely, what might this mean for faculty in writing and rhetoric where post-Fordist labor practices expose glaring contradictions between the use of outcomes assessment to demonstrate academic excellence and reliance on heavily exploited, deprofessionalized faculty, many of whom teach middle- and working-class students whose own prospects for employment are, at best, unpredictable? What does it mean for me in my role as an assessment fellow, or for my university? Tony Scott and Lil Brannon suggest that "assessments should be represented as praxis, as reflexive involvement in the vexed, complicated workings of programs and institutions," and "strive to create three-dimensional portraits . . . of the work of students and teachers" (Scott and Brannon 2013, 296). To achieve such praxis necessitates engaging in reflective conversations about issues of quality and value. It means engaging the faculty as a whole—fulltime and adjunct—in evaluating performances of teaching and learning—and the working conditions in which they take place—rather than in packaging artificial assessments into annual reports on strengths and weaknesses of student learning supposed to sum up not one complex, messy, irreducible classroom but entire academic programs in a few short paragraphs. Indeed, as a result of pushback by faculty and assessment fellows against the constrictions of the current, reductive system of assessment at LIU Brooklyn, we appear to be moving toward an inquiry-based model aimed at pursuing more interesting questions and engaging more faculty in conversations about teaching and learning.

In a paper on the measurement of economic performance and social progress requested by former President of the French Republic Nicolas Sarkozy, a commission led by Joseph Stiglitz, Amartya Sen, and Jean Paul Fitoussi concludes that "the time is ripe for our measurement system to *shift emphasis from measuring economic production to measuring people's well-being*" (Stiglitz, Sen, and Fitoussi 2008, 12, emphasis in original). This move toward a centrist left position on the part of the rightwing Sarkozy government and a similar one by British Prime Minister David Cameron a few years later indicates the broad appeal of the new metrics and the deepening contradictions of capitalism that remind officials that labor power is inseparable from those who bear it. Reporting in 2011 on the commission in the *Nation*, Eyal Press (2011) quotes Stiglitz as saying, "Any political leader wants metrics that reflect the well-being of their citizens because, to put it frankly, if their constituents are happier they'll get re-elected." Recent K–12 and higher education policies have gone in the opposite direction, bureaucratizing and commodifying teaching and learning purportedly to measure excellence while privatizing education and profiting from so-called reforms. The commission's emphasis on "people's well-being" rests on its warning that the crisis in 2008 might have been mitigated, if not averted, by different, better, statistical indicators. By analogy, it is worth imagining what sort of assessment would emphasize students' well-being instead of relying strictly on their performance on tests and rubrics, asserting that another world is possible not because we are liberal do-gooders but because such measures would be more humane, creative, just, effective, and sustainable. Whether such reforms in higher education—or global capitalism—can solve the underlying problems is a subject for further inquiry and debate for us all.

Notes

1. A third point is that ruthlessly market-driven economies tend to reduce people to statistics—among the core complaints of the 1960s student movement—and to use a cookie-cutter approach to learning that sets one rigid standard for achievement instead of acknowledging and nurturing human beings' infinitely diverse, creative capacities.

2. *Vergara v. California*, backed by wealthy Silicon Valley entrepreneur and founder of Students Matter David Welch, exemplifies this trend. In June 2014, the Superior Court struck down five state laws protecting teacher seniority and tenure. Crassly comparing the case to *Brown v. Board of Education*, the judge held that such laws keep incompetent teachers in the classroom and violate students' civil rights. *Vergara* is part of a wide net cast by anti-union, anti-teacher foundations and think tanks, dominated by donors like Bill Gates and the Koch brothers, all invoking fairness and equality in their hypocritical demands for educational reform.

3. See Stephanie Simon's (2015) "No Profit Left Behind" for a thoroughgoing exposé of Pearson's billion-dollar profits in the United States from textbooks, standardized testing, and (increasingly outsourced in large universities) online education, including a product that allows professors to track the time students spend reading Pearson textbooks.

4. Towson University School of Education Professor and United Opt-Out founder Morna McDermott traces these corporate connections: http://educationalchemy. com/2013/07/25/a-labyrinth-of-corporate-interests-in-common-core/. For a sense of the extent of corporate investment in education, see McKinsey and Company's Breaking the US Growth Impasse at http://www.mckinsey.com/insights/growth /breaking_the_us_growth_impasse. Note the rhetoric under note four: "Fully exploiting the opportunities we have outlined so far will also require business leaders to stretch their thinking and their capabilities. For instance . . . [i]n education, technology companies are seizing on the adoption by 45 states of Common Core Standards—guidelines that create a much larger and less fragmented market for new digital learning tools."

5. LIU's mission statement did not include the word "excellence" until 2002.

6. Exemplifying the ideological force and multiple forms of this attack, newly appointed Goucher College President Jose Antonio Bowen (well-respected for his

innovative ideas about teaching) claims we are now in a "knowledge-rich" era that requires professors to be "cognitive coaches" (Lewin 2014).

7. For information about United Opt-Out, see http://unitedoptout.com.

References

Adams, Peter, Sarah Gearhart, Robert Miller, and Anne Roberts. 2009. "The Accelerated Learning Program: Throwing Open the Gates." *Journal of Basic Writing* 28 (Fall): 50–69.

Bennett, Michael, and Jacqueline Brady. 2012. "A Radical Critique of the Learning Outcomes Assessment Movement." *Radical Teacher* 94 (Fall): 34–47. http://dx.doi.org /10.5406/radicalteacher.94.0034.

Bousquet, Marc. 2008. *How the University Works: Higher Education and the Low-Wage Nation.* New York: New York University Press.

Coleman, David. 2012. "At the Core of the Common Core." NewSchools Venture Fund Summit 2012. http://www.newschools.org/event/summit-2012.

Ehrenreich, Barbara, and John Ehrenreich. 2013. "Death of a Yuppie Dream: The Rise and Fall of the Professional Managerial Class." New York: Rosa Luxemburg Stiftung. http://www.rosalux-nyc.org/wp-content/files_mf/ehrenreich_death_of_a_yuppie _dream90.pdf.

Emery, Kim, and Gerald Graff. 2008. "Outcomes Assessment and Standardization: A Queer Critique [with Reply]." *Profession* 2008 (1): 255–62. http://dx.doi.org/10.1632 /prof.2008.2008.1.255.

"Fact Sheet on the President's Plan to Make College More Affordable: A Better Bargain for the Middle Class." White House Press Release. August 22, 2013.

Harvey, David. 2007. "Neoliberalism as Creative Destruction." *Annals of the American Academy of Political and Social Science* 6 (March): 22–44. http://www.jstor.org/stable /25097888.

Kozol, Jonathan. 1991. *Savage Inequalities: Children in America's Schools.* New York: Broadway Paperbacks.

Krashen, Stephen. 2011. "To Improve Schools, Fight Poverty." Lecture at Institute on Multilingualism, Graduate School of Education, Fordham University, New York, July 7.

Lewin, Tamar. 2014. "A Conversation with Goucher's New President." *New York Times*, October 31. Accessed April 11, 2015. http://www.nytimes.com/2014/11/02 /education/edlife/a-conversation-with-gouchers-new-president.html.

Ohmann, Richard. 2000. "Historical Reflections on Accountability." *Academe Online* 86 (Jan–Feb): 24–29. http://0-www.jstor.org.liucat.lib.liu.edu/stable/40252332. http:// dx.doi.org/10.2307/40252332.

O'Neill, Peggy, Cindy Moore, and Brian Huot. 2009. *A Guide to College Writing Assessment.* Logan: Utah State University Press.

Pew Research Center. 2014. "The Rising Cost of *Not* Going to College." February. http:// www.pewsocialtrends.org/2014/02/11/the-rising-cost-of-not-going-to-college/.

Press, Eyal. 2011. "The Sarkozy-Stiglitz Commission's Quest to Get Beyond GDP." *Nation (New York, N.Y.)*, April 13. Accessed May 5, 2015. http://www.thenation.com/article /159926/sarkozy-stiglitz-commissions-quest-get-beyond-gdp.

Readings, Bill. 1996. *The University in Ruins.* Cambridge, MA: Harvard University Press.

Schell, Eileen. 1998. *Gypsy Academics and Mother-teachers: Gender, Contingent Labor, and Writing Instruction.* Portsmouth, NH: Heinemann-Boynton/Cook.

Scott, Tony. 2004. "Managing Labor and Literacy in the Future of Composition Studies." In *Tenured Bosses and Disposable Teachers*, ed. Marc Bousquet and Tony Scott, 153–64. Carbondale: Southern Illinois University Press.

Scott, Tony, and Lil Brannon. 2013. "Democracy Struggle and the Praxis of Assessment." *College Composition and Communication* 65 (December): 273–98.

"Sense of the House Motion, CCCC 2011." 2011. Council on Basic Writing Blog. https://cbwblog.wordpress.com/2011/04/18/sense-of-the-house-motion-cccc-2011/.

Shaughnessy, Mina P. 1977. *Errors and Expectations: A Guide to the Teacher of Basic Writing.* New York: Oxford University Press.

Simon, Stephanie. 2015. "No Profit Left Behind." *Politico Pro.* February 10. http://www.politico.com/story/2015/02/pearson-education-115026.html.

Stiglitz, Joseph E., Amartya Sen, and Jean-Paul Fitoussi. 2008. "Report by the Commission on the Measurement of Economic Performance and Social Progress." Commission on the Measurement of Economic Performance and Social Progress. http://www.insee.fr/fr/publications-et-services/dossiers_web/stiglitz/doc-commission/RAPPORT_anglais.pdf.

Suskie, Linda. 2009. *Assessing Student Learning: A Common Sense Guide.* San Francisco: John Wiley and Sons.

Treschan, Lazar, and Apurva Mehrotra. 2012. *Unintended Impacts: Fewer Black and Latino Freshmen at CUNY Senior Colleges after the Recession.* New York: Community Service Society of New York; http://b.3cdn.net/nycss/2e01feab246663d4a8_lhm6b94lq.pdf.

US Department of Education, National Center for Education Statistics. 2013. *The Condition of Education 2013. (NCES 2013–037).* Institutional Retention and Graduation Rates for Undergraduate Students.

Welch, Nancy. 2011. "La Langue de Coton: How Neoliberal Language Pulls the Wool over Faculty Governance." *Pedagogy* 11 (3): 545–53. http://dx.doi.org/10.1215/15314200-1302777.

3
FIRST-YEAR COMPOSITION COURSE REDESIGNS
Pedagogical Innovation or Solution to the "Cost Disease"?[1]

Emily J. Isaacs

In "Laptop U," Nathan Heller (2013) asserts that higher education's move toward MOOCs (Massive Open Online Courses) has been driven by a labor efficiency problem. Productivity has increased in many fields—cars are made with lower labor costs today than in the 1950s, for example. For economists William Baumol and William Bowen, the *problem* with higher education is that teaching has become no more efficient. It still takes the same amount of professors to teach the same amount of students, an observation that seems imminently reasonable to those of us who teach. However, Bowen, the former president of Princeton, believes that the "cost disease . . . help[s] explain why the price of education is on a rocket course, with no leveling in sight" (Heller 2013, 84).

Indeed, the ever-increasing cost of higher education alarms us all, though the decision to point the primary finger at labor costs—rather than at, say, declining public dollars (Weerts and Ronca 2006, 2012), or rising expenses for non-academic campus entities and showcase projects as part of an effort to recruit students—is worth much more discussion. This "problem" view runs neatly into a hubris that exists among some of America's elite college professors: the conviction that their intellects are so great that having access to their teaching—even as one of 10,000—is worth more than instruction provided by apparently hum-drum professors at any of the 4,300 non-elite US four-year institutions that offer accredited BA degrees. Echoing the philosophy faculty at San Jose State who publicly rejected Harvard's Professor Michael Sandel's MOOC for their students ("An Open Letter to Professor Michael Sandel from the Philosophy Department at San Jose State U" 2013), MOOC critic Geoff Shullenberger (2013) aptly summarizes the problem with the elite mindset: "Perhaps within the Harvard or Stanford orbit, allowing the

DOI: 10.7330/9781607324454.c003

educationally underprivileged to watch videos of people like you seems like a great gift. But outside of that orbit, there is growing fear that monetized, creditized MOOCs will convert state and community colleges into a homogenized, intellectually impoverished simulacrum of the elite university world, in which courses consist of streaming online videos of celebrity professors combined with a robotic regime of instantly-graded multiple choice tests and software-evaluated essays." MOOCs are like Freire's banking approach to education on steroids.

Although MOOCs are getting the attention and, from most scholars, the critique, in this chapter, prompted by my own campus experience, I am exploring first-year composition course redesign efforts, which have emerged alongside MOOCs in this age of austerity. As a movement, Course Redesign may ultimately be a bigger and longer-lasting movement than the MOOC movement, and because it's quieter, frequently locally grown and not primarily organized by for-profit entities (like MOOCs' Coursera and Udacity), there is reason to hope that financial pressures will be contained, more measured, and less likely to take precedence over what should be bottom-line imperatives for high-quality instruction and rigorous assessment of teaching methodologies. Yet the following investigation of four course redesigns in first-year composition sponsored by Carol Twigg's non-profit National Center for Academic Transformation (NCAT) tempers my hopes and suggests caution is warranted. From this review it seems clear to me that a focus on "the cost disease" has resulted in what I want to call *push assessing* (think: push polling): a reinvigorated focus on grammar and other lower-order concerns, and a procedural, lowest common denominator interpretation of writing as a process.

Course Redesign couples two perennial efforts, one that has inspired our best work and one that has inspired our worst. First, there is the best work—our collective efforts in pedagogical reimagining, inspired by technological possibilities, theoretical advancement, or research (think of Linda Flower's [1994, 2008] pedagogically inspiring work). Second, there is the work of cost-saving, which is perhaps most forcefully and disturbingly represented by ever-rising reliance on adjunct faculty.[2] Nonetheless, Course Redesign is a term that Twigg has coined in reference to an approach that uses "technology to achieve cost savings as well as quality enhancements . . . Redesign projects focus on large-enrollment, introductory courses, which have the potential of impacting significant student numbers and generating substantial cost savings" (NCAT 2014c). At NCAT, Course Redesign has six formats: supplemental, replacement, emporium, fully online, buffet, and the linked workshop model. The best known is likely the emporium model, which began with developmental math at Virginia Tech and which has received some public attention and critique in the popular press (de Vise 2012; Olsen 1999). NCAT—which has received funding from FIPSE, Pew, Luminia, and (representing its biggest investor with $1.8 million) the Gates Foundation—informs its website readers that "the Emporium Model has consistently produced spectacular gains in student learning and impressive reductions in instructional costs" (NCAT 2014a). The emporium model, which Twigg reports resulted in a 77 percent cost reduction (2011), is primarily focused on developmental math instruction.[3]

In the area of writing instruction, NCAT has worked with several institutions on course redesigns that fall under the replacement model, which has limited in-class time and added more time spent online or in computer-equipped labs. Drawing primarily on NCAT's reports from four schools' experiments, and secondarily on the sparse research findings on these experiments that I could locate in peer-reviewed publications, I observe a mixed bag: one of the four schools (Brigham Young University) found that the project was ultimately infeasible, while the other three (Lincoln University in Missouri, Tallahassee Community College, and the University of West Alabama) report improved student writing, retention, and cost savings. As discussed below, beneath this summary report provided by NCAT are some serious questions about the quality of these programs. Notably, in my research review I was only able to find peer-reviewed research on BYU's experiment; for the others, as will be clear in my analysis, we can only read the reports available at NCAT. The short report describes weak assessment—or perhaps the assessments are not reported fully. Either way, what is reported should not give readers confidence in the conclusions that assert both significant cost savings and improved student learning. Successes appear exaggerated or questionable, often due to faulty cause-and-effect reasoning, as when a delivery method is claimed as responsible for basic and unrelated pedagogical improvements or cost savings (e.g., the claim that a university can replace tenure-line faculty with adjunct faculty regardless of delivery method). Limiting my review is the lack of peer review for the presentations of these pedagogical experiments. Through in-house publications at NCAT, interviews and articles in the popular press (New 2013; Panek 2005; Smith and Finney 2007), and articles in *Change: The Magazine of Higher Learning* (Twigg 2011), Twigg makes big claims about the individual and overall cost reductions and learning improvements generated by Course Redesign, but the research is poor. More specifically, as discussed at the end of this chapter, the pilot projects suffer from poor instrument choices, small samples, and a conflation of pedagogical (course method or content) changes with "redesign" alterations that leaves unclear which is responsible for the reported gains.

I have summarized NCAT's presentations of four composition redesigns, relying heavily on what NCAT reports out. As will become apparent, these presentations are fairly limited and focused on reporting gains in efficiency or effectiveness, both of which are often narrowly defined. I attempted to report out on these findings neutrally in the sections entitled "The Plan" and "Results," reserving my commentary for "Brief Analysis" and for the sections that follow my presentation of these four NCAT redesigns. I have also tried hard to be generous with these efforts, and to recognize strengths that exist alongside what most readers will see as clear weaknesses.

UNIVERSITY OF WEST ALABAMA

The Plan: To achieve the redesign, the class size of "Written English," a first-semester first-year composition course, was raised from twenty-five to thirty. The classes were divided into groups of ten who met as a group for an hour with an instructor once a week, and spent the two remaining hours in a computer lab staffed by an adjunct professor or lab assistant who provided support as students worked through "participatory, technology-centered activities such as grammar and mechanics exercises, research, drafting and peer review" (NCAT 2009b). Grammatical and mechanical instruction was online and self-paced, using *The Everyday Writer*'s online exercises and locally created quizzes. The course content was significantly revised, from a traditional modes course that required seven unrevised essays to a four-essay sequence of drafted, revised essays. Readings changed significantly as well—from a novel and a "standard rhetoric reader" to short stories and topical essays from the popular press (NCAT 2009a).

The Findings: Through comparison of two course redesign sections and two traditional sections of Written English, the redesign was reported to be more effective in terms of student writing (as measured by a diagnostic writing prompt assessment and reviews of final essays), retention rates (F rates in redesign sections were 24 percent and 11 percent, compared to an average of 36 percent), and student grammar, though in this last category, means for assessment was not specified (NCAT 2009a). Student satisfaction was also reported to be high. Finally, cost savings appears to have been realized through reducing sections (by raising class size) and through shifting from full-time professors to lecturers, which was anticipated to result in 16-percent savings (NCAT 2009b). Assessment findings appear to be reported publicly through NCAT only.

Brief Analysis: This redesign project has appealing features: the redesign related to reading (away from literature and to nonfiction) are consistent with what many in the field argue for, and the pedagogical decision to make the course into a drafting and revising program is a good move. Reported significant improvements in writing as measured by the post-test are promising. However, since the assessment methods are not detailed even briefly, it is difficult to evaluate this reported result. While it is helpful that the redesign was assessed by directly reading and assessing student writing, providing information to readers about the details of this assessment is necessary for understanding the validity of the claim of improvement. The addition of "Exercise Central," the Bedford/St Martin set of exercises associated with Andrea Lunsford's *The Everyday Writer*, is of unclear value. I can locate no research focused on *Exercise Central*, and the report suggests that this has become a major part of the course. It is reported that "lab sessions were frequently devoted to grammar," (NCAT 2009b), a significant emphasis considering that two of three class meetings were lab sessions. Heavy reliance on direct grammar instruction through exercises and testing remains troublesome given the field's longstanding concern over the effectiveness of direct, decontextualized grammar instruction and the considerable research findings against its effectiveness (see Smith, Cheville and Hillocks 2010 for a recent summary of research).[4] What is also unclear is the basis on which the designers came to the conclusion that grammar skills were "successfully strengthened by frequent use of *The Everyday Writer* grammar exercise program and by instructor-designed quizzes" (NCAT 2009b). Such a finding should be detailed and shared in peer review venues so other researchers and teachers can benefit from it.

LINCOLN UNIVERSITY

The Plan: Lincoln's "Basic English" redesign is part of a partnership between the four-year public universities of Missouri and NCAT that, at this date, has completed eleven redesigns in a variety of subjects. (NCAT 2014b). "Basic English" is a course defined by a specific (low) ACT cut score. Students meet in a computer classroom, and in classes of twenty-five (up from seventeen in the traditional class), an increase that is principally responsible for the reported 32 percent cost savings, and which is realized by "computer-graded software, adding course assistants to share grading/course management duties, and having computer lab assistants . . . in the lab portion of the course" (NCAT 2013). Other significant features of the redesign included updating an "outmoded pedagogy" that relies on "group instruction" and which varied greatly by instructor, and replacing it with a common curricula that was developed by instructors. In addition, a significant grammar component was added through the adoption of Pearson's (n.d.) *MySkillsLab*. *MySkillsLab* appears to have been selected in response to the designers' worries about students' grammatical abilities, teachers' time, and a belief in the learning value of the online instruction provided by the program: "Grammar skills are essential to assign in a developmental English class, but grading these assignments can be overwhelming" (NCAT 2013).

The Findings: The report at NCAT defines Lincoln University's redesign of Basic English as successful, with significant cost reduction (32 percent) and better-aligned grades and curricula (two goals of the redesign) (NCAT 2013). However, a close read of the report suggests that the data was more negative than positive: "It appears that there was some improvement in student learning. Two sets of pre/post-test scores were collected from students, one from a rubric designed in-house and the other from an online diagnostic designed by Pearson publishing. Students in the traditional course showed a 14-point gain on their rubric finals, whereas students in the redesigned course showed a gain of 17 points. *Students in the traditional course showed an 18-point gain on the online diagnostic, whereas students in the redesigned course showed a five-point gain*" (NCAT 2013, emphasis added). Some questions are raised here— while the in-house assessment, presumably based on readers evaluating student writing, indicated stronger writing in the redesign course, the Pearson diagnostic, presumably machine evaluated, indicated that students improved *more* in the traditional course than in the redesign course. In addition, the report notes that while students in the redesign course scored higher in the grammar and mechanics portion, Pearson's own online diagnostic indicated no difference in scores between the traditional and redesign courses. The only clear outcome of the redesign comes in cost savings: the team reports a 32 percent cost decrease through the redesign, which was achieved by a class-size increase that reduced section numbers from twenty-five to ten, along with tenure-track instructors being replaced by non-tenure track instructors and an adjunct professor.

Brief Analysis: As was the case with the redesign at the University of West Alabama, it appears as though the appealing aspects of the redesign could have been implemented independently from the redesign. A positive aspect of this redesign is the move from a lecture format to a studio environment, allowing instructors and undergraduate tutors (dubbed Undergraduate Learning Assistants or ULAs in the report) to work with students as they write. The designers note that the studio "facilitated dialogue between instructors (and sometimes ULAs) and students. . . [and] gave students more personal attention at a time when they needed it most" (NCAT 2013). This is laudable, and the kind of improvement in curricula that we might expect when pedagogical attention is paid to a long-neglected course. More specifically, the traditional course apparently suffered from inconsistency in instruction and assignments, high student absenteeism, and weak class discussion (NCAT 2013), problems that many programs have addressed without increasing class size, employing software-based assessment, or the kind of low-level, decontextualized instruction provided by *MySkillsLab*. Cost savings came primarily from class size increases, the use of undergraduate tutors, and off-loading of some aspects of assessment to *MySkillsLab*. Whether this included responding to papers is not clear, though Pearson does advertise *MySkillsLab*'s capacity to provide "Optional, automatically-graded writing prompts [which can] evaluate a student's writing skills and knowledge, providing scoring and feedback to both the instructor and student" (Pearson). On one hand, if faculty were still responding to and grading papers, then the increase from seventeen to twenty-five students would make this workload unmanageable; on the other hand, if some or all of responding was moved to automation, then students would suffer, as is documented by many researchers (for instance, Herrington and Moran 2001; Moran and Herrington 2012; Ericsson and Haswell 2006). A possible third scenario would be that the workload increase was controlled by the addition of undergraduate tutors, whose contributions the designers cite as most responsible for improvements in student learning. Including upper-level undergraduate students who have had some training in teaching writing, perhaps as part of their English Education preparation, makes some sense to me, though it is hard to imagine that the addition of undergraduate assistants could make up for a class-size increase of eight students. While this redesign has appealing aspects, it comes along with elements that are clearly undesirable—a larger class size, a greater focus on grammar, a questionable delivery model for instruction (*MySkillsLab*), and likely the inclusion of automated feedback. Finally, whether gains (or losses) have occurred in student learning is unclear at best.

TALLAHASSEE COMMUNITY COLLEGE

The Plan: Tallahassee Community College (TCC) redesigned "College Composition" to address problems with a traditional format that included a lot of class time spent "reviewing and re-teaching basic skills," a poor success rate (lower than 60 percent), and adjunct dependence (NCAT 2003d). The redesign aimed to increase consistency across sections by implementing software-based grammar assessment that would lead to individualized learning plans; web-based "interactive tutorials in grammar, mechanics, reading comprehension, and basic research skills" (NCAT 2003d); and online activities that involve interaction among students and between students and instructor. As the designers explain, "By shifting many basic instructional activities that can be readily individualized to the online environment, the in-classroom portion of the class will be redesigned so that students and faculty alike can focus on the writing process and enhance the quality of the learning experience" (NCAT 2003d). The redesign aimed to achieve cost savings by increasing adjunct faculty reliance, going from teaching 36 percent of the sections to 63 percent, and outsourcing tutoring to SMARTHINKING. The plan expected a total savings of 43 percent, a goal that was achieved during implementation.

The Findings: Tallahassee's redesign is presented by NCAT as successful in terms of improved learning (based on a six-point holistic reading of pilot and traditional course final papers), improved retention of redesign students, and cost savings (NCAT 2003d). Student learning was assessed through independent teacher evaluation using the six-point holistic scoring rubric. Students in the redesign achieved significantly higher scores than students in the traditional class. While the assessment would benefit from a larger sample, and a review of more than one essay, this is a significant finding. Students in the redesign passed at a rate of 68.4 percent, a higher rate than students in the traditional class, who passed at a rate of 60.7 percent (NCAT 2014d). The redesign team also included qualitative comments, noting that faculty believed that students were more engaged, responsible, self-sufficient, and better able to collaborate, and that writing center tutors believed students had greater understanding of the writing process. Cost savings came from shifting from tenure-line to adjunct faculty, and reducing use of writing center staff in favor of SMARTTHINKING, albeit at a cost of $33,500 in its first year, a cost that is not reconciled against the 15.2 percent drop of college writing students attendance at the writing center (NCAT 2014d), putting reported cost savings into question.

Reflection: In comparison to the two preceding reports, the TCC redesign is significantly more careful in its planning, reporting, and assessment. The benefits are documented through reasonable methods of assessment. One question I have is whether the designers made appropriate efforts to control variables to allow for reasonable comparisons. For example, were teachers selected for the pilot judged to be similar to those still teaching in the traditional sections, or were "best" teachers given this opportunity? The impact of individual teachers needs to be considered. Another significant problem lies in the pedagogical changes that were made in the redesign. What new factor(s) could be responsible for improved results on student learning or cost savings: Pedagogy and curricula? Faculty type? Use of SMARTTHINKING? Individualized instruction provided by interactive technology? It is crucial for readers to know what elements of the pedagogy were responsible for results before simply stamping approval on the whole enterprise. Finally, the cost-savings discrepancies are important to remember: across the education landscape we see reports of instructional cost savings that do not include the cost of buying, storing, and maintaining these hardware and software purchases.

BRIGHAM YOUNG UNIVERSITY (BYU)

The Plan: BYU's Course Redesign was reported to be motivated by cost savings and persistent problems with consistency due to the high turnover of instructors who mostly consisted of MA students with minimal teaching experience. The redesign of the first-year writing course aimed to provide more individual attention for students, an emphasis on independent learning, greater flexibility in student interactions with teachers, and increased consistency across sections through the sharing of best teacher resources through multi-media materials. Software-based grammar assessments were used to assist students with language usage. Further, BYU planned to increase class size from eighteen to twenty-five students, reduce teacher student contact hours per week from three to one (replacing some of those hours with mandatory teacher-student conference hours), and increase peer-tutor availability. As implemented, the plan was modified as follows: class sizes were increased to twenty-one students per section and course contact hours were reduced to 1.5 rather than 1 hour per week. In other words, the designers cut back on planned labor reductions (NCAT 2003a).

The Findings: BYU had initially predicted a savings of 40 percent after the redesign, but, in practice, according to the NCAT reports, the changes only yielded a 15 percent savings, reflecting previously mentioned design changes (NCAT 2003b). In terms of student writing, BYU's comparative assessments revealed various results, with somewhat different reports at the NCAT site, and a published article by BYU's Waddoups, Hatch, and Butterworth (2003)—differences that are likely due to being written at different points during the pilot project. Both reports suggest careful assessment, with mixed methods that include the following elements to compare the redesign and traditional courses: comparative reading of student writing, student surveys, teacher interviews, focus groups, course completion rates, and student grades. The NCAT study reports mixed results, and ultimately concludes that "a longitudinal study of successive implementations of the redesigned course suggested that student performance improved in some aspects of writing . . . but not in others" (NCAT 2003c). In addition, the designers report ongoing challenges with training and engaging faculty, particularly in respect to using the multimedia materials. On the other hand, Waddoups and colleagues' published article reports that the papers in the redesign course had a higher average score, at a 95 percent confidence interval (277). Ultimately, while Waddoups, Hatch, and Butterworth express concerns and offer recommendations, they conclude that "students performed as well in the blended course as in the traditional course" (278). BYU has since ended its involvement with NCAT.

Reflection: This redesign is the most modest in its cost savings, likely because there was not such a drastic increase in class size nor were other labor "efficiencies" implemented. It also has the most fulsome and promising assessment. Notably, this redesign does not include automated reading of and response to essays and has little emphasis on computerized grammar or other instruction. Ultimately even the multimedia support systems that BYU had initially been so invested in, and had spent so much time developing and training faculty for, weren't put to widespread, consistent, or effective use. They explain: "We have come to accept that training of instructors is a much bigger contributor to the success of this project than the design itself" (NCAT 2003a). Further, in reflecting on what worked best, the designer reports student/instructor interactions, highlighting the high value students placed on conferences and class time.

By presenting research on BYU's experimentation and assessment in a peer-reviewed venue, readers are able to gain more insights into the procedures and the assessment details. I have one question about the assessment, or at least the reporting of it. Waddoups and colleagues report that the redesigned course had two experienced instructors, but they do not provide further detail about instructors' levels of experience. If the designers did not make efforts to neutralize the effect of teacher experience or record of classroom success, the comparative assessment would be flawed. Perhaps most interesting of all is a finding from outside of these two reports: today BYU has abandoned the project and teaches first-year composition in a traditional format: "after this study, and after it dawned on all of [the designers] that they'd need to create an online curriculum—essentially an entire online semester course—they quit. We're back to the 3-a-week bricks-and-mortar model for Writing 150, and we're happy with it" (Jackson 2014).

As should be clear, I think the accomplishments of redesign efforts sponsored by NCAT are overstated in terms of student learning and cost savings, and they often ignore important considerations for the human beings who teach and learn at our schools. Central to my critique are what I consider to be low standards for assessment. Redesign efforts include many variables, but they are not assessed discretely. Because the assessments do not distinguish among various redesign elements plus changes in pedagogy, it is very difficult to know which design elements are most effective. Most prominent among these is the issue of faculty: who is participating in the redesigns? Who is not? Assessment instruments themselves vary, as do sample sizes and the range of documents reviewed. What is good writing varies vastly by the rhetorical situation. Cost-savings reports strike me as loose: sometimes the cost of the third-party computer program was included, but often it wasn't; the cost of preparing and maintaining labs appears to have been excluded as well. Start-up costs (from foundations and private money), ongoing expenses for technology (frequently from expensive for-profit entities), and technologists must be compared to the incredibly low cost that institutions incur through staffing first-year composition programs currently. As a movement, Course Redesign is about pedagogical innovation, online instruction, and cost savings; in our world these things have value, but not at the expense of teaching writing as best as we are able for the real students who come into our classes and schools.

Technology has a place in our pedagogical discussions and should not be feared. At my institution, the first-year composition program is in the midst of a three-year pilot project for the "Writing Studio," a program still evolving, but one which essentially offers a mixture of in-person discussions, workshops, and writing center-type activities and off-site online and independent activities to provide an experience that gives students independence and flexibility. I am not reporting on it here because it's too early to do so. My colleagues who are designing and teaching in the project are still revising their designs and, as the lead assessor, I don't have enough information yet. I wish Carol Twigg would likewise collect more data and be more careful in presenting successes based on brief assessments that appear to be designed to prove her mission. It may be that such an approach would require training in, or at least a commitment to, established educational research methodologies, neither of which is evident from Twigg's biography. Nonetheless, NCAT and other entities involved in Course Redesign experiments need to demand higher quality assessment programs. As faculty, we need to take a cautious, measured, and responsible response to the grant opportunities and even the internal rewards that Course Redesigns appear to offer; we must insist on independent, high-quality assessment, and reporting of results—good or bad—in peer-review venues.

Written for the popular press, Nathan Heller's "Laptop U" helped me see how seemingly limitless faith in educational technology and a fairly low opinion of the average college teacher have dovetailed with rising costs in higher education and powerful voices who point to ground-level teachers (not tech directors or super profs) as the out-of-control bacteria in the cost disease afflicting higher education. Beyond an increase in adjuncts and class size, what we see in the "redesign" of composition is an untheorized and untested return to grammar instruction simply because grammar drills provide students with something to do while a teacher attempts to work with one of the class's twenty-five or thirty writers—or even because there may be no teacher in the room at all.

Notes

1. I thank Zachary Rosenblum, a graduate assistant at Montclair State University, who helped with the research and editing of this article.
2. Thanks to the WPA (Writing Program Administration) listserv and Peggy O'Neill and Rich Haswell who mentioned Peter Elbow's "yogurt model" as a precursor redesign effort; also, Nick Carbone (2013) who cites our shared experience in the 1980s teaching at the University of Massachusetts' new "computer lab" and instructor suite, which was designed by Charlie Moran and Marcia Curtis and which "helped move students to do more writing, talking via writing and via vo[i]ce, and collaborating."
3. NCAT is not the only player in the redesign movement, but it has given significant attention to writing and Carol Twigg is a prominent and influential figure in higher education. In 2010, fastcompany.com included Twigg in their list of most creative people (in any field); a 2013 *Chronicle* article features her and NCAT as an "Idea Maker" and a 2013 "Tech Innovator" (New). NCAT is frequently cited or featured in the higher education and mainstream press, and Twigg herself has testified before congress.
4. Some research, however, supports the practice some research (AbuSeileek 2009; Oates 1981).

References

AbuSeileek, Ali Farhan. 2009. "The Effect of Using an Online-Based Course on the Learning of Grammar Inductively and Deductively." *ReCALL* 21 (3): 319–36. http://dx.doi.org/10.1017/S095834400999005X.

Carbone, Nick. 2013. "Re: The Writing 'Emporium' Model—A Class that Is Not a Class . . ." WPA List Serv, March 4.

de Vise, Daniel. 2012. "At Virginia Tech, Computers Solve Math-Class Problem." *The Washington Post*, April 23.

Ericsson, Patricia Freitag, and Richard Haswell. 2006. *Machine Scoring of Student Essays: Truth and Consequences*. Logan: Utah State University Press.

Flower, Linda. 1994. *The Construction of Negotiated Meaning: A Social Cognitive Theory of Writing*. Carbondale: Southern Illinois University Press.

Flower, Linda. 2008. *Community Literacy and the Rhetoric of Public Engagement*. Carbondale: Southern Illinois University Press.

Heller, Nathan. 2013. "Laptop U." *New Yorker*, May 20, 80–91.

Herrington, Anne, and Charles Moran. 2001. "What Happens When Machines Read Our Students' Writing?" *College English* 63 (4): 480–99. http://dx.doi.org/10.2307/378891.

Jackson, Brian. 2014. E-mail to author. "Re: trait rubric." June 6.

Moran, Charles, and Anne Herrington. 2012. "Writing to a Machine is Not Writing At All." In *Writing Assessment in the 21st Century: Essays in Honor of Edward M. White*, ed. Norbert Eliot and Les Perelman, 219–32. Creskill, NJ: Hampton Press.

NCAT. 2003a. "Round 3 Grant Awards: Brigham Young University." National Center for Academic Transformation. http://www.thencat.org/PCR/R3/BYU/BYU_Plan.htm.

NCAT. 2003b. "Round 3 Grant Awards: Brigham Young University: Impact on Cost Savings." The National Center for Academic Transformation. http://www.thencat.org/PCR/R3/BYU/BYU_FR2.htm.

NCAT. 2003c. "Round 3 Grant Awards: Brigham Young University: Impact on Students." National Center for Academic Transformation. http://www.thencat.org/PCR/R3/BYU/BYU_FR1.htm.

NCAT. 2003d. "Round 3 Grand Awards: Tallahassee Community College." National Center for Academic Transformation. http://www.thencat.org/PCR/R3/TCC/TCC_Plan.htm.

NCAT. 2009a. "C2R—University of West Alabama." National Center for Academic Transformation. http://www.thencat.org/RedesignAlliance/C2R/R2/UWA_Abstract.htm.

NCAT. 2009b. "Colleagues Committed to Redesign (C2R): University of West Alabama." The National Center for Academic Transformation. http://www.thencat.org/RedesignAlliance/C2R/R2/UWA_Abstract.htm.

NCAT. 2013. "Missouri Course Redesign Initiative: Lincoln University." National Center for Academic Transformation. http://www.thencat.org/States/MO/Abstracts/LU%20English_Abstract.html.

NCAT. 2014a. "How to Redesign a College-Level or Developmental Math Course Using the Emporium Model." The National Center for Academic Transformation. http://www.thencat.org/RedMathematics.htm.

NCAT. 2014b. "Missouri Course Redesign Initiative (2010–2013)." National Center for Academic Transformation. http://www.thencat.org/States/MO.html.

NCAT. 2014c. "Programs in Course Redesign (PCR)." The National Center for Academic Transformation. www.thencat.org.

NCAT. 2014d. "Round 3 Grant Awards: Tallahassee Community." The National Center for Academic Transformation. http://www.thencat.org/PCR/R3/TCC/TCC_Overview.htm.

New, Jake. 2013. "Fighting to Reinvent Teaching and Keep Costs Down." *Chronicle of Higher Education*, April 29. http://chronicle.com/article/Fighting-to-Reinvent-Teaching/138779/.

Oates, William, and the Urbana Language Learning Lab Illinois University. 1981. "An Evaluation of Computer-Assisted Instruction for English Grammar Review." *Studies in Language Learning* 3 (1): 193–200.

Olsen, Florence. 1999. "The Promise and Problems of a New Way of Teaching Math." *Chronicle of Higher Education*, A31–A33, A31.

"An Open Letter to Professor Michael Sandel from the Philosophy Department at San Jose State U." 2013. *Chronicle of Higher Education*, May 2. http://chronicle.com/article/The-Document-Open-Letter-From/138937/.

Panek, Richard. 2005. "101 Redefined." *New York Times*, January 16.

Pearson. n.d. "MySkillsLab: Features." Pearson Higher Ed. pearsonmylabandmastering.com.

Shullenberger, Geoff. 2013. "The New MOOC Strategy: Rise of the Higher Ed Empires." *Dissent: A Quarterly of Politics and Culture*, August 7. http://www.dissentmagazine.org/online_articles/the-new-mooc-strategy-rise-of-the-higher-ed-empires.

Smith, Michael W., Julie Cheville, and George Hillocks Jr. 2010. "'I Guess I'd Better Watch My English': Grammars and the Teaching of the English Language Arts." In *Handbook of Writing Research*, ed. Charles A. MacArthur, Steve Graham, and Jill Fitzgerald, 263–74. New York: The Guilford Press.

Smith, Virginia B., and Joni E. Finney. 2007. *"Increasing Learning, Lowering Costs: An Interview with Carol A. Twigg." Change: The Magazine of Higher Learning.* May–June.

Twigg, Carol A. 2011. "The Math Emporium: Higher Education's Silver Bullet." *Change: The Magazine of Higher Learning*, January 1, 25–34. http://dx.doi.org/10.1080/00091383.2011.569241.

Waddoups, Gregory L., Gary L. Hatch, and Samantha Butterworth. 2003. "CASE 5 Blended Teaching and Learning in a First-Year Composition Course." *Quarterly Review of Distance Education* 4 (3): 271–8.

Weerts, David J., and Justin M. Ronca. 2006. "Examining Differences in State Support for Higher Education: A Comparative Study of State Appropriations for Research I Universities." *Journal of Higher Education* 77 (6): 935–67. http://dx.doi.org/10.1353/jhe.2006.0054.

Weerts, David J., and Justin M. Ronca. 2012. "Understanding Differences in State Support for Higher Education Across States, Sectors, and Institutions: A Longitudinal Study." *Journal of Higher Education* 83 (2): 155–85. http://dx.doi.org/10.1353/jhe.2012.0012.

4
WHO'S COMING TO THE COMPOSITION CLASSROOM?
K–12 Writing in and outside the Context of Common Core State Standards

Marcelle M. Haddix and Brandi Williams

In this chapter, we explore what Common Core State Standards (CCSS) mean for K–12 teachers of writing and their learners. And, by extension, we discuss how CCSS shapes and impacts the writing of students entering college-level composition classrooms and what this means for college composition instructors. The CCSS writing standards place a strong focus on instructing students on three specific writing types: arguments, informative/explanatory texts, and narratives that are richly intertwined with research standards. The problem is not the emphasis on these three writing styles, but the de-emphasis on other writing styles that may allow for a more creative expression that youths experience through digital and other media outside of school spaces. This tension between institutionally sanctioned and unsanctioned literacies will be examined and discussed in this chapter. Specifically, we will juxtapose student writing in the context of CCSS with the kinds of writing that young people are authoring outside of school by citing examples from a local writing project for urban youth, *Writing Our Lives*. The point of this juxtaposition is not to put youth's out-of-school writing practices in direct contest with the kinds of writing practices dictated by CCSS in school spaces, but rather to emphasize the importance of moving beyond the traditional and perfunctory writing tasks oftentimes assigned in schools to make space for and legitimize the kinds of writing that are self-sanctioned by youth writers and that represent authentic purposes and interests.

DOI: 10.7330/9781607324454.c004

WRITING OUR LIVES: A MODEL FOR
SUPPORTING OUT-OF-SCHOOL WRITING

It's Saturday morning, and the final table has been set, the sign-in sheets are ready, and the volunteer workshop facilitators are in place. One by one youth, parents, local teachers, and university students come flooding into a local high school for a day of writing, creating, and sharing. This is not an extra-credit program or a financially binding educational weekend supplement. This is *Writing Our Lives*, an annual program set in place since 2009 "as a response to parents who are concerned about their students' reading and writing abilities" (Angrand 2012). The *Writing Our Lives* program is a direct response to the desires and needs of the community—a call for more opportunities for young people to write in authentic ways and to develop identities as writers.

Also informed by research on effective writing instruction for youth writers (Applebee and Langer, 2013) and on spaces for youth participatory literacy practices (Haddix and Sealey-Ruiz, 2012; Kinloch 2009), the *Writing Our Lives* program

- focuses on how urban youth writers define, understand, challenge, and use writing in and out-of their secondary and post-secondary schooled lives
- begins to theorize ways twenty-first century tools and technologies can be used to promote the writing identity of urban youth writers;
- accesses the voices of students often ignored as active agents in their own learning
- encourages, celebrates, and supports the writing of urban youth writers as critical ethnographers of their own writing lives
- provides opportunities for participants to be leaders of writing instruction for themselves, teachers, peers, and members of the community

Each year, new and returning participants come together to learn about and try different writing genres and to engage in writing practices that they feel are not always valued and affirmed in school spaces. As one participant shared, "In school you kinda contradict yourself and you kinda like, you know, cover up some stuff, like you kind of hide yourself in school but when you're outside of school, it's like you open yourself up. You unfold everything." *Writing Our Lives* becomes a space for youth writers to come out and be known as writers. This is especially evidenced at the end of each event when participants are asked to "take the mic" and share their compositions.

The *Writing Our Lives* program has connected students, artists, poets, and volunteers from the local community and school district to offer a writing space for youth in grades 6–12. Every year about ten workshops, depending on the amount of volunteers, are created to engage students in multiple forms of writing. Students are able to choose two fifty-minute writing workshops, selecting from topics such as poetry, comics and illustration, political writing, academic writing, fiction writing, self-reflection, graphic novels, and digital composing, as well as a collaborative writing workshop for students and guardians/parents. All of the workshops push students to tap into their critical literacies to uncover their voices, writing styles, and abilities to collaborate with peers on writing exercises that are not traditionally found within a classroom setting. Another important aspect of *Writing Our Lives* is the significant space and time that is given for the construction of an original piece of writing based on the topic of the workshop.

After the two workshops a free lunch is provided, catered by a local restaurant, and the participants are given a space to share their written pieces with the collective, as well as hear from professional spoken word artists from the community. Young writers and volunteers receive affirmation and leave inspired, and in many cases wanting more opportunities such as this one. Past themes include "FREE Writing," "Youth Lives Matter," and "21st Century Youth Writers, Activism, and Civic Engagement."

The student turn-out and written compositions produced at these conferences have awed not only the parents and teachers who come to support the youth, but the youth themselves as they come face to face with the realization and confirmation that they are indeed writers and are capable of merging their outside-of-school authoring skills with academic writing within a school environment. This is but one example of an out-of-school program that has created a space for teachers, families, and students to be allies in re-opening the purposes of education and writing as a way to combat the ever narrowing initiatives from the Department of Education, the CCSS, and education reformers.

K–12 WRITING IN A CCSS-DRIVEN CONTEXT

The kinds of writing that occur in contexts like *Writing Our Lives* are distinct from the kinds of writing that students are being mandated to author by CCSS. In *Writing Our Lives*, students are encouraged to use their digitally and manually authored pieces and skills without being confined to a specified one-size-fits-all model of writing. In *Writing Our Lives*, students are presumed as competent writers; they are seen as youth writers. In many K–12 contexts where curricular and pedagogical choices are guided by CCSS, student writers often do not have the time or space to author texts with breadth and depth afforded by flexing their writing skills. They are often instructed to produce writing that characterizes them as either competent or incompetent according to the standardized and timed testing measure. In addition, this fixed manner of valuing academic writing does not allow students to approach developing writing skills outside of an academic test preparation atmosphere, leaving some students "stunted" in their writing experiences and development.

The CCSS now requires that K–12 writing be focused on three specific forms: the informative/explanatory text, narratives, and opinion pieces from K–5 and then argumentative pieces from sixth to twelfth grade (National Governors Association Center for Best Practices and the Council of Chief State School Officers, 2010). What does this mean for K–12 teachers? One of the major changes is that writing is now being viewed as a demonstration of learning: writing is infused with textual support that displays the information the student has gathered about a given topic. In addition, teachers across content areas will be held responsible for teaching writing.[1]

Graham and Harris (2013) have compiled a thorough review of the CCSS with specific attention to writing in general and the impact on students with learning disabilities that provides insight on what the CCSS means for K–12 teachers and their learners. The challenges that Graham and Harris uncovered came from examining national surveys designed to capture what writing instruction looks like in classes and schools. The surveys found that elementary teachers only spent twenty to twenty-five minutes a day writing text; little instruction in writing happened after third grade; grades 4–6 only had fifteen minutes a day to teach writing; and while writing was taught in the secondary grades, it was infrequent (Cutler and Graham, 2008; Gilbert and Graham, 2010; Kiuhara et al., 2009). Teachers reported that a challenge CCSS presented to them was their lack of preparedness to teach writing (Gilbert and Graham, 2010; Kiuhara et al., 2009); in another survey, teachers reported feeling unprepared to integrate literacy and technology into their classrooms (Hutchinson and Reinking 2011).

The CCSS writing benchmarks indicate that students will have a mastery of a variety of writing skills (handwriting, spelling, typing, and good vocabulary choice), processes (planning, editing, revising), and digital tools. Yet these benchmarks, Graham and Harris (2013) caution, are

> educated guesses as to what students should be able to achieve at particular grades . . . these benchmarks lack precision and accuracy, and encourage a belief that the same standards are appropriate for all students at each grade. We contend that this viewpoint is misguided, as some

standards will be too hard and others too easy, depending upon the veracity of the benchmark and the competence of the student. (31)

Other concerns included the vagueness of some of the benchmarks (spelling and strategies for writing process from grade to grade) and the challenges that students with learning disabilities may face, such as the lack of emphasis on handwriting past first grade, motivation, sentence construction, and fluency (Troia and Olinghouse, 2013). Overall Graham and Harris (2013) emphasize the need for teachers to understand how writing develops and what contributes to its development in order to properly implement the roadmap of the CCSS.

Outcomes will also depend on when students are introduced to CCSS. Those students who are currently in the K–8th grades will have more opportunities to practice the strategies that teachers and schools are putting together to meet the benchmark standards, and have more opportunity to show gains or declines in ability to meet the standards. Those students who are already in the secondary grades, and quite possibly those in middle school, have a shorter period of time to readjust how they interact with and understand writing in an academic environment. Many of these students have had minimal writing instruction in their English language arts classes, and even less in their content area courses (Applebee and Langer, 2011).

WRITING BEYOND THE CCSS

In contrast with the kinds of writing happening in K-12 settings, the *Writing Our Lives* program not only provides an extended period of time to develop ideas and write but also deemphasizes a hierarchical mode of writing where one genre is preferred over another. In fact, the participants in *Writing Our Lives* get to interact with the academic writing genres in more authentic ways because they are being asked to produce their own self-sanctioned writing and connect it with their community and events that are important in their lives, as opposed to being assigned a topic by a third party and being asked to write in a manner that may not reflect the student as a writer, but more as a trained student. *Writing Our Lives* facilitators implement strategies that are supported by research on writing instruction (Applebee and Langer, 2013; Newkirk and Kent, 2007), yet this kind of instruction is happening outside the regular school day.

In contrast with the CCSS emphasis, the writing experiences that are encouraged in this program extend beyond using digital composing tools, like word processing, to write on demand or to respond in perfunctory ways to school-sanctioned writing prompts. Students are first and foremost considered authors in every composing endeavor, from texting, to social media discourse interactions, to the written and visually produced blogs that they create. All of these methods of expression are acknowledged and validated as authentic forms of writing. From this standpoint each facilitator is able to guide the students through a process of using their writers' voices and mediums they have outside of the classroom, and by extension, supporting the academic writing skills needed for writing in school.

CCSS largely impacts the teaching and learning culture in schools that are cited as being underperforming and that serve a majority of students from working class communities and communities of color. As a result, the CCSS's emphasis on a narrow set of writing genres, purposes, and audiences works to exclude and devalue the literacies and voices of young writers from those communities. This is critical given the articulated commitments of both K–12 and higher education contexts to both cultivate and retain racial, ethnic, and linguistic diversity and to provide access to better educational opportunities for marginalized populations. Given the disconnect between curricular goals at the K–12 level and in composition classrooms, the groups most impacted are student writers from working class communities and communities of color. That is, the implementation of CCSS in ways that are devoid of student interests and used to standardize learning is common in schools that are designated as persistently low achieving, where there is significant emphasis on raising test scores. So, those students who benefit greatly from and who desire opportunities to compose in authentic and creative ways are limited to writing instruction and practice with end goals of preparing them for the test. While they cannot alone diminish the gaps that persist for so many youth writers, programs like *Writing Our Lives* can intercede in a student's post-secondary trajectory and increase the likelihood that a student will excel in college-level writing.

HOW CCSS DOES AND DOESN'T PREPARE
COLLEGE-READY WRITERS

The CCSS provides a new context for K–12 schools and requires teachers across content areas to rethink how they teach students to write. The CCSS expects that students will write more, yet research findings suggest that students still have limited opportunities to engage in extended writing projects in multiple genres and for diverse purposes (Applebee and Langer, 2013). Instead, students are more likely to compose on-demand literary analysis in preparation for state examinations. Young people need more writing instruction, not less. More often than not, however, local, state, and federal policies hinder the likelihood for this to occur.

The students who will be entering into college will need writing support that allows them to grow as writers beyond the CCSS writing standards. This support will be needed in each course that the student pursues, in addition to out-of-class support given by writing centers and other institutional resources. Such support can encourage students to tap into more creative and expansive ways to communicate their thoughts and experiences in addition to what information they have learned. Writing could take various forms at the collegiate and K–12 levels that can range from poetic works, fan fiction, free form, journaling, and scripts to creative non-fiction. It is important not to limit students by placing a higher value in academics on particular modes (narrative, informative/explanatory, and argumentative) because it restricts the definition of writing and, for students, suggests that writing is limited to one form or one process. This practice undermines and renders invisible the multiple literacies and ways of composing that are available to young writers.

If students are being indoctrinated into a standards system that intentionally displays that it values one form, or in this case three forms, of writing, then students may believe that any writing that falls outside of this spectrum is not considered writing; and by extension, their taking on of the identities of being "writers" or "non-writers" is determined by their success, or lack of, within this spectrum. The cycle may have damaging effects on students' confidence in their writing abilities. Yet, participation among youth in social media environments continues to increase (Sadauskas, Byrne, and Atkinson, 2013). These non-academic spaces provide online environments where students are "writing their lives," sharing experiences, engaging in debates (some supported by text-based evidence), and receiving feedback from peers and followers. While this is indeed writing, it is regarded by many youth as socializing that is not welcome in the classroom.

Both K–12 teachers and college composition instructors must consider how the new context of the CCSS impacts the student writers who enter our classrooms. If writing instruction continues to emphasize on-demand literary analysis in preparation for state examinations, student writers will experience a stark and sudden shift upon entering the college classroom where other genres and styles of writing may be privileged. Because of the demands placed on K–12 teachers to support students' success on standardized assessments, there may be limited opportunities to engage in extended writing projects in multiple genres and for diverse purposes within the school context. This reality makes it even more critical that young peoples' out-of-school writing literacies are valued and encouraged, as evidenced in programs like *Writing Our Lives*. Given the new generation of youth writers being educated in this era of CCSS, it is imperative that K–12 teachers and college composition instructions engage in constant conversations about effective ways to best support the development of life-long learners and writers.

Note

1.   Before the CCSS, writing instruction would primarily be the responsibility of the English language arts instructors; however, research has shown that English language arts or English classrooms do not spend much time on writing (Applebee and Langer, 2011; Gilbert and Graham, 2010; Kiuhara, Graham, and Hawken, 2009).

References

Angrand, Ruthnie. 2012. "Writing Our Lives Gives Voice." *The Stand*, November 5. http://mysouthsidestand.com/more-news/writing-our-lives-gives-voice/.

Applebee, Arthur N., and Judith A. Langer. 2011. "A Snapshot of Writing Instruction in Middle and High Schools." *English Journal* 100 (6): 14–27.

Applebee, Arthur N., and Judith A. Langer. 2013. *Writing Instruction that Works: Proven Methods for Middle and High School Classrooms*. New York: Teachers College Press.

Cutler, Laura, and Steve Graham. 2008. "Primary Grade Writing Instruction: A National survey." *Journal of Educational Psychology* 100 (4): 907–19. http://dx.doi.org/10.1037/a0012656.

Gilbert, Jennifer, and Steve Graham. 2010. "Teaching Writing to Elementary Students in Grades 4 to 6: A National Survey." *Elementary School Journal* 110 (4): 494–518. http://dx.doi.org/10.1086/651193.

Graham, Steve, and Karen R. Harris. 2013. "Common Core Standards, Writing, and Students with LD: Recommendations." *Learning Disabilities Research & Practice* 28 (1): 28–37.

Haddix, Marcelle, and Yolanda Sealey-Ruiz. 2012. "Cultivating Digital and Popular Literacies as Empowering and Emancipatory Acts among Urban Youth." *Journal of Adolescent & Adult Literacy* 56 (3): 189–92. http://dx.doi.org/10.1002/JAAL.00126.

Hutchinson, Amy, and David Reinking. 2011. "Teachers' Perspectives of Integrating Information and Communication Technologies into Literacy Instruction: A National Survey in the United States." *Reading Research Quarterly* 46 (4): 312–33.

Kinloch, Valerie. 2009. *Harlem on Our Minds: Place, Race, and the Literacies of Urban Youth*. New York: Teachers College Press.

Kiuhara, Sharlene A., Steve Graham, and Leanne S. Hawken. 2009. "Teaching Writing to High School Students: A National Survey." *Journal of Educational Psychology* 101 (1): 136–60. http://dx.doi.org/10.1037/a0013097.

National Governors Association Center for Best Practices, and the Council of Chief State School Officers. 2010. "Common Core State Standards English Language Arts Standards." http://www.corestandards.org/wp-content/uploads/ELA_Standards1.pdf.

Newkirk, Thomas, and Richard Kent. 2007. *Teaching the Neglected "R": Rethinking Writing Instruction in Secondary Classrooms*. Portsmouth, NH: Heinemann Press.

Troia, Gary A., and Natalie G. Olinghouse. 2013. "The Common Core State Standards and Evidence-Based Educational Practices: The Case of Writing." *School Psychology Review* 42 (3): 343–57.

Sadauskas, John, Daragh Byrne, and Robert K. Atkinson. 2013. "Toward Social Media Based Writing." In *Proceeding of the 15th International Conference on Human-Computer Interaction-DUXU/HCII 2013, Part two, LNCS 8013*, edited by A. Marcus, 276–85. Las Vegas: Springer.

PART II

Composition in an Austere World

5
THE NATIONAL WRITING PROJECT IN THE AGE OF AUSTERITY

Tom Fox and Elyse Eidman-Aadahl

On March 6, 2011, President Obama signed a budget that ended the National Writing Project's (NWP) twenty-year history of receiving directed federal funds. The move threatened the very existence of the project, its over two hundred local sites, and the professional development that it offered to over a hundred thousand teachers per year. The budget cut was occasioned by the financial crisis of 2008–2012 and the related fiscal austerity measures of the 111th Congress. NWP's adaptation to this event—an ongoing task—provides an illustrative case study of an organization navigating a changing fiscal and ideological landscape of the age of austerity. This story is located in several particular histories: of federal funding, of NWP itself, and of K–12 funding as well. While NWP has continued, the age of austerity brings with it challenges: ideological muddles of simultaneous opportunities and compromises that necessitate rigorous interrogation of the consequences of NWP's fiscal decisions for the sustainability of sites and the network. These conditions, for local sites and for the national office, highlight the importance of maintaining NWP's respect for teachers' knowledge and its goals of supporting equity in education in an environment where opportunities for work often do not value teachers nor support equity.

This chapter contrasts with the others in this volume in that NWP's situation and those of composition programs housed in universities differ significantly. As a non-profit, NWP must choose among available funders, piecing together whatever funding has the potential to sustain the network and further NWP's goals. Each funder, of course, has its own desires and places its own constraints on funding. Composition programs are housed and funded by universities and rarely have multiple funders. While corporate influences on universities certainly constrain

DOI: 10.7330/9781607324454.c005

writing programs, as the contributions to this volume show, the instrumental value of composition in the university ensures their continued existence. Though, on the face of it, NWP may seem to have a greater degree of organizational autonomy because of its non-profit status, this autonomy is disciplined by the kind and amount of funding available. Finally, and most important, unlike composition programs, NWP's very existence is precarious. Though supported by the momentum of a national network with a forty-year history and sustained by a network of human resources located in and drawing strength from a variety of institutional (and geographical) locations, NWP faces the very real prospect of closure and dissolution as an entity. These contrasts are important because the responses to austerity measures by local sites and the national office have consequences, not just for the identity of the organization but for the sustainability of the network of local sites and the thousands of teachers who depend on NWP's professional community.

At the same time, though on a larger scale and in a more distributed way, NWP's work to survive the elimination of directed federal funding resembles the work of politically and institutionally savvy writing program administrators, such as those included in *The Writing Program Interrupted* (Strickland and Gunner 2009). Despite their differences, many questions for both writing program administrators and NWP that emerge in the age of austerity are similar. What alliances or partnerships would strengthen the program? What trade-offs would such partnerships entail? What will insure the continued efforts to make education more equitable? What possibilities for resistance or subversion exist? Who is at risk through such acts? And even, perhaps, when to give up and turn attention elsewhere?

THE NATIONAL WRITING PROJECT IN THE
AGE OF DIRECTED FEDERAL FUNDING

Although most compositionists now are familiar with the NWP as a federally funded project, the NWP existed for more than fifteen years without direct federal investment. The project grew from the Bay Area Writing Project in the mid-1970s to an expanding network of sites in the late 1970s and 1980s. Before federal funding, local writing project sites were self-supporting, receiving starter-support through a small National Endowment for the Humanities grant and sustaining support through their host universities. In some cases, sites received funds from their state department of education (in California, Mississippi, and Virginia for instance). Local writing projects were able to earn revenue through professional development contracts with districts and schools, fees from programs attended by individual teachers, funds from local grants, university tuition, and fee-for-service activities in their service area. Sites gathered together annually, and while there wasn't an official national office, there were experienced writing project leaders who supported universities as they started new local sites (McDonald, Buchanon, and Sterling 2004).

In 1991, through the persistent efforts of teachers and professors across the country, NWP was authorized by Congress to receive direct federal funding. Congressional authorization and appropriation made funding available to the US Department of Education to grant to the NWP with the goal of scaling the network and equalizing access to professional learning opportunities for teachers of writing across the country. Federal funding, however, required as a condition of the award the creation of a separately incorporated 501(c)3 to receive and manage the funds. The NWP national office, previously supported by the University of California, Berkeley, became a fully incorporated non-profit with full fiscal authority as well as full responsibility for its own survival.

As funding was appropriated, the national office distributed money to local writing projects and managed the federal renewal, reporting, and review process. After 1991, the award to local sites grew from a modest $10,000 or $15,000 (that sites matched three to one), to a larger and more stabilizing amount. In the final years before directed federal funding was discontinued, the award to each local site averaged $45,000. With the required one-to-one match, this money typically supported the facilitation of a four- or five-week invitational summer institute to develop local leadership for the project, stipends for teachers and professors engaged in project work related to the needs and interests of their region, reassigned time for a professor-director to manage it all, and some change left over for an administrative assistant or special programs. The professional development that the local site provided to schools paid for itself or, in best cases, earned some profit to provide additional programs for teacher leaders so that the site could maintain a strong knowledge base for service to their local communities.

The core goal of this public investment in NWP was the expansion of access, elevation of quality, and deepening of impact. During this same period of direct federal investment, and with the help of privately-funded grants, the national office began to support national programs designed to expand sites' capacities to serve rural and urban schools, support English language learners, build diverse leadership, reach content area teachers, link writing to social action projects, and create a strong presence in digital learning and literacy. In addition, federal dollars supported a broad range of technical assistance for new sites and sites that struggled as well as supporting a cycle of reporting and review designed to maintain the quality of writing project work. At its peak, the national office employed an extensive support staff, compensated teacher leaders and faculty at writing projects for leading national programs and technical assistance activities, and conducted extensive evaluation of program impact. This funding developed a wide range of resources that benefited sites and the profession more broadly, including web-based publications, books, articles, and digital communities. There is significant evidence that federal investment made possible a stronger, more developed and effective network. Both the quality and the reach of the network increased, and data show that the investment produced work at NWP that was equity focused, enacting the best intentions of the historical role of federal investments in education.

Essentially, during the period of direct federal investment the NWP fiscal model was aligned with a growing federal role in education and the tradition of tax-supported public education at both K–12 and higher education levels. The vast majority of host universities were public institutions whose state subsidies allowed for flexible spending beyond tuition-supported classroom instruction, and their expanding state budgets allowed them to invest in their local writing project sites. Writing project sites earned income from schools that drew on district or federal professional development monies or tuition dollars from teachers who often received reimbursement support for graduate courses the writing project offered on behalf of the university. Federal investment in the national network, also public money, was geared toward expanding access and improving quality along the lines of classic theory about the federal role in education.

Tax-supported public education provided the basic fiscal model that grew the NWP and also expanded composition programs and supported composition research over the final decades of the previous century. But as conservative and neoliberal ideas began to spread in the late 1980s and 1990s, the model was increasingly under assault. The resulting legitimacy crisis weakened support for public investment in education several years before the economic crisis of 2008 hit, reducing support for investment in education as a response to austerity.

AUSTERITY BEGINS

As the year broke in 2009, so did the fortunes of middle- and working-class Americans. They lost their houses by the millions, eclipsing even

foreclosures during the Great Depression. And they lost their liveli-
hoods as the economy hemorrhaged nearly two hundred thousand jobs
per week. People of color and the working class suffered the most. The
Great Recession of 2008–2012 produced the widest income gap between
rich and poor in US history and the widest wealth gap between white
and black Americans, where the average white citizen has ten times the
wealth of the average African American.

The recession also profoundly reduced funding in higher education *and* K–12 schools. It's not hard to document this: 328,000 teaching
jobs were lost (Oliff, Mai, and Leachman 2012); funding for education
decreased in thirty states (Leachman and Mai 2014); per pupil spending
on higher education fell by 21 percent (Chakrabarti, Mabutas, and Zafar
2012). Resulting from the reduction in funding was a further reduction
in the autonomy of individual teachers and professors and the schools
and universities they work in. From ballooning class sizes to accountability systems and the onerous proliferation of state and district tests,
teachers' and professors' working contexts became characterized by
limits, as described in the context of social program funding by Thomas
Edsall (2012).

The downturn challenged local writing project sites on multiple
fronts. As a result of lower revenue, state and local coffers emptied and
state support for K–12 and higher education plummeted. Real estate values tanked, and since property taxes make up 44 percent of school funding nationally, local funding for schools dried up and professional development monies disappeared (Cornman 2013). Changes in standards
and assessments added another layer of challenge. Already burdened by
draconian accountability systems from No Child Left Behind (NCLB),
teachers anticipated a brand new set of standards, the Common Core,
adopted by all but a handful of states in late 2009. While these standards may offer teachers more autonomy in creating curriculum, the
old assessments remained the same, so teachers were required to change
their practices to align with the Common Core while still being tested
on NCLB-style measures. At the same time, new laws in several states
tied student achievement to teacher pay and job security. These policy
threats occurred while teachers' spouses lost their jobs and school funding disappeared for even minimal things like pencils or books. Field
trips became out of the question unless funded by bake sales. Salary and
benefit packages were frozen at best; at worst, teachers were furloughed
and retirement funds raided. Local writing projects that typically relied
on three main sources of income—federal funding from NWP, support
from their host university, and income from professional development

contracts—were hard-hit by the unraveling of so many educational segments. By the end of 2009, university support and local school funding, two legs of the three-legged funding stool, were weakened, leaving local sites teetering financially. In 2010, the third leg was about to collapse.

During the election of 2008, one of John McCain's campaign themes was the wastefulness of "earmarks." Earmarking, a process whereby Congress could direct a funding for a particular project, quickly became a symbol of bloated government, the embodiment of pork. McCain lost the election, but earmarks remained on the political table, and the 2010 election of candidates supported by the Tea Party, especially in the House of Representatives, boosted the anti-earmark sentiment as a symbol of commitment to deficit reduction. When, finally, a budget was passed in 2011, most non-military earmarks were banned. Earmarked funding for NWP (traditionally sponsored by Democrat George Miller in the House and Republican Thad Cochran in the Senate), along with all other national literacy programs and programs such as the National Board for Professional Teaching Standards, was cut entirely. For local writing project sites, the third leg of the funding stool was eliminated.

THE AGE OF AUSTERITY COMES TO THE
NATIONAL WRITING PROJECT

The age of austerity had arrived on NWP's doorstep: *$25 million to $0 in the span of three months.* By anyone's definition of the word, NWP's national office and the local sites faced a crisis and some very difficult decisions. At the national office, where federal funding constituted over 90 percent of the total budget and where neither state/local support nor direct tuition payments were possible, the situation was most acute. The national office laid off over two-thirds of the staff, reduced funding promised for sites out of the current budget (without knowing if any more funding would be forthcoming), ceased site support activities except through ad hoc and informal phone calls and email, and ended the national programs that were supported by the federal appropriation. Since NWP's federal funding was designed as *forward* funding, meaning funding in a federal fiscal year supported programming in the next year, the organization had funds in hand from the previous budget year to provide for about a year of scaled-down activity before it faced the necessity of closure. Local sites, for their part, had to figure out how to survive in an economic climate that rivaled the worst times in US history without the prospect of an annual support grant from NWP. In many ways, the historic role of the National Writing Project—to be at the side of teachers, especially in the most desperate of situations in the most needy of schools—was threatened because local sites and the national office no longer had resources to help.

NWP's response to funding conditions brought by fiscal austerity is ongoing. Even though the NWP apocalypse didn't happen, there was far less routine support for local sites from the national office. For the most part, local sites were supported by their universities, who worked with them to reinvent programming, signaling a surprising willingness on the part of universities to support writing projects even during a period of reduced state funding. Sites reworked course credit arrangements, recalculated reassigned time, and started grant writing and fundraising campaigns. Most universities stepped up despite their own financial crises and said, *yes, we do want a writing project*. Teacher and university leaders volunteered their time to keep writing projects going.

At the national level, the organization was required to test and retest emerging models of funding that represent paths that social efforts might take as they move from classic models of liberal tax-supported institutions (think Great Society programs of the 1970s) to now-taken-for-granted elements of neoliberal economic principles. What is NWP learning? As an organization, NWP has had to reposition itself rhetorically in relation to funding opportunities, emphasizing, for instance, expertise in rural education, science writing, technology, or civic education. Receiving two major federal grants and extending partnerships with private foundations has given local sites a modicum of financial stability so they can continue to support teachers and students in their local service areas.

AUSTERITY AND NETWORK CHANGES

NWP's survival of austerity was possible because of a decades-long history. Routines of communication, habits of knowledge-building, existing partnerships with universities and school districts, built up and out during directed federal funding, kept the network going while everyone looked for new sources of support. While this history was important to NWP's continuation, austerity has demanded change in the network as well. Since 2011, sites have had to rely less on the national office and more on each other. For instance, the network of urban sites now is handled by individual sites managing a conference through fees, university support, and, occasionally, commercial sponsors, instead of money from the national office. Other writing projects have transformed or developed yearly conferences, inviting the network to exchange smart and thoughtful ways to implement the Common Core State Standards. There are many other examples.

Another significant change across the network came from invitations for educators to participate in nation-wide conversations and activities that build knowledge around using technology to support learning. For instance, "Educator Innovator" involves educators in maker events, web-making, gaming, coding, Massive Open Online Collaborations around connected learning, and other activities. Thousands of educators participate in these events, networking with each other to build new knowledge and experience new forms of learning and teaching. These activities are funded through a variety of partnerships, including with Mozilla and MacArthur. The technology initiatives build the NWP network more through connecting individual teachers and less by connecting local writing project sites. Networked individuals weren't a sudden response to loss of federal funding; NWP began to build a network of technology-focused teacher leaders as early as 2001. However, the absence of directed federal funding combined with the simultaneous growth and visibility of NWP technology initiatives has highlighted the networking of individuals.

In these ways, the NWP network has shifted to a rhizomatic network structure among and between local writing projects and individual teachers for both funding and knowledge sharing. The consequence of this shift is more connectivity, increased agility, and the ability to switch directions and pull together people and resources quickly. Technology can serve connecting purposes in a network. One of the consequences of work with technology is that approaches to teaching with technology can be profoundly destabilizing, challenging basic assumptions about teachers' roles, students' agencies, and the materiality of writing itself. Such challenges—and the people who revel in them—have the consequence of reformulating and simultaneously stabilizing the network by diversifying the ways that people and writing project sites connect with each other.

ACCOUNTABILITY SHIFTS IN FEDERAL FUNDING

Although the National Writing Project and the vast majority of local sites survived the loss of directed federal funding—an achievement not to be underestimated—a series of conditions and constraints characterize this new environment (Baez 2009; Daza 2012). These include a narrow definition of evidence in evaluation and an increased emphasis on competition. If NWP is to maintain support to local writing projects, it will need to manage these changing conditions and constraints at the federal level. While NWP continues to diversify its funding beyond the federal government, there are few other sources of funding for education large enough to support a national network. For now, US Department of Education grants are key to providing support to local writing projects across all regions of the country. Because supporting local sites is an equity issue, successful federal grant writing remains an important means for NWP to reach teachers of underserved students.

Shifting educational policy over the past two decades has been described in different ways by a variety of scholars (Baez 2009; Daza 2012; Passow 1992). Passow perhaps most straightforwardly described this as a shift from *fiscal accountability* to *educational accountability* (Passow 1992). We would add that since Passow's article, there is another shift, particularly in the current administration, which emphasizes competition. Many, if not most, federal educational programs were originally designed for the purposes of equity and access, traditionally the role of the federal government in education. Title I funding, for instance, was designed to be given to schools where 40 percent of students qualify for free and reduced school lunches. Accountability that accompanied Title I funds needed to show that federal funds were spent on educational programs for low-income students and not on other students, and that the purpose of the funding was honored by the program and the services provided. This is fiscal accountability. When critics began to worry that Title I did not actually improve the education of low-income students, accountability shifted from simply proving that schools spent the money on low-income students to proving that the school's Title I program helped narrow the achievement gap between low- and high- and middle-income students. To measure effectiveness, then, federal funding was tied to *educational accountability*. Educational accountability was understood to require targets more specific than measures of services provided; instead, it would require the development of achievement metrics related to educational outcomes.

Title II funding shifted in similar ways. Title II is the section of the Elementary and Secondary Education Act that provides federal funds for professional development of teachers and principals, the funding sources for much local writing project programming. In the 1980s, the federal indicators of high quality programs accepted teachers' self-reports of improvement and change as evidence of the program quality. Programs had to document numbers of teachers and numbers of hours to demonstrate provision of services and cost effectiveness as part of presenting themselves as high-quality programs. Over time, however, policy makers wanted to know if professional development improved students' achievement. As with the shift in Title I funding, the shifts in Title II funding was from fiscal to educational accountability.

This shift applies to NWP's funding history as well. The stability of the directed funding relied on the commitment of some key senators and representatives and yearly lobbying efforts of teachers and writing project leaders. NWP's authorizing legislation was remarkably simple and did not itself require detailed means of evaluation. Nor did the legislation specify content other than a focus on the improvement of writing, leaving sites open to respond to local needs and priorities. Evaluation measures were not specified in the legislation, allowing the NWP to negotiate changing evaluation requirements with the federal Department of Education itself. The changes from fiscal to educational accountability occurred for NWP before defunding as a part of the ideological shift accompanying No Child Left Behind at the Department of Education. So NWP had to work hard to maintain funding through various evaluation projects in the latter half of the directed funding period. It's important to be clear that the shift toward educational accountability accompanied by strict metrical measures of student outcomes did not apply directly to the national office. NWP is a national non-profit and, strictly speaking, is not "accountable" in the ways that schools and districts are. Local sites felt the shift toward educational accountability much more directly than did the national office.

In the age of austerity, large funding sources seek to scale programs that prove educational gains, and of course, educational gains are the point of professional development programs. The question is what constitutes evidence of gains. The Department of Education grant programs, beginning in the Bush administration with NCLB and accelerating in the Obama administration with Arne Duncan's tenure, focus educational accountability on specific outcomes and require educational programs to provide particular types of evidence for impact. One of Duncan's signature programs, Investing in Innovation (i3), funds initiatives at three levels based on a hierarchy of evidence for program impacts on student achievement. The highest levels are reserved for programs with gains verified through well-conducted randomized control trials, or RCTs. These programs are then added to the What Works Clearinghouse (http://ies.ed.gov/ncee/wwc/), a list of programs recommended to states and districts, as well as private funders.

This growing significance of "evidence-based education" with its preference for RCTs has been associated with the Institute of Education Sciences, founded by Grover J. (Russ) Whitehurst, Assistant Secretary, Educational Research and Improvement for the Department of

Education. Whitehurst promoted the RCT as the "gold standard" for educational research, modeling the approach on agriculture and medicine where RCTs are used in drug trials, for instance. RCTs require scaled measures that are comparable across contexts, typically meaning data are translated into numbers for comparisons. In fact, a limitation of RCTs is that they "can only take a specialized type of evidence as input," input that is typically data translated into numbers (Cartwright 2007).

For writing teachers and researchers, RCTs feel foreign. Scholars in writing studies see language production in general and student writing specifically as highly contextualized social practices. Therefore, scholarship in writing studies typically appreciates the influence of context in contrast to the RCT, which seeks to reduce the influence of context. Although an emphasis on the improvement of student outcomes or student achievement is not unwise, from the perspective of composition scholars, the comparison of writing performance across contexts—to compare teacher with teacher or school with schools—requires contextual information that RCTs cannot accommodate.

In addition to specific definitions of evidence and evaluation, Arne Duncan's Department of Education has emphasized competition more than that of his predecessors. For example, the second of Duncan's signature programs, Race to the Top, required states and districts to compete with each other in hopes of winning much larger grants than were available in previous administrations. This culture of competition has not always been the case in federal education policy. In earlier periods, federal intervention in education focused on equalizing access and funding through desegregation, school busing, and the Elementary and Secondary Education Act, which was part of Lyndon Johnson's portfolio of programs for the War on Poverty in the 1960s. Duncan's programs shift the understanding of equity by prioritizing systemic reform and work in high-need schools. NWP's work funded by the Supporting Effective Educator Development Program of the Department of Education concentrates on work with schools in high-poverty communities.

Taken together, the intent of these policies is to promote equity by assisting "high-need schools and communities" to access "programs that work." This focus on equity, however, is in the context of a strong emphasis on competition for a decreasing pool of resources, as demonstrated by the newest Race to the Top competition, "Race to the Top— Equity and Opportunity." Critics have noted what seems to be a contradiction between competition and equity, between the ideas that there are winners and losers in a race and that money be equally distributed to schools and districts in need (Strauss 2014).

This is the funding world that NWP and NWP sites face, a marketplace of grant opportunities that require specific evaluation measures, ones that may not accurately measure student writing ability. People in the NWP network and in the national office understandably proceed with caution and a set of several concerns in this landscape. Agency for sites and for the organization presents itself as a series of complex questions with constrained choices: should NWP apply for these funds even though it would prefer other means of evaluation? Would teachers and students be better off if NWP did or did not receive the funding? Does this funding source compromise NWP's principles to the extent that it would no longer *be* a writing project? The answers to these questions involve a strategic design of the work promised to the funder and a constant interrogation of the work as it proceeds. This sense of agency, described by Marilyn Cooper as "emergent and enacted" depends on a dialogic relationship with both the funder and the response to the work (Cooper 2011). In this way, NWP retains its sense of itself as an organization that works for the values teachers respect and equity in education. These questions are not new, but as NWP seeks financial stability and continuity in the absence of directed federal funding, they are more urgent.

NWP is not alone in feeling this urgency. Progressive educators from all parts of the system have lost ground in the last forty years, mainly to corporate interests that not only influence funding opportunities but profit from textbooks, programs, and assessments (Kohn 2000). These well-financed interests influence federal policy, state textbook adoptions, assessments, and district-level instructional materials (Davis 2013). As implementation proceeds both of the Common Core and of other newly-designed state standards (because many states have now rejected the Common Core), commercial programs compromise the potential of the standards. NWP's history of customizing professional development, drawing upon teachers' expertise, and co-designing curriculum with teachers and schools is at odds with this environment.

The sense that ordinary people have lost autonomy to "systems"—corporate, educational, governmental, institutional, or other—is a theme in postmodern culture. Educational research and theory reflects this theme, resulting in a variety of studies that document what power is available to ordinary students, teachers, and other educators. These include, as brief examples, Bourdieu and Passeron's generous understanding of cultural capital (Bourdieu and Passeron 1977), Giroux's (1983) resistance studies, new arguments against deficit theories (Ahlquist, Gorski, and Montaño 2011; Gorski 2010), de Certeau's (1984) exploration of tactics, James C. Scott's (1987) explorations of the array of discursive (and non-discursive) "weapons" that Malaysian peasants employ, Gerald Vizenor's (1999) concept of *survivance* and most recently, studies of hacking culture (Coleman 2012; Galloway and Thacker 2007). This set of scholarship emerges from knowledge that human agency finds a way, even in contexts where institutions and policies limit autonomy. In the hands of scholars such as these, neoliberal values, such as opportunism, entrepreneurialism, and innovation are turned upside down into values of subversion, hacking, *la perruque*, and resistance. The skills necessary for survival are primarily rhetorical, articulating an individual's or an organization's own goals and principles within the discursive territory of someone else.

NWP's sense of agency has shifted since the loss of directed federal funding, again, distinguishing its situation from those of composition program in universities. Instead of focusing on a single funding source, NWP interrogates an array of funding sources, each with its own set of constraints and its own set of possibilities, each defining the work in ways to a greater or lesser extent that differ from NWP's own definition. Where funding partnerships can be developed, they are made available to the network and local sites are able to pick and choose among offerings according to their interests. Understanding this environment is not a particularly new concept for any non-profit or for grant-savvy composition scholars, but poses challenges to NWP to retain its identity as an organization: keeping its principles of equity and social justice at the center, and honoring teachers' knowledge about the teaching of writing. As a consequence, NWP, embodying the skills explored by the scholars mentioned above, has been both opportunistic and cautious in seeking funding opportunities on behalf of the network of sites.

There are risks, to be sure: risks that NWP will be defined by measures of student outcomes assessed in ways not supported by the organization; risks that constraints in the manufactured federal marketplace will become so tight that NWP will be ineligible for competition; risks that the exhausting search for dollars year after year will be unsustainable. Working in the age of austerity is *more work*. Austerity has reduced the workforce so there are fewer human resources and increased demand for professional, ethical, and political vigilance. NWP's work in this new era brings with it the intensified vigilance required of a principled organization in times of austerity. Is this work good? Can the organization live with the compromises it entails? Will students and teachers be better off because of this work? Will NWP's work respect teachers and the knowledge they produce? Will NWP be able to continue to support work with teachers and schools in economically poor communities? These questions, and others, guide NWP's work and help local sites and the national office make decisions about programs, funding, and partnerships.

As a networked organization, NWP has been able to reposition itself in a competitive funding environment better than some expected, focusing on the critical elements that maintain some support for local sites around areas deemed critical: local leadership development and work with high-needs schools that off-sets the "rich get richer" nature of market solutions. At the national level and in each individual site there is an equivalent set of tensions over what to invest in from a diminishing pool of resources. While NWP has achieved some financial stability, the organization faces a future where its survival will depend on the skillful management of these tensions. How we all learn to deal with these tensions is both what it means to teach and work in an age of austerity and also a window into whether Edsall's view of an acrimonious zero sum game plays out in local lives as well as in the halls of Congress.

References

Ahlquist, Roberta, Paul C. Gorski, and Theresa Montaño, eds. 2011. *Assault on Kids: How Hyper-Accountability, Corporatization, Deficit Ideology, and Ruby Payne Are Destroying Our Schools.* New York: Peter Lang.

Baez, Benjamin. 2009. *The Politics of Inquiry: Educational Research and the "Culture of Science."* Albany: SUNY Press.

Bourdieu, Pierre, and J. Passeron. 1977. *Reproduction in Education, Society and Culture.* London: Sage.

Cartwright, Nancy. 2007. *Are RCTs the Gold Standard? Technical Report, Contingency and Dissent in Science.* London: Centre for Philosophy of Natural and Social Science.

Chakrabarti, Rajashri, Maricar Mabutas, and Basit Zafar. 2012. "Soaring Tuitions: Are Public Funding Cuts to Blame?" *Liberty Street Economics.* September 19. http://liberty streeteconomics.newyorkfed.org/2012/09/soaring-tuitions-are-public-funding-cuts-to -blame.html#.VAyzpmRdWoM.

Coleman, Gabriella. 2012. *Coding Freedom: The Ethics and Aesthetics of Hacking.* Princeton, NJ: Princeton University Press.

Cooper, Marilyn. 2011. "Rhetorical Agency as Emergent and Enacted." *College Composition and Communication* 62 (3): 420–49.

Cornman, Stephen Q. 2013. *Revenues and Expenditures for Public Elementary and Secondary Schools Districts: School Year 2010–11 (Fiscal Year 2011).* http://nces.ed.gov/pubs2013 /2013342.pdf.

Davis, Michelle R. 2013. "Ed. Companies Exert Public-Policy Influence." *Education Week,* April 22.

Daza, Stephanie Lynn. 2012. "Complicity as Infiltration The (Im)possibilities of Research With/in NSF Engineering Grants in the Age of Neoliberal Scientism." *Qualitative Inquiry* 18 (9): 773–86. http://dx.doi.org/10.1177/1077800412453021.

de Certeau, Michel. 1984. *The Practice of Everyday Life.* Trans. Steven Rendell. Berkeley: University of California Press.

Edsall, Thomas Bryne. 2012. *The Age of Austerity: How Scarcity Will Remake American Politics.* New York: Anchor.

Galloway, Alexander R., and Eugene Thacker. 2007. *The Exploit.* Minneapolis: University of Minnesota Press.

Giroux, Henry A. 1983. "Theories of Reproduction and Resistance in the New Sociology of Education: A Critical Analysis." *Harvard Educational Review* 53 (3): 257–93. http://dx.doi.org/10.17763/haer.53.3.a67x4u33g7682734.

Gorski, Paul C. 2010. *Unlearning Deficit Ideology and the Scornful Gaze: Thoughts on Authenticating the Class Discourse in Education.* http://www.edchange.org/publications/deficit-ideology-scornful-gaze.pdf.

Kohn, Alfie. 2000. *The Case Against Standardized Tests: Raising the Scores, Ruining the Schools.* Portsmouth, NH: Heinemann.

Leachman, Michael, and Chris Mai. 2014. *Most State Funding for Schools Less than Before the Recession.* Washington, DC: National Center on Budget and Policy Priorities.

McDonald, Joseph, Judy Buchanon, and Richard Sterling. 2004. "The National Writing Project: Scaling Up and Scaling Down." In *Expanding the Reach of Educational Reform: Perspectives from Leaders in the Scale Up of Educational Intervention,* ed. Thomas K. Glannan, 81–106. Santa Monica: RAND Cooproration.

Oliff, Phil, Chris Mai, and Michael Leachman. 2012. *New School Year Brings More Cuts in State Funding for Schools.* Washington, DC: Center on Budget and Policy Priorities.

Passow, Henry A. 1992. *Title I ESEA/Chapter I ECIA: A Quarter Century Effort to Provide Educational Equity and Equality.* ERIC 367724.

Scott, James C. 1987. *Weapons of the Weak: Everyday Forms of Peasant Resistance.* New Haven, CT: Yale University Press.

Strauss, Valerie. March 7 2014. "Obama's New Race to the Top Context for 'Equity.'" *The Answer Sheet.* http://www.washingtonpost.com/blogs/answer-sheet/wp/2014/03/07/they-still-dont-get-it-obamas-new-race-to-the-top-contest-for-equity/.

Strickland, Donna, and Jeanne Gunner. 2009. *The Writing Program Interrupted.* Portsmouth, NH: Boynton/Cook.

Vizenor, Gerald. 1999. *Manifest Manners: Narratives on Postindian Survivance.* Lincoln, NE: University of Nebraska Press.

6
OCCUPY BASIC WRITING
Pedagogy in the Wake of Austerity

Susan Naomi Bernstein

EVERY ACADEMIC'S WORST NIGHTMARE

To imagine pedagogy in the wake of austerity, imagine bearing witness to suffering. Imagine the promise of occupying hope for the future by creating ephemeral if imperfect communities that foster hope and connection. This fostering presents a pedagogy of non-attachment. Not detached pedagogy, but unattached—ego surrendered. Educators become united as much as possible with the cause of students in pursuit of education.

The work of this pedagogy began for me long before Occupy Wall Street, through teaching and theorizing the teaching of Basic Writing at the University of Cincinnati and the City University of New York (CUNY). Basic Writing served as a metaphor and material reality for creating a better world through collective responsibility for active and engaged learning, described in Adrienne Rich's recently recovered papers from her experiences in Mina Shaughnessy's SEEK program at CUNY (Reed 2014; Rich 2014).

Yet in higher education—even as colleagues argued that Basic Writing and open admissions were "cash cows" that couldn't be touched—Basic Writing became one of austerity's first victims. CUNY served as one of the early testing sites for corporate and philanthropic grants to "accelerate remediation." My professional identity and personal passions were so deeply intertwined with Basic Writing that when austerity began, hydralike, to make its presence felt, I wrestled with twenty years of hard work seemingly coming to an end. A timeline of these events might resemble the timelines of many others who lost their jobs after the crash of 2008. My personal situation often seemed to call up every academic's worst nightmare. But the details, in the wake of the material realities

DOI: 10.7330/9781607324454.c006

of economic inequality made visible by Occupy, offer a broader, more historical context for understanding job loss. An acquaintance from Queens, a woman who had emigrated from the former Soviet Union, said to me in the midst of it all: "People are living in the streets—in America. Now we can see what we have become."

TIMELINE

2007 In the spring of 2007, representatives of the faculty union at the University of Cincinnati met with the faculty of our successful developmental education program. They told us that if the program was cut (already the rumors were flying), we could not be guaranteed our jobs. The union could neither save us nor fight for us. I was offered a position at CUNY, which I decided to accept.

2008–2009 Just after the crash of October 17, 2008, I received a "letter of concern" regarding my employment at CUNY. In the spring of 2009, the beginning Basic Writing class, to which I had devoted the largest share of my time, was eliminated. Meanwhile, back in Ohio, a dear friend in the developmental program won an award for Tutor of the Year. He was so devoted to the students, and so modest about his own gifts and accomplishments, that I would not find out about this achievement until well after the fact.

2009 In the fall of 2009, CUNY eliminated open admissions at the community colleges, a surprise move which gave New York City high school counselors no time to prepare their students for alternative choices. My tenure-track contract was not renewed, and my initial appeal to the president was denied. Conditions at CUNY remained toxic for Basic Writing, undermined by a severe testing regime that served a gatekeeping function intertwined with race and class. I decided not to appeal my case.

2010 In the next year, CUNY outsourced Basic Writing to staff whose hourly pay was much lower than adjunct pay, not to mention assistant professor salaries. Accelerated classes, funded by corporate sponsors, were offered to first-time enrolled students with test scores that just missed the cutoff for English 101. Everyone else received the regular test-prep courses, with no beginning classes for students who needed additional preparation. In Ohio, the developmental education program, including my friend's writing center, was cut.

2011 In the fall of 2011, I faced a second academic year without employment. That summer, my friend, who had lost his writing center job in Ohio when the developmental program closed, killed himself. The national news spoke of permanent unemployment for people over fifty. On September 17, Occupy Wall Street began an encampment at Zuccotti Park, across the street from the World Trade Center site. I was tired of protests that offered nothing concrete after the rallies were over. I decided to attend a matinee showing of the *The Black Power Mixtape 1967–1975* (2011), a Swedish documentary of the Black Power Movement. I mourned the consequences of decades of eliminating the very social policies that had made my own education possible.

FACING THE HUDSON RIVER

The job interview in Westchester County was a cattle call. Sitting en masse in a large room, we filled out our applications for adjunct positions, while off to the side the interviewers questioned applicants. We could hear every question and every word, and we could hear that the interviewers greeted applicants differently based on age and rank of graduate school. We also could hear that the interviewers did not have standard procedures and that each applicant was asked different questions. "How would you relate to our students?" they demanded of an older gentleman who was dressed in tweeds despite the humidity. "Who's your favorite jazz musician?" they inquired of a very young woman, leaning toward her as if to more fully appreciate her response.

When it was at last my turn for an interview, one of the interviewers offered a rant about the necessity of teaching "skills instead of content." The interviewer decried the "low-level" competence of the students, as well as the students' "low-level" potential for future achievement. Rather than hold back, I offered them the theories and practices that I was working on that summer as I composed the fourth edition of *Teaching Developmental Writing* (Bernstein 2013).

Later I waited nearly alone on a train platform facing the Hudson River, watching a thunderstorm and feeling the spray of rain underneath the platform awning. I tried to imagine my friend not dead. I tried to imagine that he had run off to Atlanta or San Francisco, cities he was interested in but had never visited, cities where he could easily blend in with the crowds. Perhaps he would even show up in New York, which he had never visited either. But these thoughts were fleeting and offered no comfort. I could not feel his presence anywhere in the world. Watching the gray of the Hudson fade into the gray of the sky, I felt the nightmare of that moment encompassed in a line from Yeats: "A terrible beauty is born."

My friend had won recognition for his work as a tutor, but at the time of his death he had been unemployed and underemployed for just over a year. The future that my friend and I had imagined together over the phone seemed to end at the moment of his passing. For the rest of the summer, the mainstream media offered news reports of government budget deficits and still more homilies on the new realities of permanent unemployment. One evening, while watching television evening news, I began to shake uncontrollably. My spouse turned off the television.

My story of austerity might have ended at that point, without a job or the hope of a job, or any other organizing principle, other than unmitigated sorrow. By the time Occupy arrived, I felt my resilience had been tested to its limits and I had found this new movement terribly wanting. As if Occupy could resurrect either my friend or Basic Writing from the dead.

Take a break from writing, my editor suggested. Come back when you feel ready. I was not in any position to refuse her offer.

RESURRECTION CITY

The Occupy Wall Street encampment began in New York City's Zuccotti Park on September 17, 2011, almost two months to the day after my friend's suicide. On September 24, the Occupiers held a demonstration in Union Square. I watched the demonstration unfold in live stream on my laptop, then on the local cable channel New York 1. It was from New York 1 that I learned the police had, without provocation, corralled several young women and then hit them with pepper spray. The women and the movement had responded non-violently. My heart crept up to my throat. In that moment, my reticence and despair took a leap of faith. The next day, I visited the encampment for the first time and began again to shake, this time from unexpected joy.

That day, Sunday, September 25, 2011, I took the subway from Queens to Lower Manhattan, exiting at Cortlandt, a station that had newly reopened after sustaining severe damage from the World Trade Center attacks a decade before. The sound of drums and the humming of a thousand conversations led me to Zuccotti Park, otherwise known as Liberty Square. I found the information table and met a young man who instantly reminded me of my friend, with that same intense hope that another world was possible, that the future would hold moments of awakening that we could not dream of now.

The park easily recalled Resurrection City, the encampment begun by the Poor People's March on Washington the spring after Martin Luther King was assassinated. I was ten years old then, and I knew of Resurrection City only by watching the evening news in the midst of another terrible spring, my mother pregnant and frail with the last of her five children. From the sorrow and the anger that felt inescapable that year, I watched the reports of Resurrection City day after day, hoping for some change that would make my mother's condition easier to bear and that would eradicate the impossible frictions of white segregated schooling.

The racial hatred of ten-year-old white children had been difficult to fathom—and the silence of my teachers even more difficult. "Why don't black people live in our neighborhood?" I had asked at home and at school after Dr. King had died. "Because," adults told me, "people choose where to live, and black people choose not to live here." But I had seen the underserved neighborhoods of Chicago on endless road trips from the near north suburbs to visit grandparents in the south suburbs. I found the adults' explanation incomprehensible. Not until years later would I discover the deliberate policies of redlining and protective covenants and the impact those policies would have not only in shaping my own history but also on future patterns of urban and suburban migration and the uprisings that, throughout my lifetime, have ensued (Wilkerson 2010; Coates 2014).

Resurrection City did not last, but at Occupy I found its reincarnation—a phenomenon that I had never expected to see again. I trembled and wept. The young man working at the information table directed me to the kitchen at the center of the park. "We have food," he said, "and you can find something to drink."

ONE MUST IMAGINE SISYPHUS HAPPY

All autumn I returned to the park, to meditate with Meditation Flash Mob and to take part in mass demonstrations. We meditated behind police barricades with NYPD helicopters buzzing overhead, and each meditation ended with an invocation to those Native Americans who had inhabited the land where we now were sitting. In meditation at Zuccotti, I felt the deepest peace I had ever known.

In time, I would become active in the Women's Circle with Occupy's Consciousness Committee (Writers for the 99% 2012) and would take part in the Free University of NYC and Occupy Sandy. My affinity with the movement came in large part from our diversity. We were a group diverse in age, race, class, sexuality, and political persuasion. In the cross-dressing men I met at Zuccotti, I found another incarnation of my friend. "He would have loved New York," I said to my spouse. "He would have loved Occupy. He could have lived freely here, discovered who he was becoming." But that was not possible now. Somehow those of us that had survived would need to move forward.

Later, when I found enough concentration to return to writing, I expressed gratitude to my editor for her compassion. We spoke about

Troy Davis, whom the state of Georgia, overlooking the many pleas for his innocence and his life, had recently executed. My editor told me that her father was a pastor and she had many times born witness to his work with people in mourning. As we discussed the centrality of race to the book's revision, my editor added another detail: her grandfather was pastor to Daisy Bates when she was head of the Arkansas NAACP and mentor to the Little Rock Nine, the African American students who integrated Central High School in Little Rock. Once more I felt deep affiliation. At the end of 1957, in the vast middle of that critical school year in Little Rock, I was born in a segregated Chicago suburb. Racism and segregation would shape my own schooling and would give rise to the complexity of the work of Basic Writing.

Perhaps the most compelling complexity was the hope of resilience and connection that I found embodied in the work of Occupy Wall Street at Zuccotti Park. So many people had lost so much, but the mainstream media ignored those losses and focused instead on the supposed necessities of austerity. The encampment deconstructed the very notion of austerity's necessity. Occupy Wall Street made our losses visible and also bore witness to suffering.

Albert Camus (1955) writes of the man, Sisyphus, condemned for eternity by the gods to roll a heavy stone up a mountain, only to watch the stone roll down again each time. As the man retrieves the stone, he comes to understand the absurdity of his fate, and this understanding brings the man to a moment of conscious awakening: "He is superior to his fate. He is stronger than his rock." Camus offers this moment of consciousness in the difficult time of the French resistance. Yet this moment also accurately describes my experiences of Occupy Wall Street: "One must imagine Sisyphus happy" (123).

Although there was no empirical evidence for optimism, Occupy Wall Street offered the material reality of what happens when everyday people not only bear witness to suffering but also work together to attempt to ameliorate suffering. Not all of these efforts will bear fruit; the non-hierarchical structure of these efforts proves simultaneously empowering and frustrating. Yet when the sufferer joins with others to acknowledge and to alleviate the situation, she can begin to claim a stake in the future.

Such a structure might appear untenable in an institutional environment focused on outcomes and assessments. Yet for Basic Writing pedagogy, this approach offers possibilities for resilience, recognized so many years ago by Mina Shaughnessy and Adrienne Rich as the worthy, if difficult, work of creating democracy in a war-torn economy. Indeed, as bell hooks (1994) has suggested about feminist scholarship, such work must bring a seemingly marginalized field to the center of discussion.

TIMELINE

2012   By the early summer, I had one job offer: an adjunct position teaching Basic Writing at a small private college's satellite campus in the Bronx. The satellite campus was housed in a repurposed office building between a credit union and an abandoned party store. I was offered a position, the pay very low because the college was tuition dependent, almost as soon as I walked in the door. My spouse, meanwhile, had been laid off from his part-time position and was growing increasingly frail. He found another position in a location that would require an extraordinarily long commute. The week before his job began, he landed in the hospital with lithium poisoning. He was taken off all of his medications, including his psychiatric medications. When Free University began soon after in Madison Square Park, I taught a course called "Writing for Home, School, and Everyday Life." Other writers—a young Occupier, a recent immigrant from the former Yugoslavia, and two black activist poets from Harlem—joined me at a small green table. We read aloud Margaret Walker's poem "I Want to Write" and then wrote our own "I Want to Write" poems. We discussed activism and writing from the heart. My spouse also joined us. He was growing increasingly confused, and we could not find anyone to prescribe his psychiatric medications. A few days after a visit to the emergency psych ward, my spouse received a registered letter telling him he had lost his job. The next evening, the winds and high tide flooding of Hurricane Sandy began in New York City.

PEDAGOGY IN THE WAKE OF AUSTERITY

How does this experience of trauma and collective action translate to Basic Writing classrooms? In terms of theory, we refuse to essentialize our students. Mina Shaughnessy (1977), Adrienne Rich (1995; 2014), Mike Rose (1989), Marilyn Sternglass (1997), Mary Soliday (2002)—all have written of the need to identify what students can do rather than presume who students are. To identify any human being only by the surface features of his or her writing ignores the great potential that human beings bring to the classroom. No human beings are "basic writers." Instead, such human beings are students enrolled in classes called "Basic Writing."

The human beings enrolled in classes called Basic Writing, as human beings anywhere, are people that endure suffering. This suffering, so often invisible to teachers and others, may appear as excessive absences or late, incomplete, or unfinished homework—or it may appear as perfect attendance, stellar participation, and brilliant writing always submitted on the due date. Any human being may have parents or grandparents who face deportation and who need their American-educated multilingual child to translate for them at meetings with Immigration and Customs Enforcement (a.k.a. ICE). She may be a mother to six children who lost her own mother when she was a child. He may be a single man with a job in industry and an undiagnosed cognitive processing difference. She may be a young woman coming of age who lost a parent in Afghanistan or a veteran who lost her fellow soldiers in a firefight in Iraq. He may have survived a hurricane or a tornado or the poisoning of his water by a coal or oil company.

We need, as bell hooks long ago suggested, to teach the students who meet us in our classrooms—not who we think the students are or who we want the students to be, but the actual students. We must treat all students as our intellectual equals. Because all of our students are connected to us—their futures are intertwined with our futures. Rather than claiming "Everyone is a basic writer in some situations," we need to argue that no human being is a basic writer, even as some human beings may benefit from courses called Basic Writing.

The pedagogy that evolves from such a stance is informed by the critical pedagogy of Paulo Freire (1970), Ira Shor (1992), and Henry Giroux (1992)—and also by the feminist rhetorical practices of Jacqueline Jones Royster and Gesa Kirsch, while taking a page from Amy Winans's work in contemplative pedagogy to cultivate critical emotional literacy (Royster and Kirsch 2012; Winans 2012). Such pedagogy also invokes the notion of community—of critical partnerships between teachers and learners to work together in encounters with writing processes and products. I call this pedagogy Action/Mindfulness Research. Action/Mindfulness Research involves principles of non-judgmental awareness, thinking outside the box, whole-body awareness, active group work, extended writing time, and building community inside and outside of the classroom. These principles invite us and the human beings with whom we work to engage trauma that disrupts education and to work actively to shape a future that offers resilience and hope. This chapter serves as one example of this research.

Earlier iterations of this pedagogy evolved in Bronx classrooms where I taught as an adjunct instructor. That year overlapped with the onset and aftermath of Hurricane Sandy and all of us in those classrooms had experienced some aspect of natural disaster, whether it was living without the public transit upon which we depended or losing our homes to the flood. When we returned to school after the missed classes and citywide trauma of Hurricane Sandy, the writers in Basic Writing and I developed a culminating writing project in Action Research/Non-Judgmental Awareness. We created this assignment to offer opportunities for writers who had experienced the storm as material and emotional losses that were difficult to measure in straightforward terms. Materially, we had endured the losses of home, water, electricity, cable, and Internet. Emotionally, we had experienced losses of everyday lives we had once taken for granted. Those losses took visible form as long lines for gas rationing, children who could not attend school because public transit did not run its regular routes, and illnesses suffered by ourselves and our family members. Before the storm we had lived through difficult conditions, and we saw these conditions exacerbated in the storm's aftermath.

This writing project asks writers to bear witness—and to research and to write to persuade the audience to act—just as Aristotle urged. All my teaching life I have experimented with assignments like this, with varying degrees of success. But after Hurricane Sandy, I felt a deep need to create conditions that would make writing more purposeful for all students. This Action/Mindfulness Research and pedagogy differs from service learning because it focuses on mutual aid. As students and teachers, we participate in our communities—at work, at home, through activist and spiritual practices—in order to become mindful in our daily lives and to create changes that offer as much benefit to us as they do others in our communities. Our service acknowledges suffering—our own and that of others—and takes on projects that offer us possibilities for transformation in everyday moments to which we might not usually pay attention.

EDUCATION IN THE BRONX

In the spring of 2013, I taught another Basic Writing course at the same school in the Bronx for very low pay. During the long commutes from a majority white neighborhood in Queens to a largely black and Puerto Rican neighborhood in the Bronx, I planned classes and wrote in my teaching journal. I called on Occupy's experiences of compassionate action to inform the work I undertook with students living in the poorest congressional district in the United States.

Some students had lost their homes in Hurricane Sandy, and others worked several low-wage jobs in addition to attending school and raising families. The intricate balance of school, work, and family could easily unravel through a child's illness or a flare-up of a student's chronic illness, or through homelessness, job loss, or other life-threatening emergencies. I learned to not ask too many questions, to listen with empathy, and to respond with the firmness that the students expected from me. Students insisted on their right to learn, and together we negotiated and renegotiated the precarious terrain of our learning together. My teaching journal recounts one such negotiation:

> One morning, Kay greeted me with these words, "There's a downside to education. There are consequences for college that no one talks about." As a result, Kay explained, her final essay for the course would be critical.
>
> "I have a video that you might like," I replied, cuing up Suli Breaks's "Why I Hate School but Love Education" (2012) on YouTube. After the second showing, I wrote with the class. The discussion that followed was volatile and at the same time deeply earnest. Students offered critiques of the costs of their schooling, both financial and emotional. They questioned the purpose of the writing course.
>
> "What do we need it for?" some students asked.
>
> "Because we need writing for everything," other students responded.
>
> Many students questioned Breaks himself. "If we weren't so confident, this video would persuade us to drop out of school."
>
> "No," still other students insisted, "that's not the point of what he's saying. He just wants people to be mindful of their education."

Many students copied the video's citation information to include in their final papers. Then students told me that Tee, another student, had written his own spoken-word piece that morning on the bus. It was a remix of "Richard Cory" by Edward Arlington Robinson, a poem about the moral failures of material wealth. The students had read "Richard Cory" together in one of their other classes.

Tee recited his piece, and I remembered the Simon and Garfunkel song by the same name. "It's by two old white guys, though," I said. "Please play it," the students asked. After we listened, class ended, and Tee told me that he enjoyed the song. "I'm going to pick that up," he said. That was the last class Tee attended, and I never saw him again.

TIMELINE

2013 I accepted a full-time, non-tenure-track position co-coordinating a Basic Writing program in Arizona, 2,500 miles away from New York City. In three years of applying and interviewing, this was the only full-time offer that I received. We had four months to prepare, and in three of those months, Free University of NYC created new actions, two at Cooper Square adjacent to Cooper Union (a small private school that had offered free tuition for over 150 years but starting Fall 2014 would impose tuition) in the East Village and one at Marcus Garvey Park in Harlem. At the second Free University at Cooper

Square, I focused on Mina Shaughnessy and Adrienne Rich's work at the City College of New York (CCNY), in the days when tuition was free. Participants wrote and spoke about their experiences with education, focusing especially on the burdens of high tuition and personal debt. These participants were in their early twenties, and they learned for the first time on that day that tuition at CCNY and at the other CUNY schools had once been free. For the last Free University, at Marcus Garvey Park, my class resembled an all-ages women's studies class as we analyzed a short excerpt of Angela Davis's *Autobiography*, in which she addresses her motivation for writing and her concern with connecting her life's work to larger historical concerns (Davis 1974). In early evening, participants in all of the classes gathered together in a large circle to discuss Edward Snowden's revelations of the NSA's extensive and secret surveillance program. We ended with a potluck vegan dinner donated by a local restaurant, and continued the circle to plan for the future. That future would take me out of New York City. Yet I began to understand that the work was portable and sustainable beyond this circle and beyond this city, even if the form of the work could not yet be predicted.

OCCUPY BASIC WRITING

On the first day of the 2014 fall semester, I taught my first Basic Writing class in an American Indian community in central Arizona. The students in this class, already working as education paraprofessionals, were studying for bachelor's degrees in education so they could teach language and culture in their community. We spent the last hour of class writing together, and then I was asked by my peer reviewer, the program's coordinator, to read my writing aloud. The coordinator suggested that the writing explained why I had come to this community, and how much I valued writing as a means of connection and forming community. I read aloud and we discussed the writing.

> "On behalf of the class," a student said, "I want to welcome you to the Community. Now we know why you are here."
> "We love to laugh," another student said, "it's part of our culture. And we love to eat, so we should all bring food next time."

As class was ending, another student said that a dust storm was in progress. The coordinator and I walked out to the car, and our mouths filled with grit. Neither one of us had ever driven through a dust storm before. We drove slowly through a section of highway out beyond the urban sprawl, with no malls and no office buildings. We were amazed at the clarity of cloud-to-ground lightening, at the illumination of the sky, at what could be seen for miles and miles from the highway.

Several nights later, my friend appeared in a dream. In the dream I felt immense joy when I realized that he had returned. When I awoke, I picked up my phone from the side of the bed, found the "notes" app, and tapped out the message of the dream:

Portable writing center as home
    You've got to help people express what I couldn't express in my lifetime.
Lift people up!!!!!!! Sing it. It's a necessary path toward consciousness.

The next week in class, we discussed possible significant issues that students might focus on for their first writing project. We discussed the civil unrest in Ferguson, Missouri. "What about Robin Williams's suicide?" asked a student. I am sure my body language changed. I did not want students to write about celebrities, and this was how I began my rebuttal. But the student persisted and was joined by others. Students in the class had lost siblings within the last several months. "This is a problem in our Community. We are studying to become educators—and we want to learn so that we can help our students."

I took a quick breath. We had already spoken that evening about the rhetoric of dreams, and I had mentioned in that discussion that I had recently had a visit from a friend. Recapitulating that discussion became a place to begin.

"That visit I told you about?" I started, "It was from a friend who also committed suicide. He was American Indian, from the Midwest, but none of us knew until he died. I found out when I went to the gathering at his family's house. My friend tutored in my classes and he helped me edit my writing. The visit came after driving home through the dust storm. He reminded me of why I was teaching, of what is important."

"That is why you came to teach here," a student said.

"Yes," I said. "And obviously, Robin Williams stays on the list."

CONCLUSIONS IN THE WAKE OF AUSTERITY

My most important guides to teaching and living—Freire, Rich, Davis, and others—remind us that we cannot stop at merely identifying the unequal distribution of our own privilege. Instead we must act to change conditions. So we must write and must speak—we must bear witness to austerity and we must recognize human suffering—including our own suffering. Acting to alleviate suffering brings us back to resilient space, in mutual aid, helping each other as we help ourselves and allowing ourselves to be helped in return. These efforts do not rely on the binary roles of teacher/student or victim/advocate. Instead, like Occupy Wall Street and Occupy Sandy, practices evolve in public space—whether in our classrooms or on our beaches or in our streets—as each of us takes on tasks that fit our talents and allow us to stretch our skills beyond the bounds of what we once believed were our limited capabilities. This work holds great challenges and also remains fraught with the same hierarchies that contradict the purity of our ideals. But, much like Basic Writing, it is necessary work. And we begin to realize that we do it together, from the most difficult places of confronting our deepest vulnerability—and from the equally uncomfortable spaces of recognizing our greatest strengths. Through that recognition, we can begin to Occupy Basic Writing and to consider the implications of our occupation—and our full presence—for the future.

In *Therapy After Terror*, Karen M. Seeley (2008) writes that after September 11, 2001, New York City psychiatrists found that the theories and practices of their training were disrupted, or at least quickly became inadequate. In the midst of so much human suffering, including that of the therapists themselves, it no longer seemed appropriate to inquire, "What does this event symbolize to you? Does this event remind you of an occurrence in your childhood?" In the wake of the attacks, such questions seemed not only irrelevant but also out of touch with the indescribable grief of what had become everyday life.

Ten years after the attacks, I sat in my therapist's office in the last week of September, and recounted to him my first visit to Zuccotti Park. In the past, other therapists had dismissed my activism by asking what these experiences represented to me. But my therapist had served as a volunteer emergency psychiatrist after 9/11. On this day in late September, 2011, my therapist said to me, "I don't see why you're not down at Zuccotti more often." The deep, ethically embodied perspective of his words propelled me forward.

Everyone who spent time at Zuccotti Park undoubtedly has a different story. I share my own story here—of Occupy Wall Street to Arizona—because, despite all empirical evidence to the contrary, I still believe that a better world is possible—and I especially believe that a better world is possible for Basic Writing. Because of this belief, I want to suggest that Basic Writing needs a revised epistemology, ways and means of knowing based on material realities and embodied events of everyday life in the wake of austerity. If a better world is possible, then all of us, working in and beyond Writing Studies, hold responsibility for creating this world for the future.

References

Bernstein, Susan Naomi. 2013. *Teaching Developmental Writing: Background Readings.* 4th ed. Boston: Bedford/St. Martin's.

The Black Power Mixtape 1967–1975. 2011. Directed by Göran Hugo Olsson. Sundance Selects.

Breaks, Suli. 2012. "Why I Hate School But Love Education: Spoken Word." YouTube .com. December 2.

Camus, Albert. 1955. *The Myth of Sisyphus and Other Essays.* Trans. Justin O'Brien. New York: Vintage International.

Coates, Ta-Nehisi. 2014. "The Case for Reparations." *The Atlantic,* June. http://www.the atlantic.com/magazine/archive/2014/06/the-case-for-reparations/361631/.

Davis, Angela Y. 1974. *Angela Davis: An Autobiography.* New York: International Publishers.

Freire, Paulo. 1970. *Pedagogy of the Oppressed.* Trans. Myra Bergman Ramos. New York: Seabury.

Giroux, Henry. 1992. *Border Crossings: Cultural Workers and the Politics of Education.* New York: Routledge.

hooks, bell. 1994. *Teaching to Transgress: Education as the Practice of Freedom.* New York: Routledge.

Reed, Conor Tomás. 2014. "'Treasures That Prevail': Adrienne Rich, the SEEK Program, and Social Movements at the City College of New York, 1968–1972." In *Lost and Found: The CUNY Poetics Document Initiative, Series IV,* ed. Iemanjá Brown, Stefania Heim, erica kaufman, Kristin Moriah, Conor Tomás Reed, Talia Shalev, Wendy Tronrud, and Ammiel Alcalay, 37–65. Berkeley, CA: SPD Books.

Rich, Adrienne. 1995. "Teaching Language in Open Admissions." In *On Lies, Secrets, and Silence: Selected Prose 1966–1978,* 51–68. New York: Norton.

Rich, Adrienne. 2014. "What We Are Part of: Teaching at CUNY 1968–1974, Part II." In *Lost and Found: The CUNY Poetics Document Initiative, Series IV,* ed. Iemanjá Brown, Stefania Heim, erica kaufman, Kristin Moriah, Conor Tomás Reed, Talia Shalev, Wendy Tronrud, and Ammiel Alcalay, 37–65. Berkeley, CA: SPD Books.

Rose, Mike. 1989. *Lives on the Boundary: The Struggles and Achievements of America's Underprepared.* New York: Free Press.

Royster, Jacqueline Jones, and Gesa E. Kirsch. 2012. *Feminist Rhetorical Practices: New Horizons for Rhetoric, Composition, and Literacy Studies.* Carbondale: Southern Illinois University Press.

Seeley, Karen M. 2008. *Therapy after Terror: 9/11: Psychotherapists, and Mental Health.* New York: Cambridge University Press. http://dx.doi.org/10.1017/CBO9780511551239.

Shaughnessy, Mina P. 1977. *Errors and Expectations: A Guide for the Teacher of Basic Writing.* New York: Oxford.

Shor, Ira. 1992. *Empowering Education: Critical Teaching for Social Change.* Chicago: University of Chicago Press.

Soliday, Mary. 2002. *The Politics Of Remediation: Institutional and Student Needs in Higher Education.* Pittsburgh: University of Pittsburgh Press.

Sternglass, Marilyn. 1997. *Time to Know Them: A Longitudinal Study of Writing and Learning.* Mahwah, NJ: Lawrence Erlbaum.

Wilkerson, Isabel. 2010. *The Warmth of Other Suns: The Epic Story of America's Great Migration.* New York: Random House.

Winans, Amy E. 2012. "Cultivating Critical Emotional Literacy: Cognitive and Contemplative Approaches to Engaging Difference." *College English* 75 (2): 150–70.

Writers for the 99%. 2012. *Occupying Wall Street: The Inside Story of an Action that Changed America.* Chicago: Haymarket Books.

7

AUSTERITY BEHIND BARS
The "Cost" of Prison College Programs

Tobi Jacobi

I remember the things my teachers used to say to me: "James, you're special. Smarten up." "James, you have so much potential. Please, don't blow it." I wonder what they would say now. (Castrillo 2013, 279)

James Castrillo, "Every Morning"

How can so many never have heard of an outline? Or a thesis statement, a semicolon, or a run-on sentence? I had never met so many intelligent adults whose basic writing skills were so poor and whose early educational experiences had been so utterly dysfunctional." (Lewen 2008, 691)

Jody Lewen, "Academics Belong in Prison: On Creating a University at San Quentin"

The term *austere* might come to mind before one considers how *austerity* has affected the more than 2.4 million people behind bars in the United States: a monochromatic wardrobe; a bland and barely nutritionally-sound diet; a strict schedule for movement, sleep, even speech; an education—as Castrillo and Lewen suggest—arrested, perhaps, by circumstance. Yet, while the lack of material and physical freedom might indeed point to an austere existence, the systemic measures taken to construct such an existence are anything but simple and plain with an annual price tag that is well into the billions.[1] One might say that austerity formally unlinked higher education from prison in 1994 when Clinton's Violent Crime Control and Law Enforcement Act eliminated Pell grant access for the prison population. What had been a robust and progressive system of US prison college programs was effectively shut down, falling from over 350 to fewer than 10 within a few years (Fine et al. 2001). Such programs had been growing and transforming educational access since the 1970s, offering a stronghold of prisoner

DOI: 10.7330/9781607324454.c007

access to associate's degrees in the humanities and social sciences and, perhaps more importantly, contact with engaged teachers and peers who were committed to intellectual rigor and continuing education. As a recent Rand report documents, the 2008 recession further decimated the prison education opportunities that remained; in California, for example, funding was reduced by 30 percent resulting in the loss of 712 teaching jobs and forcing the implementation of new modes of instruction that reduced both contact hours and frequency of classes (Davis et al. 2013). What remains of prison education, as Doran Larson so aptly states in his 2013 collection of prison essays, is "a tattered map of private charitable work and the exceptional instances of progressive, state-sponsored efforts" (257).[2] Amid those tatters we often find writing courses, composition teachers, and a highly motivated set of students.

As this brief essay argues, prison offers a complex site for analyzing the relationship between writing, higher education, and austerity. The promise of education behind bars itself is enticing, so rich with promise that it often risks forwarding what Harvey Graff (1987) calls "the literacy myth," as various publics seek to claim its agentive power. *It will counter repressive prison policy. It will deter recidivism. It will combat years of abuse. It will free.* Such lofty narratives suggest tensions between the institutional use and release of prisoners' words (e.g., required disclosure of crime, scrutinized research) and the motivations of college programs (e.g., democratizing missions, reciprocal learning aims). As a required class for almost any degree, composition courses are often part of the core curriculum in these prison college programs. Indeed, writing—whether in composition classes or as part of other coursework—was and is central to the work of higher education behind bars. And as perennial underdogs, it is hardly surprising to find a cadre of composition and literacy teachers at the heart of many (re)emergent programs.

PRISON + AUSTERITY = FUELING RECIDIVISM IN THE PRISON INDUSTRIAL COMPLEX

The prison experience is integral to American culture, H. Bruce Franklin (1978) has argued, "not just to the culture of the devastated neighborhoods where most prisoners grew up and to which they return but also to the culture of an entire society grown accustomed to omnipresent surveillance" (643). This seeming comfort has resulted in a selective blindness that allows the "free" to adopt an often unconscious tossing of the keys to the cells that hold millions hostage at inadequate educational levels. Yet rather than safeguarding the wider population from physical

and moral harm, this mass celling of our citizens has rather dire consequences for a democratic society. Employment projections for the coming decades suggest that academic or at least vocational training will be
mandatory for most job applicants.[3] Yet the United States has insisted on
withholding those critical skills from a significant segment of the population at a historical moment when unskilled labor demands continue
to diminish. This lack of educational attainment is not, as some might
assume, due to lack of aptitude, since prisoners are drawn from every
geographic and cultural background. Indeed, many federally incarcerated people choose to enroll in GED classes repeatedly simply because
the GED is the only mandated education program that cuts across state
and federal facilities.[4] When they do find access to advanced coursework,
imprisoned students perform well, achieving higher retention rates than
their traditional campus peers[5] and eventually lower recidivism.[6]

While we might view the loss of the college programs as an early
attempt at sociopolitical austerity, it is also clearly linked to an ideological regression in approaches to punishment. Though we have not
returned to sixteenth- and seventeenth-century corporal punishment
practices and tradition of public spectacle, we have indeed returned to a
model of incarceration based more fully in isolation than rehabilitation.
As Angela Davis (2003) eloquently argues, "The contemporary disestab-
lishment of writing and other prison educational programs is indicative
of the official disregard today for rehabilitative strategies, particularly
those that encourage individual prisoners to acquire autonomy of the
mind" (57). And in a democratic society "autonomy of mind" is highly
valued. The repression goes far beyond job and reentry readiness to
shape the very direction of our nation's trajectory. The systematic denial
of voting rights for people with felony convictions for at least five years
in Florida, a state with some of the strictest regulations on how people
return and reintegrate after prison, for example, may easily have influenced the vote for George W. Bush over Al Gore in 2000.[7]

There are other indicators that link austerity to prison and complicate the possibility of education as a key to individual and social
freedom. Many universities are inextricably tied to the prison industrial complex through everything from investment in Corrections
Corporation of America (CCA) market shares to UNICOR (Bureau of
Prisons) dorm furniture contracts. Many share board of trustee members with, and accept research funding from, large-scale private prison
corporations.[8] These entanglements further complicate calls for universities to increase their commitments to serving diverse populations in
ethical ways. Until universities agree to divest corporate ties (to prison

profiteers and predatory distance learning programs) and reinvest through committed college programs, the austere life that many experience behind bars and upon reentry will be unlikely to change.

RECLAIMING A PLACE FOR HIGHER EDUCATION BEHIND BARS

It is, perhaps, a sign that change is on the horizon when conservative *Forbes* magazine forwards a pro-prison education editorial. In their 2013 article, education editorial writers Skorton and Altschuler (2013) argue that prison college programs offer "a humane, comparatively cheap and effective alternative to the discipline-and-punish approach that all too often breeds only hopelessness and recidivism." Since the demise of more widespread programs, a small but stable group of mostly private programs have emerged through support from private sponsors, invested faculty, institutions, and committed groups of student volunteers.[9] These prison writing programs are often launched by a committed group of faculty and students at well-established liberal arts colleges or state universities with a history of reaching out to communities and peoples without traditional access to college and with an emphasis on earning associate's degrees in the liberal arts. In the section that follows, I've highlighted several prison college programs and literacy initiatives; each represents a response to both the stunning loss of decades old college programs and the compelling need for writing and literacy education called for by prisoners themselves.

One particularly strong program is the Bard Prison Initiative (BPI) in New York. Imagined and established in 2005 by then Bard student Max Kenner, BPI has granted more than 275 degrees with an additional five hundred students enrolled. Their mission promises attention to both intellectual rigor and social justice with a track record that boasts both post-incarceration employment and low recidivism through liberal arts education.[10] Bard teacher and writing program coordinator Delia Mellis (2014) describes their first-year seminars and writing-intensive advanced courses in ways familiar to compositionists with an emphasis on process, revision, academic research training, and building communities of writers. Innovative components include student-compiled topical research libraries (to assure students that instructors advocate unbiased positions) and (inside and outside) peer tutors assigned to writing and writing-intensive courses.

Another exemplary prison college program is the Education Justice Program (EJP) based at The University of Illinois, Champaign-Urbana. Through program development, EJP commits "to building an open, inclusive learning environment and to transparent, collaborative governance [based on the belief] that critical self-reflection is an important part of creating and sustaining a healthy program climate."[11] A distinctive feature of EJP is its broad commitment to learning through credited courses and a stunning number of other opportunities, ranging from a prison justice radio show and reading and writing workshop series to an ESL language partners group and outdoor landscape/food production laboratory. Writing teacher Vanessa Roullon characterizes her experience as "a personal and intellectual experience with mature individuals in a space where we teach each other."[12] It is also noteworthy that many of the teachers and volunteers in the program are graduate students, including several enrolled in the doctoral program in writing studies; these teacher-scholars often continue their work with the justice system after graduation through scholarly pursuits and/or program development in new locations.

Finally, the San Quentin Prison University Project (PUP) is also worth highlighting. Through an ongoing connection with California's Patten University, PUP facilitates a rigorous college program for student prisoners. Moving from volunteer to coordinator to executive director, Jody Lewen (2008) has grown the program significantly despite a prevailing assumption that mediocre written performance is an acceptable norm for prison students. She notes that not only do some programs feel uncertain about the intellectual capacities of incarcerated students, but they also question the need for rigorous and challenging coursework for students who may not pursue work beyond an associate's degree (693). With renewed emphasis on quality education in the arts and humanities, PUP now requires four writing and communication classes as part of an overall sixty-credit degree program and currently enrolls more than three hundred students. PUP is particularly concerned with breaking the cycle of incarceration that often spans both lifetimes and generations; as Lewen told National Public Radio, support for the program is "an argument in favor of universal access to higher education" (Lewen qtd. in Gonzales 2014).

The success of programs like the three represented here has fueled the desire for professional connection and support. Several established programs have also been working to establish themselves as models that might be replicated by others. The Bard Initiative, for example, has led the establishment of the Consortium for the Liberal Arts in Prison whose members—private schools in Connecticut, Iowa, Maryland, and New York—"share the view that a liberal education can transform the lives of individual students, and our public institutions, in ways that far exceed the prevailing responses to crime, punishment, and the need for change."[13] Such efforts support the possibility of prison college programs gaining wider and deeper support across institutions of higher education. They also make possible more creative fundraising, more efficient management of paid and volunteer teachers, tutors, and staff, and the establishment of standards that align with conventional postsecondary expectations for learning and degree work that will be recognizable by both correctional and college/university administrations.[14]

There are also extracurricular, non-credited writing and literacy opportunities that support motivated students inside (and sometimes move toward social justice).[15] More than seventeen states host at least one Books through Bars project to get reading materials into the hands of men and women in prison.[16] To complement their upper division course offerings, the Education Justice Project offers a series of writing workshops on topics ranging from "practically painless English" to "composing introductions and conclusions" to "creative writing." They also offer regular creative nonfiction workshops and publish a collection entitled *Winter Harvest*. The Inside-Out Writers group in southern California similarly targets juvenile populations by offering writing as a means of reflection and a catalyst for change as youth learn how to integrate into their home communities. The SpeakOut writing workshop series that I coordinate in local youth and adult detention centers in northern Colorado is similarly situated, offering incarcerated writers opportunities to explore writing as a means of communicating, learning, reflecting, and making their voices public through the *SpeakOut Journal*. Our program, like many creative and expository writing workshops, works to complement college programs by employing familiar writing heuristics and introducing writers to a range of writing processes in a non-evaluative setting. This is often an intentional effort to offer alternatives to the negative school—and writing—experiences that prisoners recount in their educational histories.

College programs, prison-college collaborations, and other prison literacy projects might be well situated as responses to austerity measures. We might recognize in their mission statements an alternative rhetorical platform for prison activists and radical prison abolition groups whose work and ideology remains valued, but whose voices receive less attention in mainstream media, academic, and political landscapes. They insert hope and possibility through the creation of sustainable and accessible prison college and educational programs where women and men can develop the communication skills they need to both survive individually and contribute to healthy communities and governance.

On the other hand, admirable as these programs are, they are not without flaw. Funding often comes almost fully from private donations and fundraising events, effectively sidestepping a public call for social responsibility for reentry work and a justice (and education) system built upon democratic notions of community care and investment. Worse yet, others thinly veil an entrepreneurial spirit endorsed, if not mandated, by the recruitment desire for increased tuition dollars. Prisoners can gain admission—if they have advocates who can complete paperwork and documentation for them. Prisoners can enroll in online or correspondence classes—if they can pay tuition and textbook fees. Prisoners earn degrees—if they can complete all requirements within ten years. Cost alone prevents many prisoners from entering college programs. Beyond the material, the stigma and ongoing repercussions of one's crime are difficult to escape. Adams State College, for example, requires incarcerated applicants to submit an application, previous transcripts and "hand-written explanation of crime/felony";[17] while the former are expected and commonplace, the requirement to handwrite an explanation of prior life experience, particularly one that may elicit trauma, is unusual, perhaps cruel. Writing, it seems, is not only restricted and monitored inside prison but also used as a tool to maintain the power differentials between prisoners, guards, and college admissions committees.

IMPLICATIONS FOR COMPOSITION PEDAGOGY AND CURRICULA BEHIND BARS

In his lauded prison memoir, Jimmy Santiago Baca (2001) champions the power of writing inside:

> Language gave me a way to keep the chaos of prison at bay and prevent it from devouring me; it was a resource that allowed me to confront and understand my past, even to wring from it some compelling truths, and it opened the way toward a future that was based not on fear or bitterness or apathy but on compassionate involvement and a belief that I belonged. (5)

In the last fifteen years, numerous creative and critical narratives have emerged from the US justice system in the form of edited collections, scholarly analyses, memoirs, documentaries, web collectives, and blogs. As Baca claims, an invitation to speak often releases a textual floodgate from women and men behind bars. If nothing else, we might credit austerity measures with invigorating the prison writing community.

My own years of experience as a prison and jail writing teacher confirm that inside writers are eager to face the blank pages and ready to take on the sometimes significant challenge of learning to communicate beyond prison walls (e.g., engaging academic, public, and legal audiences). Courses focused on basic and academic writing and communication are often central to prison college programs. As we know, such courses are often vital building blocks for students who have not followed a traditional educational trajectory and/or timeline. Writing itself—whether academic, public, creative, or personal—is well-positioned to make meaningful interventions for incarcerated people seeking to advance their communication and critical thinking skills.

Necessary as this work is, it does not come without complication when enacted inside our repressive prison system; writing teachers' efforts to engage common "free world" pedagogical practices are regularly stymied by the institutional and peer pressures that are unique to life behind bars. The observations that follow suggest that significant operational and material barriers exist in educational programs, imposed in part by contemporary climates of austerity.

- *Disclosure and self-censorship:* Like traditional college students, incarcerated students may experience heightened anxiety about academic and personal disclosures that sometimes come with written assignments; unlike traditional students, however, they may also feel concerned about choosing paper topics that will call attention to their "privileged" status as a college student or that might suggest work that violates prison or legal protocols. Common topics like legalizing marijuana or gun control may draw attention to prisoners in ways that result in confiscated writings or restrictions on research materials.
- *Heuristics on lockdown:* While many composition teachers and administrators ascribe to shared practices for program development and administration (e.g., WPA guidelines), prison regulations and funding may pigeonhole prisoners into course or pedagogical models that make the development of a strong set of rhetorical and writing skills difficult for many students. Traditional practices such as collaborative writing and peer review sessions become complicated by dynamics that are beyond the control of the teacher. The community formed in a traditional class that meets two or three times weekly is shifted when the students live with each other twenty-four hours a day and might have trouble shifting into "student" mode during a weekly class session. Peer review sessions might be particularly vexing if out-of-class dynamics are present; alternatively, sessions might be greatly enhanced by students' deep investment in each other's success. Perhaps the worst case scenario lies in a reliance on distance learning, correspondence courses, or even Massive Open Online Courses (MOOCs); as many writing teachers have argued, these platforms can make the collaborative and recursive nature of writing and peer review nearly impossible to emulate.

• *Institutional and disciplinary realities of prison*: Traditional academic expectations must often be reconsidered in a prison classroom. Preparation for writing strong academic texts—a skill that many prisoners would like to develop—might be limited by institutional restrictions on how research materials are accessed as well as access to basic word processing equipment. Bard Prison Initiative teachers have grappled with this issue by limiting course reading requirements to several key texts or gathering strong source samples in a course packet for students to use as they learn how to produce academic prose. There are other material limitations as well. Teachers might be turned away by a new or overzealous guard. Students might be unable to attend class due to lockdowns, court dates or legal meetings, visits, or conflicts with other classmates. Few of us, for example, who teach in conventional college programs have run into student excuses like these recounted by Bard College Prison Initiative student, Deshawn Cooper (2013): "I cannot turn in my paper today because the facility's academic supervisor didn't feel up to printing any of our papers this morning," or "I couldn't do the paper because the prison administration hasn't allowed the books for the course into the facility yet" (263).

While we might shrug such pedagogical challenges off as the reality of teaching inside, they are likely heightened by the weight of austerity measures placed on both prison staff (often forced to juggle multiple jobs such as the simultaneous supervision of classes, visitations, and inmate workers) and teachers (often volunteering at least a portion of their labor). Further, it is easy to imagine backlash from prison staff, some of whom may support educational rehabilitation but stop short of supporting college access. While many contemporary students have concerns about job prospects, students behind bars face significantly higher challenges since most jobs require disclosure of felonies and do not look favorably upon prison history. Those that don't require disclosure likely still face employment gaps that create uncertainty about stability and commitment. While getting a degree does motivate and excite, it can also lead to a sense of despondence if release (and thus job prospects) seems slim. Too, as prison teacher Doran Larson (2013, 257) argues, "[o]nce released, even those who have enjoyed effective prison programming face obstacles to employment, housing, and other basic needs that few of us could overcome." While we would be remiss in perpetuating a myth that writing or a few college classes alone can adequately address these material realities, those of us who work with writers behind bars recognize a motivation and will that we long for in our traditional campus students. Even with limited material and community resources, students in prison often engage critically and far more deeply than students pressed to fit in three more credits or build their resume for upcoming career fairs. We see that writing coursework and pedagogies based in rhetorical practice find ready minds and willing pens. We see emergent voices ready to participate in movements that resist simple band-aiding of the justice system through occasional classes and that want to contribute to collective resistance to educational inequality and mass incarceration.

CONCLUSION

In early 2014, New York Governor Andrew Cuomo made national headlines with his public show of support for increased access to higher education for prisoners in ten state prisons ("Gov. Cuomo's Bold Step on Prison Education" 2014). Those of us invested in prison education cheered, then held our breath, then shook our heads as the New York State legislature rallied support to crush the proposal before it ever got a chance to gain public traction. The booming prison expansion and privatization of New York State Prisons in the 1990s and early 2000s promised economic stability to regions that were otherwise losing industry to competitors abroad. Prisons kept small towns afloat in many cases and any threat to the stability of the state prison population (in addition to perceived privileging of inmates over staff in terms of educational access) was quick to fuel opposition to educational reform behind bars. Yet austerity behind bars would better serve people inside and out by replacing costly (and inhumane) solitary confinement or heavy-handed medication regimes with educational programs with both breadth and depth to foster the critical thinking and technical skills men and women need to find meaningful work upon their release.

We might question the wisdom of confronting a monolith like the justice system at a time when many composition programs struggle for institutional equity within campus walls. Yet—as Tony Scott's chapter in this volume points out—there is little guarantee of reward for the current push to produce career-minded and entrepreneurial student populations; likewise there is often little recognition for a carefully wrought rhetoric or handbook in tenure and promotion committees or in annual reviews. Community-based learning partnerships are often asked to create sustainable (e.g., financially self-sufficient) projects and relationships. On my own campus, I've often seen lauded the entrepreneurial approach to partnerships that result in reciprocal social and financial profit. And while exclusion of other forms of community partnership aren't explicit, even the grant applications require applicants to anticipate how sustainability will be achieved after the grant cycle, suggesting that ongoing support for work that requires some financial and faculty commitment are a bit lower on the priority list than those that will result in tangible products or services. My own position is this: we can tactically resist the urge to serve as pawns—willing or silent—of institutions beguiled by the promise of entrepreneurial survivalism. Our small writing program in a county jail has resisted the move to charge participants or distribute prisoners' words for profit. We in composition face similar choices when we decide when and how to write textbooks, when and where to pursue research funding.

The question is how can we justify not working with people who desire and need access to advanced education? How might we create conditions that demand attention to these sites of access and education? Writing program administrators regularly face impossible choices about labor and compensation, curricula and assessment. We experience the joys of announcing wage increases and the dismay of enforcing rising class sizes. We build relationships with textbook companies who stand to benefit enormously from our expertise and access to undergraduate wallets and benefit ourselves when small revenues come back into our pockets and programs. We fund conference travel and research agendas. At what point do we ask this system to engage issues of justice beyond our own labor and on-campus students' needs? Where and when will we advocate and for whom? The fact remains that we incarcerate more people than any other nation, and as educators we have a responsibility to them. Such tactical support might take the form of encouragement for community-based teaching and research through course reassignment or mini-grants, leveraged support from textbook companies in the form of reduced or free books to traditionally marginalized populations, or advocacy for institutional support with higher administration through the establishment of awards or revised tenure policies. In late spring 2015, The Vera Institute, a Washington DC-based prison justice group, launched a five year targeted study aimed at supporting and examining the impact of higher education for prisoners two years before and after release (Vera Institute of Justice 2015). They encourage their participants "to create a continuum of education and reentry support services that begins in prison and continues in the community after release until the student has achieved a degree"; too, we might look to the prison education program at Saint Louis University, a unique associate's degree program for both prisoners and prison staff, an innovative model of restorative justice that invites (and perhaps insists upon) shared responsibility for increased access to and leveraging of education as a response to social and economic austerity.[18] It is through these kinds of initiatives that we might track meaningful evidence of learning and change for formerly incarcerated people (and justice industry employees) who have accessed higher education and who will enter job markets with the kinds of rhetorical and communication savvy that composition courses prepare them for.[19]

Working within prison college and writing programs will not erase the stain that the prison industrial complex has become on the American landscape. The United States embroils seven million citizens in the justice system (as well as the countless family and friends who struggle to support them).[20] Whether one is serving multiple life sentences or completing a short community service requirement, the justice and corrections process interrupts life trajectories and often access to advanced education. And the responsibility of those of us in higher education moves beyond mere access. As Lewen (2008, 695) advocates, "Across the disciplines, the opportunities to intervene beneficially in this situation are nearly infinite. But what people in prison most urgently need are people who genuinely care about them." College programs like those highlighted here—and the significant writing instruction that they entail—begin to address the revolving door of the US justice system by humanizing those behind razor wire. Writing opportunities, in short, can and should move beyond an entrepreneurial stance by contributing to a regime of collective care for all people. This remains a significant opportunity for writing teachers and theorists to participate actively in the healing our justice system.

Notes

1. Annual reported figures range from 74 million to over 52 billion depending on which incarceration categories and services are included. See Henrichson and Delaney (2012) and Kychkelhahn (2011).
2. Numerous studies have called for renewed access to education, and the Second Chance Act of 2007 sought to improve opportunities for rehabilitative prison and post-prison services, though results from this effort are emergent. See Gorgol and Sponsler's (2011) recent survey of post-secondary education in state prisons for a catalog of existing programs.
3. The Obama administration and White House ("Education: Knowledge and Skills for the Jobs of the Future" n.d.) have indicated a strong desire for skilled workers in coming decades, projecting that post-secondary degrees or certifications are the prerequisites "for the growing jobs of the new economy . . . of the thirty fastest growing occupations, more than half require postsecondary education."
4. Jails are not held to that same requirement, though most do have GED programs available.
5. The Goucher Prison Program reports that their prison retention rate in 2012 was 19 percent higher than their main campus rates (Mayhugh n.d.).
6. Davis et al. (2013) found that participation in educational programming resulted in a 43-percent drop in recidivism (xvi). Also see Jake Cronin (2011).

7. For more on this matter, see Meredith and Morse (2014), "Do Voting Rights Notification Laws Increase Ex-felon Turnout?" *The Annals of the American Academy of Political and Social Science* 651 (January 2014): 220–49.
8. For a brief snapshot of dubious ties between higher education and the prison system, see Hannah Gold's (2014) *Rolling Stone* essay, including reference to prohibitive admissions policies for people with convictions and tuition breaks for family members with a corporate prison connection.
9. Harvard faculty Kaia Stern and Bruce Western have begun to chart the growth of available post-secondary education prison programs. See their map of current programs at http://prisonstudiesproject.org/directory/.
10. See http://bpi.bard.edu/what-we-do/.
11. http://www.educationjustice.net/home.
12. http://www.educationjustice.net/home/ejp-stories/vanessa-rouillon/.
13. http://consortium.bard.edu/.
14. In addition to offering credited coursework to students inside, some programs have also worked to establish collaborations across institutions and student groups. These experiences range from collaborative learning initiatives to peer tutoring opportunities to an adapted service learning-style set of outreach experiences. While there is always a risk of prison tourism and service-learning-gone-wrong in such efforts, the aim to create space for reciprocity is often embraced by "inside" students who welcome the opportunity to mentor and influence peers at traditional institutions. For examples that result in credit and non-credited experiences, see the Inside-Out Prison Exchange Program (http://www.insideoutcenter.org/college-prison-courses.html), Grinnell College's Liberal Arts in Prison Program (http://www.grinnell.edu/academics/centers/liberal-arts-prison), and Arizona State University's Prison English Program (http://english.clas.asu.edu/prisonenglish).
15. Writing experience and activity is wide-ranging in US prisons, ranging from academic course assignments and legal writing to letters home and personalized children's books.
16. See a map of current book programs here: http://www.booksthroughbars.org/pbp/.
17. "Adams State Admissions FAQs." http://www.adams.edu/extended_studies/undergrad/prisoncollegeprogramfaqs.php
18. See the Saint Louis University Prison Program for more details: http://www.slu.edu/prison-program.
19. See the Vera Institute of Justice (2015) "Pathways from Prison to Postsecondary Education" report for more detail: http://www.vera.org/project/pathways-prison-postsecondary-education-project.
20. See the useful Pew Center on the States (2009) report on US prison populations: *One in 31: The Long Reach of American Corrections.*

References

Baca, Jimmy Santiago. 2001. *A Place to Stand.* New York: Grove Press.
Castrillo, James. 2013. "Every Morning." In *Fourth City: Essays from the Prison in America,* ed. Doran Larson, 279–80. East Lansing: Michigan State University Press.
Cooper, Deshawn. 2013. "Notes from the Underground." In *Fourth City: Essays from the Prison in America,* ed. Doran Larson, 262–5. East Lansing: Michigan State University Press.
Cronin, Jake. 2011. "The Path to Successful Reentry: The Relationship Between Correctional Education, Employment, and Recidivism." Truman Policy Research Report 15. https://ipp.missouri.edu/publications/the-path-to-successful-reentry-the-relationship-between-correctional-education-employment-and-recidivism/.

Davis, Angela. 2003. *Are Prisons Obsolete?* New York: Seven Stories Press.

Davis, Lois M., Robert Bozick, Jennifer L. Steele, Jessica Saunders, and Jeremy N. V. Miles. 2013. "Evaluating the Effectiveness of Correctional Education: A Meta-Analysis of Programs that Provide Education to Incarcerated Adults." https://www.bja.gov /Publications/RAND_Correctional-Education-Meta-Analysis.pdf.

"Education: Knowledge and Skills for the Jobs of the Future." n.d. http://www.white house.gov/issues/education/higher-education.

Fine, Michelle, et al. 2001. "Changing Minds: The Impact of College in a Maximum-Security Prison." City University of New York Graduate Center and Bedford Hills Correctional Facility. Available at http://sfonline.barnard.edu/prison/minds_01.htm.

Franklin, H. Bruce. 1978. *The Victim as Criminal and Artist: Literature from the American Prison.* New York: Oxford University Press.

Gold, Hannah. 2014. "Five Links between Higher Education and the Prison Industry." *Rolling Stone,* June 18. http://www.rollingstone.com/politics/news/5-links-between-higher-education-and-the-prison-industry-20140618.

Gonzales, Richard. 2014. "Inside San Quentin, Inmates Go To College." June 20. http://www.npr.org/2011/06/20/137176620/inside-san-quentin-inmates-go-to-college.

Gorgol, Laura, and Brian Sponsler. 2011. "Unlocking Potential: Results of a National Survey of Postsecondary Education in State Prisons." Institute for Higher Education Policy Issue Brief. May. http://www.ihep.org/sites/default/files/uploads/docs/pubs /unlocking_potential-psce_final_report_may_2011.pdf.

"Gov. Cuomo's Bold Step on Prison Education." 2014. *New York Times,* February 18. http://www.nytimes.com/2014/02/19/opinion/gov-cuomos-bold-step-on-prison -education.html?_r=1/.

Graff, Harvey. 1987. *The Legacies of Literacy: Continuities and Contradictions in Western Culture.* Bloomington: Indiana University Press.

Henrichson, Christian, and Ruth Delaney. 2012. "What Incarceration Costs Taxpayers." Vera Institute of Justice/Center on Sentencing and Corrections. January. http://www .vera.org/sites/default/files/resources/downloads/Price_of_Prisons_updated _version_072512.pdf.

Kychkelhahn, Tracey. 2011. "Justice Expenditures and Employment, FY 1982–2007-Statistical Tables." December. http://bjs.gov/content/pub/pdf/jee8207st .pdf. 1–10.

Larson, Doran, ed. 2013. *Fourth City: Essays from the Prison in America.* East Lansing: Michigan State University Press.

Lewen, Jody. 2008. "Academics Belong in Prison: On Creating a University at San Quentin." *PMLA* 123 (3): 689–95. http://dx.doi.org/10.1632/pmla.2008.123.3.689.

Mayhugh, Jess Blumberg. n.d. "Lessons Learned: Goucher College Brings Its Faculty, Students, and Courses into Maryland Prisons." *Baltimore Magazine.* http://www .baltimoremagazine.net/2014/6/goucher-college-offers-courses-inside-maryland -prisons.

Mellis, Delia. 2014. Bard Prison Initiative. Phone Interview, June 17.

Meredith, Marc, and Michael Morse. 2014. "Do Voting Rights Notification Laws Increase Ex-felon Turnout?" *Annals of the American Academy of Political and Social Science* 651 (1): 220–49. http://dx.doi.org/10.1177/0002716213502931.

Pew Center on the States. 2009. "One in 31: The Long Reach of American Corrections," 1–48. March. Washington, DC: The Pew Charitable Trusts.

Skorton, David, and Glenn Altschuler. 2013. "College Behind Bars: How Educating Prisoners Pays Off." *Forbes,* March 25. http://www.forbes.com/sites/collegepr ose/2013/03/25/college-behind-bars-how-educating-prisoners-pays-off/.

Vera Institute of Justice. 2015. "Pathways from Prison to Postsecondary Education Project." April. http://www.vera.org/project/pathways-prison-postsecondary -education-project.

8
BUSKERFEST
The Struggle for Space in Public Rhetorical Education

Mary Ann Cain

Some teaching moments couldn't be better if we staged them. My Creativity and Community class had voted to conduct our final meeting at a coffeehouse one student, Holly,[1] had used for her final project on creating public space. With only four students, it was easy to come to consensus about going "into the field." Having only four students allowed much flexibility and also drew us closer together than previous semesters when the enrollment minimum of ten was met. We decided to see for ourselves if Holly was correct in her assessment that this coffeehouse provided a "third place," urban sociologist Ray Oldenburg's (1997) concept that had helped frame the semester's discussion. Conversations in such places, writes Oldenburg, are characterized by social "leveling": "[q]uite unlike those corporate realms wherein status dictates who may speak, and when and how much, and who may use levity and against which targets, the third place draws in like manner from everyone there assembled" (28).[2] I hoped our coffeehouse experience would do something similar and leave students with a powerful final experience of how public space can level hierarchical social relations and foster creative expression within and between diverse social groups.

As my eyes adjusted to the dim setting, I scanned the long, narrow, brick-walled room for signs of my students. Two were already seated at a massive antique oak bar, recycled from one of many nineteenth and early twentieth century establishments crafted by German immigrant cabinet makers. The old building leaned a bit with age and unspoken history. The coffeehouse was simply the latest iteration of over a century of industrial and commercial use. My German ancestors would likely approve. I was thinking of those ancestors as I searched for my students. But before I greeted them, my eyes suddenly met those of the barista. We burst out in exuberant surprise.

DOI: 10.7330/9781607324454.c008

"Coco was a student in this class a few years ago," I offered to the two students listening in. As Coco and I caught up, the other two students arrived to overhear a lengthy conversation about her life to date.

"She used to play with the Three Rivers Jenbe Ensemble," I said. The students nodded; I had spoken frequently about that group—a West African drumming, dance, and cultural education forum for young people—and its later formation as the Three Rivers Institute of Afrikan Art and Culture. Until this semester, Three Rivers had been a service learning option for the course.

"Are you still connected with Three Rivers?" I asked.

Coco proceeded to describe how her troupe of hula-hoop artists had been collaborating with Three Rivers. The upcoming street fair BuskerFest was next on their calendar. My students and I listened keenly to Coco's description of her troupe, of BuskerFest (I had to ask what a busker was), and eventually to her memories of our class.

"So is this place a third place?" I asked. I was fairly sure Coco would remember that term.

"Most definitely," she said.

I turned to my students. We were all sipping drinks Coco had prepared and were ready to move to a table in the corner near the empty, ad hoc stage in the back. She had already opened the door to a "leveling" of our talk.

It is tempting to continue this story with such celebratory moments juxtaposed against the foreshadowing of a fiscal storm. For instance, while for some reason administrators had allowed the class to run despite its low numbers, I will not be able to count on such benevolence in the future. Enrollment benchmarks are just one of many neoliberal strategies that rein in not only costs but curricula. However, the aim of this chapter is not celebration or mourning. Instead, my purpose is to provide here-and-now observation of micro-moments of public space-making in and beyond writing classrooms as a way to understand how public space is created by claiming it. Writes social geographer Don Mitchell (2003, 35), "The very act of representing one's group (or to some extent one's self) to a larger public creates a space for representation. Representation both demands space and creates space." I also seek to illustrate what's at stake when such spaces grow ever more fragile and elusive. "No one is free to perform an action," states Jeremy Waldron, "unless there is somewhere he is free to perform it" (qtd. in Mitchell 2003, 27). Nancy Welch similarly notes that the increasing privatization of public space makes the claiming and creation of such space ever more difficult (Welch 2008). I want to show how a close reading of such spaces might provide ways to think about how to claim/create them and also what they do and how they function. If we know what we have when we occupy public spaces, we may become more adept at sustaining them—critical knowledge in an age when neoliberalism is dispossessing people of both material supports and spaces in which they can voice visions and needs.

I will perform this reading through both the austerity struggles of my service learning partner, Three Rivers, and through (the topic of my current book project) the legacy of Dr. Margaret T. G. Burroughs, an African American artist-teacher-activist and institution builder on Chicago's South Side, in a neighborhood known by its residents as Bronzeville. Burroughs's earliest activism centered on the creation of the South Side Community Arts Center, a Depression-era project assisted by the Federal Arts Project/Works Progress Administration. The Art Center's formation provides a useful lens through which to understand how public space has been, and can be, claimed. Bronzeville's efforts in claiming/creating public space during a dire economic moment also runs counter to current claims that privatization is the key to reviving the economy and "saving" education. But again, I seek to not simply celebrate Bronzeville's success in establishing a truly public space. Instead, I want to provide some historical perspective of how such a space was created, for the insights we might find as we go forward in our own struggles to forge public space in university writing classrooms and for community-based education.

In this discussion of public versus private space, I want to emphasize that by public, I mean spaces where "representation," as Mitchell says, as well as the kind of identity building that Burroughs, the Art Center, and Three Rivers supported, are foremost in its function. Public funding, such as in education, does not in and of itself guarantee public space. Nor, as Oldenburg points out, do privately owned places entirely preclude it. But as I will discuss, when those who claim and create a public space are also equal participants in how that space is formed and run, then such spaces can provide more sustainable locations for social transformation.

The parallel histories of the Art Center and Three Rivers go beyond simply two struggling arts centers focused on African American history and identity-building. Three Rivers began as an arts organization focused on Afrocentric culture, history, and experience for children in a community where virtually no such education had been available. Artistic activity, in this case Western African drumming and dance, became the vehicle for this push to establish African American identity not merely as a neutral addition to a multicultural melting pot but instead as an oppositional space for critical and creative resistance to white domination. While larger urban cities had fought more visibly militant battles for such spaces, the history of Fort Wayne, Indiana, presents a much more muted, even surreptitious stance toward anti-racist activism. The lessons that Three Rivers sought to extract from its Art Center predecessor was how to build bridges across diverse racial, ethnic, and class groups that would provide a sustainable center for social interactions of the "leveling" sort described by Oldenburg, a "leveling" that would provide the necessary conversations for individuals and groups to reidentify themselves as part of a larger enterprise of more visible resistance and counterpoint to white hegemony. Art was instrumental in creating those spaces.

Similar to the Arts Center, Three Rivers was able to launch its efforts to bring identity-building Afro-centric art to a community that was largely Eurocentric in its arts focus, and it was able to do so through young people. As with many working class and poor communities, art in Fort Wayne in general is considered largely a past-time activity, subordinate to earning a paycheck, raising a family, and, in some cases, supporting a church. But arts education for young people is more accepted, even as it, too, remains susceptible to across-the-board cuts in school and community programming with every budgetary downturn. Thus Three Rivers found ready audiences and resources.

Spring Semester 2014 was the first time since I began teaching the course in 2006 that Creativity and Community was offered without a service learning option. My partner, Three Rivers, had lost its home base the previous December. They could no longer afford rent for the building they had occupied for several years. The artistic director's fiscal vision had been to shift from government and foundation grants, which tied them to specific types of programming as well as outcomes accountability, to a community-based funding source that would support Three Rivers's vision of a space for building African and African American identity. He had hoped the local community would step up, understanding the benefits of the nonprofit, non-privatized approach to cultural and anti-racist education through diverse, largely Afrocentric programming that spoke in direct opposition to white-dominated institutions, politics, and economics and was run by the people for whom it was formed.

Three River's vision of community support was more than just a daydream; Bronzeville's Art Center set a precedent for community-run, identity-building arts centers that from the beginning included artists and ordinary people as a significant voice in its establishment, management, planning, programming, and educational outreach. Three Rivers's vision of community-based support attempted to extend the legacy of the Art Center and of Black Nationalist resistance to capitalist economics based on racial oppression. By attempting to bypass the standard practices for most arts organizations of grant writing and corporate gifting, Three Rivers sought to connect more directly to its primary audience, the local African American community, and thus be more responsive to community needs, interests, and concerns. At the same time, Three Rivers quite consciously sought to educate all of its participants in African and African American history and culture, subjects still given short shrift in local schools and in the local culture at large. Unlike granting agencies and corporate sponsors who routinely ask for targeted projects as well as outcomes assessment as "proof" that a group is meeting its goals, a community-based operation would go directly to local citizens and would be accountable through people's participation and support. Disengaging from privatized funding would provide Three Rivers with a stronger base for its anti-racist, pro-African, and interracial agenda. Being anti-racist required an independence that Three Rivers's forerunner, the Art Center, had achieved, however briefly, in its early years of operation.

At first, Three Rivers scraped by on memberships plus donations from individuals and local businesses. The new, larger space allowed a greater breadth and depth of programming than in their previous formation as a West African drumming and dance ensemble. But with the 2008 recession, Three Rivers reversed course and began applying for grants as revenues for rent, electricity, and heat steadily shrank. By December 2012, when it was clear the group could no longer maintain its multi-year lease, the building's owner was persuaded to provide the space rent free for the next year, with the understanding that Three Rivers would develop new revenue streams. Instead, by December 2013, the group was officially homeless—not their term but mine, depicting my own sense of displacement as the loss of a dedicated physical space changed my ability to offer my Creativity and Community students a service learning option.

On the surface, Three Rivers's partnership would seem a minor loss. The Three Rivers service learning option was always just that—an option. In fact, most students elect to develop other public spaces for their final projects. But its presence was much more important than simply providing an option. Early each semester I invited Three Rivers's participants to class to describe their experiences. Sometimes students received a drum lesson. Sometimes former students who had taken the service learning option would also visit. Students were also invited to attend the group's performances, workshops, and social events for extra credit. By the time the semester ended, Three Rivers was a known quantity to everyone. Since Three Rivers is one of the few anti-racist and Afrocentric cultural education groups in the community, it provided a striking example of the presence and ongoing struggles of African Americans in a city that, like many northern destinations of the Great Migration, continues to be highly segregated. The very fact of Three Rivers's existence—as a place where students could go and be welcomed by familiar faces, a place where their received notions of "appropriate" discourse about race and class could also be challenged, on a side of town that they might not know well, if at all—brought an awareness to students of the community's racial, ethnic, and social diversity, as well as its persistent segregation. Part of the familiarization with Three Rivers occurred because I maintained a narrative about the group's creation and use of public space. Three Rivers illustrated how public spaces were available beyond profit-driven institutions and businesses or private homes. It also showed, in a culture that tends to value profit over people, how fragile such spaces are. Ultimately, whether students participated in, or even agreed with, Three Rivers's profile and mission, they were aware in very material ways that some people really do make the effort to go against the mainstream for the sake of public space.

At first it might appear that Three Rivers's struggle to claim and hold an oppositional space in its white-dominated community has little in common with the Depression-era founding of the South Side Community Art Center. Yet like Three Rivers, the Art Center's history is one of struggle to keep its doors open in the wake of fluctuating community economics and politics. One important distinction between the Art Center and many other art institutions is that artists have always held a prominent role in its operations, an aim shared by Three Rivers. But this role has, from the beginning, sparked tensions between those who produce the art and those who consume it. Class tensions, mixed with political and ideological oppositions, had shaped the struggle for this public space in Bronzeville well before the Art Center was proposed. Thus, the difficulties in creating/claiming public space with the Art Center are a microcosm of the larger issues in the community, then and now, and aptly forecast the struggles of Three Rivers.

We have two accounts of how the Art Center came to be. In Burroughs's telling, George Thorpe and Peter Pollack, an Illinois Art Project staff member and north-side gallery owner, "called together a small group of 'leading' black citizens including a few young artists like myself to talk about this proposed Art Center. Our first meetings were held at the south-side [*sic*] Settlement House at 32nd Street and Wabash Avenue" (Burroughs 1991, 2). A much different account by James Graff holds that Pollack approached Dr. Metz Lochard, editor of the premier African American newspaper the *Chicago Defender*, about "arranging for Chicago businesses to display some of the fine but largely unrecognized work of local black artists," with Lochard bringing Pollack "unannounced" one Sunday to meet society maven Pauline Kigh Reed (Burroughs 1991, 1). Graff characterizes this meeting as the origins for the Art Center idea. It is perhaps, as Bill Mullen points out, no surprise that in this alternative narrative artists "found themselves pushed to the margins by the numerous black socialites who had come to attach themselves to this sudden institutionalization of black culture" (Mullen 1999, 85). Tensions between artists and society people, Mullen writes, were part of an ongoing struggle within the South Side over political aims and affiliations.[3] Despite these tensions, the shared goal of the Art Center brought together, however tenuously, artists, businesspeople, citizens, and society leaders in a powerful way. As a result of their fundraising campaigns, membership drives, and galas, the Art Center raised about $8,000 from within Bronzeville itself, enough to purchase the Georgian-style 1893 house of grain merchant George A. Searverns Jr. without white donors (Hine and McCluskey 2012) and thus without direct threat of reprisals for its more radical, anti-racist leadership among the artists and their labor union partners.

The inauguration of the Art Center still stands as a significant milestone in African American history. Its first year of operations saw, according to Burroughs, an "auspicious start," with twenty-five exhibitions seen by twenty-eight thousand visitors, along with twelve thousand children and adults attending art classes (Burroughs 1991, 10). The Art Center continued to be a place where everyone from Bronzeville and beyond, rich or poor, white or black, of various ethnicities and political persuasions, could meet, mingle, and come together for the sake of community. It was also a meeting place for unions and political groups sympathetic to the anti-racist thrust of the Center, groups who directly and indirectly influenced Burroughs and other artists in the arts of political organizing and direct action. As famed photographer and Art Center artist Gordon Parks remembers, "It seemed that half of Chicago was there [for his 1941 exhibit]. The elite, dressed in their furs and finery, rubbed elbows with some of the people I had photographed in the poor quarter; I had invited as many of them as I could find" (qtd. in Mullen

1999, 91). The Art Center also from the start embodied the tensions of competing visions and sponsors. For its 1941 dedication, the Art Center—now operating with a full-fledged board, including artists such as the twenty-three-year-old Burroughs who served as secretary—invited Eleanor Roosevelt, a key force in the establishment of the Federal Arts Program (FAP). Excluded from the banquet honoring Mrs. Roosevelt was Bronzeville's J. Levert Kelly, president of the Waiters and Bartenders association and a generous donor to the Art Center but also, according to Burroughs, "a well-known gentleman around town whose activities caused him to be considered not quite in the pale of society by some people" (Burroughs 1991, 6). When Kelly let people know he "might just break up the whole party, First Lady or no," Chicago police—"by some miraculous coincidence"—picked him up two hours before the First Lady's arrival, holding him until ceremonies were completed and Roosevelt had departed (7).

Burroughs draws a comparison to Kelly's fate with that of artists who were invited to but shut out of speaking at the dedication ceremony, and she highlights the same strategy of threatening disruption to create/claim space: "Mr. Kelly was not the only one shut out of the Dedication Ceremonies. We artists were just about shut out as well. However, because of the fact that (we) the artists also threatened to disrupt the proceeding one David Ross was granted five minutes to deliver the following statement which I had prepared on behalf of the artist" (7). The speech that follows contains often-cited passages that illustrate Burroughs's keen political consciousness about the role of art and the community. In particular, she makes a point to address stereotypes that she likely viewed the "society" people as holding regarding art and artists:

> We were not then and are not now complimented by the people who had the romantic notion that we liked to live in garrets, wear off [*sic*] clothes and go around with emaciated faces, painting for fun; living until the day we died and hoping that our paintings would be discovered in some dusty attic fifty years later and then we would be famous . . .We believed that the purpose of art was to record the times. As young black artists, we looked around and recorded in our various media what we saw. It was not from our imagination that we painted slums and ghettos, or sad, hollow-eyed black men, women, and children. There [*sic*] were the people around us.
>
> We were part of them. [T]hey were us. Thus, the coming of this Community Art Center has opened up new hope and vistas to all of us. (Ibid., 8–9)

The South Side Community Arts Center was one of over one hundred such community-based centers begun during the Great Depression. However, today it is the only arts center of that era still remaining, largely because the Bronzeville community bought the building through its "Mile of Dimes" campaign and for years was able to maintain a more egalitarian approach to its operations. For many decades, the Art Center has provided public space for creative expression to populations that have long been denied. In this way, participants have been able to claim/create public space through self and collective representation. As Burroughs's story of exclusion and disruption at the inaugural banquet underscores, however, this claiming of public space has never been without struggle, never secured once and for all. Within a year of the Art Center's inauguration, the war effort shifted federal funds away from the FAP. Furthermore, tensions between the Roosevelt administration and conservatives came to a head. The FAP, belittled for paying artists, was accused of harboring Communists and their sympathizers; the conservative Red Scare mentality persisted well into the 1950s (Mullen 1999). Burroughs, while not a party member, publicly held the great singer/actor/activist Paul Robeson up as her role model. Robeson would be banished from the United States for many years after testifying before the House Committee on Un-American Activities, and Burroughs herself would be called before the Chicago Board of Education and pressured to name fellow teachers at DuSable High School. Even her beloved Art Center at one point targeted her by returning her annual dues, thus denying her membership in the institution she had worked so hard to found.

During parallel times of stress, Three Rivers and its predecessor, the South Side Community Art Center, exerted creative effort to create public space. But unlike the Art Center, which started in large part because of the Federal Arts Project's interest in employing artists, particularly those in the inner cities burgeoning with first- and second-wave migrations from the South, Three Rivers never had any such substantial backing, public or private. When it reached a crossroads in terms of funding, Three Rivers elected to move away from funding sources that might compromise its oppositional, anti-racist stance. Artistic director Ketu Oladuwa noted that the subsequent collapse in funding and the disappearance of a dedicated space for the groups was more a matter of cycles in the larger scheme of nonprofit group, cycles that come and go with community support and concerns. In today's Bronzeville, too, the Art Center faces constant challenge among shifting community winds. Local community and other forms of public and private sponsorship currently support the Art Center, but not in the way of its founding, when public monies provided an opening for the creation of a truly public space. However one views the reasons for Roosevelt's creation of the

FAP, whether pressures from labor, a gesture to win black votes from the Republican party, or Eleanor Roosevelt's forceful stances on the cultural fronts of social justice, the FAP daringly opened opportunities for the creation of public spaces that the war economy and later, the Red Scare of the 1950s, would challenge and nearly break. This was a moment when public will trumped austerity politics, when public money helped create public space rather than being used to simply control it, in large part because of the organization and activism between artists—mostly young people at the time—and labor organizers skilled in staging direct community action. It is a lesson worth remembering in the face of an emergent entrepreneurialism (read "BuskerFest') that, instead of drawing upon lessons from a collective past, is in danger of forgetting them because of an enforced "homelessness" in current neoliberal economies that pushes more and more workers into contingent positions within an increasingly unequal distribution of wages and wealth.

Thus it is in much changed conditions that my students in Creativity and Community face the requirement, for their final public project, to create space for their work as writers and rhetors. Attempting to do so, students start to understand how closely tied the available spaces for public expression in the United States are to private, often corporate ownership and control, as well as how crucial organization across diverse individual and group identities is for claiming such space. For instance, one student sought to gather classmates of her daughter's elementary school class to talk and write about concerns and questions they had about their experiences in school, including bullying. The student planned to publish and distribute the girls' work at a local event and through relevant campus offices at my university. However, elementary school officials denied her permission to conduct group meetings at the school, claiming that state law prohibited unlicensed persons from working with students on school grounds, away from teacher supervision. While the school is a public one, the effects of privatization are evident even in this example; the kinds of conversations supported by "third places," and/or by spaces that do not fall directly under institutional control—a control exercised by the larger capitalist economy—are difficult to cultivate. So, for instance, the girls wanted a space of "leveling" where they could discuss their experiences at school, most notably about bullying, and they wanted to do it with an adult who was not part of their classroom space and thus someone who would not control the discussion or deliver negative consequences for what was said, or even feel compelled to report the discussion to others in authority for security purposes. The girls simply wanted their own space without adults dominating directly or indirectly. When my student brought that group of girls to our university's student lounge and library spaces, they were not only able to articulate their concerns with their elementary school experiences but also began to critique them. Action plans were not far behind. Thus, from the contradictions within a second institution's privatizing spaces came conversation and expression to generate, strengthen, and support a developing identification within and between the girls for their view of their school and their educational experiences.

Just as my student's group of girls found important, but temporary refuge, Three Rivers remains without a home base and thus endlessly in search of refuge—a busker constantly on the move. In contrast, the South Side Community Art Center has, despite ongoing financial struggles, maintained this public space, this refuge, this home space, without giving up its artists' and community-driven focus and programming. Yes, the Art Center struggles, but its struggles at least have a place, an identity, and a purpose known to Chicago and much of the nation and the world by virtue of its historical significance and its longevity, as well as its continuing function as a place of "social leveling." It maintains a home for anti-racist, anti-elitist, community-based activity—a home created in an earlier era of public commitment and public funding.

In the coffeehouse's public space my students and I, however temporarily, created and claimed, our discussion, along with light from the large paned windows off the street, is waning as the sun travels west. The conversation settles into a comfortable silence. Linda remarks how she's glad to have had the opportunities offered by this class to go "outside the box." Ashton offers how she can't *not* think of public space and third places when she goes around her small town one-hour north. We are all letting our guards down; the leveling seems to have taken hold. More silence. We want to linger, but we feel the pull of other obligations.

"This is why I teach," I say, in a rare moment of disclosure. I am used to keeping the conversation's focus on the students. "This is what really matters. I just hope we can hang on at the university." Pause. "Tell everyone you know why this matters. Get people to understand how public education gave you something you could never have gotten anywhere else."

Hope may not be the right word, tied as it is to the more celebratory aspects of "success." But I do feel, for a moment at least, hopeful. We are all now connected in ways we never could have imagined on our own. And we can all tell others about why they should want to be, too.

As I say goodbye to Coco and tell her I'll be looking for BuskerFest, I remember her spontaneous hula hooping for us that afternoon in the middle of the coffeehouse. Then I picture her in the city streets, a performance artist claiming public space along with other buskers. I think of Three Rivers and how it is following the trends of many arts groups around the world, hosting "pop-up" events in the available spaces. I think about the young Margaret's Art Crafts Guild and how they, too, were "homeless" in similar ways before the Art Center (Bone and Courage 2011). I look back at the silent, leaning brick building before I get into my car and know I will keep telling (and writing) these stories to whoever will listen.

Notes

1. All names have been changed for confidentiality.
2. While Oldenburg's "third places" included private businesses such as coffeehouses, taverns, and the like, what I am arguing for is the importance of public space beyond private ownership, where people from diverse backgrounds can meet and have contact through the "leveling" conversations that Oldenburg advocates, but who also share responsibility and power in the administration and oversight of that space.
3. Burroughs herself did not dismiss this struggle within the Art Center; in her 50th anniversary account of its founding as well as elsewhere she credits women such as Reed and Frances Matlock (a teacher who had also led young Burroughs to protest in the streets with the NAACP Youth Leadership Council) for their assistance and resources. But no matter how the idea for an art center began, it is clear from Art Center minutes that artists, including Burroughs, were involved in the planning stages from the very beginning (Cain 2014).

References

Bone, Robert, and Richard A. Courage. 2011. *The Muse in Bronzeville: African American Creative Expression in Chicago, 1932–1950.* New Brunswick, NJ: Rutgers University Press.

Burroughs, Margaret T. G. 1991. "Saga of Chicago's South Side Community Arts Center (1938–1943)." Personal copy.

Cain, Mary Ann. 2014. Archives South Side Community Art Center, Box 1.

Hine, Darlene Clark, and John McCluskey, Jr. 2012. *The Black Chicago Renaissance.* Urbana: University of Illinois Press.

Mitchell, Don. 2003. *The Right to the City: Social Justice and the Fight for Public Space.* New York: The Guilford Press.

Mullen, Bill. 1999. *Popular Fronts: Chicago and African-American Politics, 1935–46.* Chicago: University of Illinois Press.

Oldenburg, Ray. 1997. *The Great Good Place: Cafes, Coffee Shops, Community Centers, Beauty Parlors, General Stores, Bars, Hangouts and How They Get You through the Day.* New York: Marlowe and Company.

Welch, Nancy. 2008. *Living Room: Teaching Public Writing in a Privatized World.* Portsmouth, NH: Boynton Cook.

9
FIRST-YEAR WRITING AND THE ANGELS OF AUSTERITY
A Re-Domesticated Drama

Nancy Welch

ACT I: "WRITING CANNOT BE A TAX ON THE UNIVERSITY"

Picture this: a new provost arrives at your mid-size public university—a new provost whose record-setting compensation package makes headline news. Within a few weeks he is moving forward with his priorities. These priorities include speedy approval for building a new STEM (Science, Technology, Engineering, Math) complex. These priorities also include forging ahead, as urged by the governing board and regional accrediting body, with new General Education requirements, including for foundational writing. For the STEM project's initial planning, the provost instantly identifies $2 million (soon to increase to $5 million); he gains the governing board's approval for a building budget of $100 million beyond. When it comes to General Education, he also goes to work: that is, he directs his office to downsize the budget for the newly created first-year writing program and seek ways to "flex" the just-approved foundational writing requirement—even before the program and the requirement have been launched.

This scenario, which played out at my university over the spring and fall of 2013, is likely familiar to readers of this collection because we are all living to varying degrees under the twin banners—distinct but mutually reinforcing—of corporatization and austerity. In public college and university writing programs, steep declines in state and federal support intensify the cost-cutting, labor-squeezing measures of lean production and just-in-time staffing that have characterized contemporary composition. As university administrations direct greater budget shares away from general education and toward those centers thought capable of supporting the university in hard funding times, pressure mounts for first-year writing directors to convert program

DOI: 10.7330/9781607324454.c009

activities into revenue generators—or else go without. Years ago Steve North, with characteristic bluntness, said to me, "Everyone thinks writing is a good idea, but no one wants to pay for it." In the corporatized university, the adage becomes, "Everyone thinks writing is a good idea, but it has to pay for itself."

Yet even though evidence of higher education's market makeover abounds on my campus, when it comes to characterizing and justifying the cuts to first-year writing, corporate terms have been conspicuously absent. Rather—what will come as no surprise to feminist readers of this collection—writing program work is presumed to be a set of activities separate from the market sphere, embodying an ethos aloof to the pettiness, the grubbiness of money. For example, although the faculty senate president was visibly disturbed when the provost rescinded pledged resources—senators would not have approved the new requirement had they known this was another unfunded mandate—she nevertheless urged writing faculty to make do because canceling the requirement would be "disastrous for our students." Similarly, when a faculty senate budget committee inquired into the underfunding of this and other initiatives, a General Education committee co-chair argued that the true obstacle to curricular reform was not insufficient funding from the administration but insufficient concern for teaching from faculty. A signature of the proposed first-year writing program at the University of Vermont (UVM) is that most sections will be taught as first-year seminars by full-time continuing faculty across the disciplines. More than forty faculty members with tenure-track and senior lecturer appointments had participated in revising and piloting these seminars when the provost announced his intention to cancel funds to support such activities. This is the context in which the General Education committee co-chair claimed faculty in Biology, Geography, and Studio Art don't need material supports for learning to teach first-year writing seminars; they just need to *care* more.

At first glance, these sentiments seem to position first-year writing squarely in the domestic rather than the market sphere. Such sentiments seem to mark the continuing saga, as detailed in Eileen Schell's (1997) still-essential *Gypsy Academics and Mother-Teachers*, of teaching labor equated with maternal selflessness, writing instruction presumed to be carried out by angels in the university architecture who work for psychic rewards or pin money. From this perspective we might say that the corporatizing winds blowing through higher education herald nothing new for writing instruction because writing instruction was privatized—consigned to the domestic sphere—long ago.

But note the words of the provost himself. "Writing," he declared, "cannot be a tax on the university." He charged writing faculty with pushing for a "Cadillac program." On the face of it, such a charge was puzzling since faculty across campus had agreed to transform their already existing first-year seminars into courses promoting foundational writing; the costs in question were for a handful of course releases and some summer stipends for faculty revising their first-year seminars to become writing seminars. One General Education committee member even did a per-pupil cost comparison with other university writing programs and concluded that ours was not a Cadillac but a Yugo.

The program's make and model, however, made no difference. At stake was a principle—a principle not specific to this administration but hard-wired into neoliberalism. Neoliberalism seeks to resolve the persistent crisis in capital accumulation not only by expanding the reach of the market but also by shedding financial responsibility for all areas of life, including in education, that cannot be easily packaged and sold. On principle, so the neoliberal logic goes, one should favor institutional supports and infrastructure for those university centers that might produce lucrative exchange values. On principle, one should reduce as much as possible—or move from the realm of formal to informal, waged to unwaged—any supports that resist commodification; those supports are no longer imagined as a public good but instead, in the (frequently racialized) rhetoric of taxpayer resentment, as an unsustainable *drain*. This logic and the restructuring it engenders proceed regardless of how little or how much is in a university's coffers. In fact, UVM matches the financial profile of public colleges and universities that, reports *Inside Higher Ed*, have imposed cuts while dramatically increasing net unrestricted assets (Kiley 2011). Hence the response of one administrator when a faculty member asked if it really was the case that UVM couldn't afford stipends for faculty across disciplines taking on the work of retooling—reprovisioning themselves—as writing teachers. "My understanding," replied the administrator, "is that the decision was not financial." Or as my college's dean put it, "Why should we pay faculty to do what they should be doing anyway?"[1]

The problem, in the view of these administrators, is that composition is *not already* in the domestic sphere; it has *not yet* or *not yet fully* been cast into the realm of unwaged domestic labor. That composition instead would occupy a position in the university commons—indeed, the very idea of a university commons—is what struck my provost (who used the same aggrieved voice I hear on my neighborhood listserv whenever a school budget is up for approval) as cause for complaint. Mass literacy programs and supports are just a piece of the social goods and rights won through the expansion of public higher education following World War II and, especially, the democratization brought by 1960s civil rights struggles and campus rebellions. Over that thirty-year "American Dream" period, literacy education (albeit fitfully, partially, and vulnerable to underfunding and ideological constraints and attacks) moved from the largely private realm of individual responsibility and social class inheritance to public concern and even public right. Today's corporatized administrations and governing boards are schooled in the imperative of rolling back those thirty years of post–World War II socializing gains. To such minds, any social-good positioning of literacy and socially shared responsibility for literacy acquisition is an accountability-and-efficiency flaw to be corrected: here is a program that needs to be *reassigned* from public good *back* to private up-to-the-individual, leave-it-to-the-family responsibility. Compositionists should be thrifty and all writing teachers self-provisioning. Composition work should be shouldered with the spirit of cheerful voluntarism. In the age of austerity, the adage becomes, "Composition is a good idea but no one should *have to* pay for it."

There is nothing about the provostial logic at my university that is idiosyncratic. Rather, this campus drama is underwritten by neoliberalism and its drive across economic sectors and social institutions to palm off provisioning while doubling down accountability: "centralizing power" while "decentralizing blame," as socialist feminists Kate Bezanson and Meg Luxton put it (Bezanson and Luxton 2006, 4). When this provost deems the writing program an unfair *tax* on the university—a term this administration also applies to other socially necessary but costly supports such as the university libraries—he is associating it with and also lamenting it as *social provisioning*, as among the social services, social programs, and social supports that in a Keynesian economy are funded by taxes on private wealth, property, and profits. When the provost decries this *tax* and characterizes the writing program as a *Cadillac*, he taps not only into the toxic rhetoric of taxpayer resentment but also into racist caricatures of Cadillac-driving "welfare queens," a rhetoric that has provided potent ideological fuel for defunding and dismantling social programs. This is not to suggest, however, that this administration plans to dismantle the new writing requirement itself. To the contrary, the provost's office is eager to assess it and to demonstrate to the governing board and accrediting bodies that desired course outcomes are being measured and met. Instead, being dismantled or, more accurately shifted—from formal to informal, from waged to unwaged, from social to private—are program provisions and faculty support.

ACT II: COMPOSITION IN A LEAN WORLD

For anyone coming to grips with composition in the age of austerity, the past decade's exposés of higher education's market transformation are indispensable.[2] While it can appear that the "Open for Business and Up for Sale" rebranding of US colleges and universities has been borne of necessity, driven by steep declines in federal and state support, this literature details a situation at once more complex and more stark. Corporatization has proceeded over the past quarter century whether the economy is in bust or in boom with short-term budget crises giving the gloss of exigency to what is a wider, long-term project to transfer public resources and services to the market sphere.

My concern in this chapter, however, is not with the stem-to-stern corporatization and commodification of university life. Instead, I am puzzling over what seems to be a silence in the otherwise comprehensive literature on higher education's restructuring: silence about what this restructuring has also meant for the vast areas of university work, including much of the work of composition programs, that cannot be easily brought to market, regardless of whether market conversion is promoted through carrots or through sticks, regardless of whether compositionists embrace or shun entrepreneurialism. I am not speaking, of course, of the killing that has long been made in the composition textbook industry, nor of the niche markets that a handful of composition programs will indeed be able to cultivate by branding writing studies majors or peddling peer-review services. My concern is instead with mass literacy instruction—from basic and first-year writing to prison-writing programs, pre-service language arts teacher education, writing centers, community-based and service-learning literacy programs, and the National Writing Project—that defines for most practitioners what it means to do the work of composition. Such programs, along with the courses and activities of General Education more broadly, are among the core teaching activities of a university. Yet because this is costly work that does not bring ready market returns—as Christopher Newfield (2008) notes in *Unmaking the Public University*, public undergraduate education is unavoidably expensive (194)—it represents a *limit* on the market conversion of higher education.

This limit on corporatization can help explain why especially at public colleges and universities, neoliberalism is characterized both by privatization as commodification and profiteering *and* as reassignment of socially necessary work to the unwaged, voluntarist sphere. As administrations try to offload the costs of core educational activities, they create bubbles of re-privatized domestic or unwaged labor among a university's profit-oriented centers. In these bubbles, the work of education is to be carried out by angels in austerity's architecture, shepherding programs without monetary support and formal workload recognition. For instance, California State University, Chico's Thia Wolf, Jill Swiencicki, and Chris Fosen describe resorting to uncompensated committee service to direct a first-year writing program that by 2008–2009 had seen an increase in course caps to twenty-seven and the cancellation of course releases for a director (Wolf, Swiencicki, and Fosen 2010, 158). Similarly, an associate provost at UVM asked me if directing a writing program, including providing summer writing institutes and ongoing guidance for faculty across the disciplines teaching first-year writing seminars, could be done as "service."

What we find in these bubbles of re-privatized and re-domesticated labor is the reordering not only of the terms of production but of social *reproduction* and social *provisioning*. To cut to the bone the costs of writing instruction, and general education more broadly, the neoliberal university depends not just on the mechanisms of lean production but also on lean social reproduction: the offloading of program supports and faculty provisions. Program positions are cancelled, budgets are reduced or eliminated; growing numbers of faculty go without university-provided offices, computers, supplies, journal subscriptions, and conference travel and without health care, retirement, and a basic needs-meeting wage. There is, to be sure, stratification within the ranks of writing faculty, widely varying degrees to which tenure-eligible and contingent faculty are provisioned. All told, however, the neoliberal trend—which across the academy has transformed the professoriate from 75 percent tenure-track at the start of the 1970s to 25 percent today (Coalition on the Academic Workforce 2012)—is decidedly in the direction Marx (1990) describes in *Capital*: "the lot of the laborer, be his payment high or low, must grow worse" (799).

Within composition's bubbles of re-privatized labor, a writing program's social reproductive work—that is, the work of tending to the minds, skills, outlooks, and attitudes of the current and next generation of students—is carried out but by a faculty increasingly expected to self-provision. For example, even as my university rolls out elaborate instruments for quantifying and measuring teaching effectiveness, the administration has cancelled a popular summer grant program that encouraged groups of faculty to collaborate on pedagogical and curricular development. Such summer work will still need to occur—assessment will make sure of that—but it will go unpaid. Under university austerity regimes, students likewise bear mounting pressure to self-provision. That is the understanding we need to assess the "innovation" of writing studios. When a first-year program like Arizona State's responds to the shock of budget cuts by asking students to make their own way through online assignment modules supported by "faculty-produced videos, audio lectures, and other digital supplemental content" (Bourelle et al. 2013), the responsibility—and cost—of literacy learning is shifted onto students.

As the cases of Arizona State and my own university show, it is not that austerity threatens to bring the *end* of composition's work—or not an end to composition's work narrowly imagined as the delivery of writing instruction servicing functionalist literacy needs. Far from it: my university's provost applauds the new first-year writing requirement (implemented Fall 2014, initally without program supports) and remains eager for evidence of its results. Likewise, in this volume's accounts of eviscerated college writing and community-based literacy programs (see Bernstein, Cain, Fox and Eidman-Aadahl, and Jacobi), what is most striking is how, defunded and even "homeless," the work continues. We can take heart from stories of resourceful and tenacious survival. But if we consider that the neoliberal restructuring of higher education is a long-term project to reorder *permanently* the terms and costs of education, something disturbing comes into view: the increasingly widespread and naturalized expectation that writing programs can endure without provision, can endlessly adapt to terms of increasingly lean social reproduction.

ACT III: HOME ECONOMICS

In critical pedagogy and literacy studies, the term social reproduction is typically understood as ideological: the ideological apparatus, including institutions of schooling, that ensure what Jean Anyon (2011, 3) sums up as "the reproduction of social classes, the economy, and racial and gender exclusion and subordination." Here social reproduction theory draws from the Marx of *The German Ideology*; it is concerned with the superstructure, with the institutions through which ruling ideas are inculcated and reproduced from generation to generation.

Contemporary socialist feminists—particularly in the work of Canadian feminists such as Kate Bezanson (2006), Meg Luxton (2006), and Lise Vogel (2013)—are likewise concerned with the reproduction of ideas: with the daily and generational replenishment of workers "not just in adequate quantities but with appropriate 'skills' and 'aptitudes'" (McNally and Ferguson 2013, xxxi, xxvi). But turning from the Marx of

The German Ideology to the Marx of *Capital*, these feminists further spotlight the premium Marx placed on the "maintenance and reproduction of the working class" as the "most indispensable means of production" and "a necessary condition for the reproduction of capital" (Marx 1990, 711, 718). From this understanding that "the production of goods and services and the production of life are part of one *integrated* process" (Luxton 2006, 36; my emphasis), socialist feminists examine how social reproductive labor involves inseparably the cultivation of bodies and minds: "the provision of food, clothing, shelter, basic safety, and health care, *along with* the development and transmission of knowledge, social values, and cultural practices" (Bezanson and Luxton 2006, 3; my emphasis). Doing so, they identify the interdependency between what may otherwise be cast into the separate spheres of base and superstructure; they probe how the reproduction of capital depends on the social reproduction of labor power, "the aggregate of those *mental and physical capabilities* existing in a human" (Marx 1990, 270; my emphasis).

By accounting for how labor power itself is produced, this fuller story of *Capital* thus reveals that the care-taking, provisioning labor commonly dismissed as women's work or bemoaned as a tax is, in fact, central to capital accumulation. Yet that centrality, writes Lise Vogel (2013), is also "deeply veiled," in part because such labor most frequently takes place "noncapitalistically" outside the market (192, 157).[3] Historically this extra-market labor has been assumed by the family, thus increasing the rate of exploitation as capitalism offloads onto the domestic sphere the costs of preparing the bearers of labor power for another day, another year, another generation of work. Under pressure from social movements and labor, the twentieth century also saw responsibility for social reproductive labor increasingly assumed by the state.[4] Chief among neoliberalism's features is its drive to increase profit at the point of production (of both goods and services) by reassigning caretaking and provisioning obligations from the state *back to* family, volunteer, and other unwaged realms, including through commodified care work that is "gendered, often racialized, and poorly remunerated" (Bezanson and Luxton 2006, 6).[5]

Neoliberalism's offloading of public programs and supports does not, however, mean that the state has withdrawn from the picture. Instead, socialist feminists emphasize, the state has become all the more necessary to muster the "political mobilization" required to "reroute the state-household-market-third-sector circuits" (Bezanson 2006, 175)—mobilization assisted by celebrations of bootstrapping and self-provisioning family values as well as by rhetorics of resentment and blame. Consider how President Barack Obama (2013) promoted his College Scorecard in speeches that at first explicitly named diminished state funding as a chief driver of skyrocketing tuition but then called not for restored public funding but for colleges to be more accountable regarding the value of their product and students to be more responsible consumers. Here is a state not sidelined by but assisting higher education's marketization. But neoliberalism requires the state to do more than play the role of free-market cheerleader. Given the centrality of social reproduction to the economic system, the state is also needed as watchtower, accountability and assessment measures increasing as public funding decreases. "In the absence of public investment for social supports," explain Bezanson and Luxton, the state steps up bureaucratic oversight and accountability requirements to ensure that "social reproduction is sufficiently completed" and so that "pubic outcry is minimized" (6). As John Clarke and Janet Newman detail in *The Managerial State*, a study of the neoliberal reconfiguration of social welfare arrangements, "While the state has withdrawn in some ways, its powers and apparatuses have been extended in others—transferring responsibilities but simultaneously creating the capabilities of surveillance and enforcement to ensure that such responsibilities are being fulfilled" (Clarke and Newman 1997, 29). Here, too, we can consider the Obama administration's College Scorecard and other accumulating accountability and assessment measures delivering higher education's version of No Child Left Behind and Race to the Top: government will indeed remain involved in higher education, not as supporter and primary funder but as monitor and judge of its social reproductive results.

Through the lens of reprivatized social reproduction, we can understand the shared crisis of today's debt-burdened college students and the adjunctified faculty—mostly women and disproportionately African American and Latin@ (Curtis 2014)—charged with provisioning their minds. Lean social reproduction offers us, too, a framework for grasping how higher education's tragic headlines—an eighty-three-year-old French lecturer living in such penury, she was referred shortly before her death to Pittsburgh's Orphan Court (Kovalik 2013); my own composition colleague who, diagnosed with stomach cancer and shut out of the university's health-care coverage, taught extra classes to pay for two rounds of chemotherapy (Bousquet 2008a)—are more than signs of Dickensian hard times; they are revelations of how far neoliberal capital has proceeded in reassigning caretaking and provisioning work from the state back to the individual and family. Socialist feminist critiques of political economy can also help compositionists in particular to grasp the paradox, observed by Richard Ohmann (2004) in *Tenured Bosses and Disposable Teachers,* that the field's accumulating markers of professionalization—including compositionists who have moved into provostial ranks, charged with overseeing "student success" and "teaching excellence"—have grown hand in hand with its worsening labor conditions (43–44). After all, the *management* of social reproductive work remains highly valued even when, or especially when, financial responsibility for that work is being cast off. At the same time a socialist feminist framework might provide a more precise understanding of where most writing program directors reside within the corporate university's political economy: *not* as powerful boss compositionists but as dutiful wives practicing small economies with a shrinking purse.

CURTAIN CALL: MALTHUS IN THE WINGS

What difference could it make for compositionists to approach austerity challenges—our field's professionalization and growing precarity proceeding side by side, a writing requirement launched but its basic-needs budget defunded—through a socialist feminist lens? For starters, when we consider how neoliberalism reorders the terms of production *and* of social reproduction, we bring into view the relationships between professionalization and casualization, between administrative spending bonanzas and program cuts. These relationships, however, are correlational or structural rather than causal: both borne from a larger neoliberal reordering that aims to expand the realm of commodity production *and* to reduce or eliminate compensation for social reproduction. Likewise, when my university's administration cancels $9,000 in summer stipends for faculty revising their first-writing seminars *and* offers grants of $20,000 to $50,000 to help faculty "advance a discovery/technology toward a commercial application" and cultivate "an exciting new culture of faculty entrepreneurship" (Rosowsky and Galbraith 2014), the link is correlative rather than causal. The faculty teaching development stipends are not cancelled *because* the administration seeks money to launch the new product-licensing grants; the faculty teaching development stipends are cancelled in a climate where capital accumulation is fueled by new avenues for profit-making and minimal care-taking and provisioning obligations.

Thus there is no point in arguing back and forth across the table and over email, as I did with my provost's office for a full year, that if you have money for this priority and that priority, you should have it for writing and General Education as well. It was never, for the provost, a question of whether the program was affordable; whether the price tag for faculty development was $9,000 or $900, he was not to be persuaded.

There is, however, a point in joining with others, on my campus and beyond: to fight the re-privatization of the social programs and supports won through the past century; to figure out the complexities of solidarity across a campus workforce that is both stratified and shares in common diminished means to care for ourselves and do our work; to create a mass socializing logic that can rival neoliberalism's ruling ideas.

At the same time, given the rapidity with which university administrations are divesting themselves of financial responsibility for faculty and staff supports, socialist feminist analysis can keep us mindful of the material constraints we face. Even in a program like mine that is staffed entirely by union-represented full-time continuing faculty, teaching loads of up to eight courses a year, mounting audit-and-accountability requirements, and cancelled staff support all spell exhaustion. They also point to approaching breaking points across spheres of social reproduction. "Households," warns Bezanson, "cannot . . . manage social reproduction on their own, and women's labour . . . is not endlessly elastic. Without sufficient support, standards of living drop, the most vulnerable households typically collapse, and a crisis in social reproduction is produced" (2006, 38).

To be sure, an entrepreneurial few will strive to resolve this crisis in provisioning the house of composition through market solutions. But to suggest what the work of composition will look like for most—what tasks will be set for the angels in the neoliberal architecture—I offer one anecdote more.

Not long ago, I was a finalist to direct a writing program at a midsize public university. On the second day of a packed campus visit, when I had my first and only opportunity to talk with the current program director, I asked, "What else can I tell you? What else would you like to know?" I expected questions about scholarship, teaching, and philosophy. I did not expect this reply: "Have you ever fired anyone? I need to know if you can fire people. We have a lot of lecturers who are aging out."

That program director's burning question makes starkly visible the material conditions and also the political, philosophical choices and commitments before us. Must composition in an austere world take the shape of the corporate, brass-tacks WPA ready to put "aged-out" teachers out to pension-less pasture? Can we find images of our work instead in the students and faculty who, as I write, are striking to save public higher education in Quebec and Ontario and in the new Civil Rights activists who from Ferguson to Baltimore are rising up against austerity and racist dispossession? Much of the work of composition is social reproductive work for the society at hand *and* the society to come. As social reproductive work, education can train minds and bodies for the needs of capital, including equipping people with racist, sexist, and chillingly Malthusian ideas. But education can also, Jean Anyon (2011, 21) reminds us, produce "critics, rebels, and radicals"—the critics, rebels, and radicals who have ever been necessary to challenge and change the terms of education and whose arguments and movements are needed—are possible—now.

Notes

1. My university thus provides the public university's example of a larger pattern in neoliberalism identified by British Marxists Neil Davidson (2013) and Bill Dunn (2009)—a pattern of *reallocation* rather than reduction. In the larger economy, reallocation is fundamentally obscured by real and painful cuts to programs and provisions (housing, health care, and more) that many people depend on; in the university, reallocation is obscured too by the real budget cuts and staff reductions that many departments face. In the neoliberal era, observes Davidson, "It is not the *amount* of state expenditure and areas of state intervention that have changed but *where* the money is spent and how activities are carried out" (2013, np) through a process that Dunn sums up as "reorientation rather than decline" (2009, 29).

2. Of particular note are Bousquet's (2008b) *How the University Works*, Newfield's (2008) *The Unmaking of the Public University*, Slaughter and Rhoades' (2004) *Academic Capitalism and the New Economy*, and Tuchman's (2009) *Wannabe U: Inside the Corporate University*.

3. Marx himself was so eager to enter the "hidden abode of production" (Marx 1990, 279) that he left the hidden abode of social reproduction unexamined.

4. Although some social reproductive activities can be commodified for market purchase, the price can be dauntingly high—as is evident when even the very rich seek cheap immigrant labor to meet their childcare, eldercare, and housekeeping needs.

5. Of course, higher-education administrations, and the owning class more broadly, do not seek to reduce or eliminate the costs of their own provisioning. In fact, if we look at such elements of executive compensation packages as housing, car, and wardrobe allowances, what becomes visible is not only a campus wage gap but a campus provisioning gap. If we are surprised that Gilded Age excess seems to cause these administrators no shame, we might consider how much the abode of social reproduction is hidden from view—and how much capital accumulation depends on it remaining so—so that such administrators perceive themselves to be *self*-provisioning and *self*-perpetuating. The claims of a writing program—like all forms of provisioning labor—thus become a double problem to be warded off: this *tax* on university coffers is also an *attack* on capitalism's central and enabling myth—the myth whose full restoration neoliberalism seeks—of the self-reliant, self-made man.

References

Anyon, Jean. 2011. *Marx and Education*. New York: Routledge.

Bezanson, Kate. 2006. "The Neo-liberal State and Social Reproduction Gender and Household Insecurity in the Late 1990s." In *Social Reproduction: Feminist Political*

Economy Challenges Neo-Liberalism, edited by Kate Bezanson and Meg Luxton, 173–214. Quebec: McGill-Queens University Press.

Bezanson, Kate, and Meg Luxton. 2006. "Introduction: Social Reproduction and Feminist Political Economy." In *Social Reproduction: Feminist Political Economy Challenges Neo-Liberalism*, ed. Kate Bezanson and Meg Luxton, 3–10. Montreal: McGill-Queens University Press.

Bourelle, Tiffany, Sherry Rankins-Robinson, Andrew Bourelle, and Duane Roen. 2013. "Assessing Learning in Resigned Online Composition Courses." In *Digital Writing Assessment and Evaluation*, ed. Heidi A. McKee and Dànielle Nicole DeVoss. Logan, UT: Computers and Composition Digital Press.

Bousquet, Marc. 2008a. "But I Need This Class to Pay for My Chemo." *Daily Kos*, February 13.

Bousquet, Marc. 2008b. *How the University Works: Higher Education and the Low-Wage Nation*. New York, NY: NYU Press.

Coalition on the Academic Workforce. 2012. "A Portrait of Part-Time Faculty Members." http://www.academicworkforce.org/CAW_portrait_2012.pdf.

Clarke, John, and Janet E. Newman. 1997. *The Managerial State: Power, Politics, and Ideology in the Remaking of Social Welfare*. London: Sage.

Curtis, John. 2014. "The Employment Status of Instructional Staff Members in Higher Education, Fall 2011." American Association of University Professors. http://www.aaup.org/sites/default/files/files/AAUP-InstrStaff2011-April2014.pdf.

Davidson, Neil. 2013. "The Neoliberal Era in Britain: Historical Perspectives and the Current Era." *International Socialism* 139 (July 5).

Dunn, Bill. 2009. *Global Political Economy: A Marxist Critique*. London: Pluto Press.

Kiley, Kevin. 2011. "So You Say You're Broke?" *Inside Higher Ed*, May 27.

Kovalik, Daniel. 2013. "Death of an Adjunct." *Pittsburgh Post-Gazette*, September 18.

Luxton, Meg. 2006. "Feminist Political Economy in Canada and the Politics of Social Reproduction." In *Social Reproduction: Feminist Political Economy Challenges Neo-Liberalism*, ed. Kate Bezanson and Meg Luxton, 11–44. Montreal: McGill-Queens University Press.

Marx, Karl. 1990. *Capital: A Critique of Political Economy*. vol. 1. New York: Penguin Classics.

McNally, David, and Susan Ferguson. 2013. "Capital, Labour-Power, and Gender-Relations: Introduction to the Historical Materialism Edition of *Marxism and the Oppression of Women*." In *Marxism and the Oppression of Women* ed. Lise Vogel, xvii–xl. Chicago: Haymarket Books.

Newfield, Christopher. 2008. *Unmaking the Public University: The Forty-Year Assault on the Middle Class*. Cambridge, MA: Harvard University Press.

Obama, Barack. 2013. "Remarks by the President on College Affordability." http://www.whitehouse.gov/the-press-office/2013/08/23/remarks-president-college-affordability-syracuse-ny.

Ohmann, Richard. 2004. *Tenured Bosses and Disposable Teachers: Writing Instruction in the Managed University*. Ed. Marc Bousquet, Tony Scott, and Leo Parascondola, 36–45. Carbondale, IL: Southern Illinois University Press.

Rosowsky, David V., and Richard Galbraith. 2014. "Expansion of Faculty Grant Program: SPARK-VT." Memo, November 12.

Schell, Eileen. 1997. *Gypsy Academics and Mother-Teachers*. Portsmouth, NH: Heinemann-Boynton-Cook.

Slaughter, Sheila, and Gary Rhoades. 2004. *Academic Capitalism and the New Economy: Markets, State, and Higher Education*. Baltimore, MD: John Hopkins University Press.

Tuchman, Gaye. 2009. *Wannabe U: Inside the Corporate University*. Chicago: University of Chicago Press. http://dx.doi.org/10.7208/chicago/9780226815282.001.0001.

Vogel, Lise. 2013. *Marxism and the Oppression of Women*. Chicago: Haymarket Books. http://dx.doi.org/10.1163/9789004248953.

Wolf, Thia, Jill Swiencicki, and Chris Fosen. 2010. "Students, Faculty, and 'Sustainable' WPA Work." In *Going Public: What Writing Programs Learn from Engagement*, ed. Shirley K. Rose and Irwin Weiser, 140–59. Logan: Utah State University Press.

PART III

Composition at the Crossroads

10
WHAT HAPPENS WHEN IDEOLOGICAL NARRATIVES LOSE THEIR FORCE?

Jeanne Gunner

The literature of anti-austerity arguments in higher education over-all and rhetoric and composition in particular is extensive, especially as austerity measures have immiserated labor beyond what was once a more narrowly "working conditions" set of problems of office space and computer access. Typically these arguments adopt a frame of ideological critique. The ideological frames have not been monolithic; the human-ist defenses of a "save the liberal arts" and "nurture the citizen" variety regularly accompany political economy perspectives, Marxist analyses, feminist readings, and pragmatic responses. Nonetheless, the neoliberal regime has imbued composition theories, pedagogies, and administra-tion, inevitably implicating us all in complicity with corporate values, labor problems, and growing social inequality. Embodied forms of con-sent—for example, the tenured ranks' consent to a system of privilege bought through the exploitation of contingent workers—make up the material practices of our day. We teach in classrooms or online formats that are increasingly part of a class differentiation of student oppor-tunity. We manage and are managed according to institutional values increasingly difficult to distinguish from corporate values. Consent and critique come to seem the wearing contradiction of an academic life.

But what if this issue of consent, of our field's collective collabora-tion with austerity measures, itself suggests less a false consciousness or inevitable interpellation and more a broad fraying of certainty regard-ing ideological critique and its ability to produce effective forms of resistance? For those of us who have been sympathetic to it, ideologi-cal critique has seemed far preferable as an ethical and intellectual program than has a pragmatic, self-serving strategy of collaboration; actively engaging in critical questioning of the field as it is enveloped

DOI: 10.7330/9781607324454.c010

in the hegemonic narrative of austerity has seemed to offer the hope of progressive change. We hope to do meaningful work; we hope to open up resistant stances. And, unquestionably, ideological protests have had some positive material results. Often, however, these can seem mainly symbolic registers of discontent; the approval of a union in one place is (over)matched by the expansion of a radically less organized, less visible material workforce in a non-profit enterprise. Sometimes the effect, and the affect, is intellectual and ethical exhaustion.

Just as in the last decade in English Studies overall we have experienced a theory fatigue, some in rhetoric and composition today seem to be approaching an ideology fatigue, and a related loss of belief in the material efficacy of discursive and rhetorical modes of resistance, the result of ambiguous results in the face of often monumental efforts. In this discussion of austerity and composition, then—and in living the daily reality of austerity measures that impinge on students and teachers and enrich the expansion of entrepreneurial programs and offices—I focus on scholars who are searching for an "outside" to the ideological construct of resistance. As progressive, conservative, or otherwise oriented ideological narratives intended to promote material change come to seem less and less productive, and as discourse and rhetoric themselves come to seem less and less certainly functional in a communications system more and more characterized by heterogeneity rather than knowledge regimes, it seems time to play Peter Elbow's (1998) "believing game" with emerging theories that question near-naturalized disciplinary and critical constructs in the field. It may be that, as one result of a growing ideology fatigue, austerity measures are fueling potentially creative and productive disruptions of our own by impelling composition theorists to seek ways of thinking that may transcend the hegemony of hegemony.

CONSENT WITHOUT POWER

Many strands of the hegemonic austerity narrative frame disruption of the conventional educational structure as not only a necessity, but a silver lining, a bright promise in dark economic times, even a democratic set of bootstraps. An embedded libertarian message encourages students and workers to speed up the educational process, bypassing conventional forms, their own experience and initiative the biggest-bang investment they can make. Passive public acceptance of a fully instrumentalized model of teaching and a commodified notion of knowledge/expertise help disrupt the social relation of teacher/student, furthering a key element of the austerity agenda in erasing the cultural and economic power of faculty, repositioning them as barriers to educational progress. Each week if not each day, the higher education online newsletters carry stories detailing the superannuation of the conventional teacher model. The 2013 Pearson-Texas A&M-Commerce-South Texas College collaboration on a competency-based hybrid degree program is just one example. Instead of teaching faculty, students would draw on an academic coach, an "academic adviser on steroids," according to the "director of innovations in higher education." The teacher-free program will "help first-time students who may feel like they may be better served by a go-at-your-own-pace curriculum" that is "not designed to keep them chained to a seat" (Winston 2013).

From a perspective critical of this hegemonic austerity narrative, the proliferating programs buoyed by similar discourses of breakthroughs, innovations, and progress under the banner of austerity enable a higher education structure that is also a class-tracking system (as analyzed in, for instance, Armstrong and Hamilton's [2013] *Paying for the Party*) and a solidification of white privilege in elite private institutions at a demographic time of white minorification. Many proposed disruptive measures invoke a kind of nano-learning that happens beyond classrooms and without teachers, the final stage in the disposable-teacher revolution. And clearly, at a time of intense political polarization, external assessment/accreditation organizations that claim objective measures and unbiased data offer control over "leftist" faculty, enhanced by the apparent objectivity of technology deployed to the end of controlling curricula and faculty both. The ideological environment produced by the austerity narrative is captured well by the shorthand that has been used to justify extreme austerity measures in European nations: TINA, or There Is No Alternative, Margaret Thatcher's famous phrase. Within this context of crisis and inevitability, formerly unpalatable options become routine practices. And yet . . .

Despite the near-daily appearance of books, articles, opinion pieces, blog postings, speeches, local demonstrations, and other commonplace genres of professional and public discourse, arguments analyzing and resisting the above realities seem not to constitute a motivating material counter-agenda. Parents and students, dissatisfied as they may be with immediate conditions, have not categorically risen up to decry the casualization of academic work, the reduction in face-to-face education, the social tracking produced by reduced access to traditional four-year schools. Popular opinion has been as much against traditional disciplinary practices and structures—and against faculty, with their presumed laziness and undeserved job security—as against financial tuition increases, aid reductions, and capacity problems. The real dismantling of conventional higher education, on the other hand, has been highly effective in the material ways we know too well. The power seems to be with the mega-monied side: even the California teachers' union could not successfully battle the Silicon Valley-funded initiative that prevailed in a recent court action against the public school tenure system. Rhetorically positioned as an issue of the constitutional right to a quality education, the successful suit paves a path for further privatization of the K–12 system, an expansion of charter schools, and the disempowerment of faculty (and, of course, of unions, too). The most persuasive rhetoric seems to be the argument backed up by vast capital.

And so consent, even from within. In its Summer 2013 issue of *Peer Review*, the Association of American Colleges & Universities sponsors a highly unusual foray into Realpolitik in the topic it addresses—"The Changing Nature of Faculty Roles"—and the arguments it presents. While heavy on critique of the austerity-induced reduction of tenure-line faculty, the article authors accept that the necessary path is accommodation—"Just as liberal education itself is changing in the twenty-first century, this century demands a new faculty model, one that is flexible and dynamic for our times" (Albertine 2013, 5)—and that resistant efforts such as unionization campaigns "implicitly or explicitly recognize that we are unlikely, save in a few elite places, to see the traditional faculty role restored" (Paris 2013, 17). Sometimes consent is less intentional and more a matter of unforeseen strategic cooptation. As a field, composition has promoted writing without teachers; decentered classrooms; service learning; online writing courses; outcomes, common cores, and assessment; managerialism: these have been "repurposed" into some of the primary building blocks in educational "reforms," such as competency-based learning, pre-packaged curricular "deliverables," and other mechanisms of improved delivery systems through faculty erasure.

In hindsight, it certainly is easier to see a cooptation of strategy rather than its triumph in producing alternatives to exploitative practices and corporate/state control; Ed White's (2005, 33) strategically intended argument that the field should take the lead in developing writing assessment measures, for instance, morphed into active leadership on the part of our professional organizations in promoting outcomes and common core formulations of composing skills. We find ourselves the victim of our own habitus; from our earlier pursuit of cultural capital— the attempt to align with the research university model—to the manifest conservatism of the field today, we have been seeking a berth in a sinking ship. Critique becomes gestural, an epideictic rhetoric that does not materially move. As ideological narratives lose their force, academic capital further diminishes, and the disciplinary power of rhetoric itself is called into question. How many of our colleagues and former students now work for corporations that sponsor events such as the Bainbridge Educational Summit to which I, like many administrators, were electronically invited and whose rhetorical claims—of possessing "deep functional and industry expertise in every part of the education chain," of preparing its "clients" for "future disruptive trends in the K–12, Higher Education, English Language Learning, and Workforce Learning Markets" (Bainbridge Education Summit 2014)—reflect the field back to us fully subsumed to a corporate venture.

Although doubts about a unified field theory for rhetoric and composition have been with us for decades, more recent, I think, is a sense of increasing entrapment in what it has become as austerity transforms it—even when that transformation is another creative form of disruption, such as the challenges ushered in with new forms of technology and how best to understand their effects on what it is we (think we) do. In giving rise to theories of posthumanism, technology has disrupted the foundational position of humanistic rhetoric especially, thus helping to accelerate a changing sense of writing. In a *College Composition and Communication* review essay, Elizabeth Wardle criticizes a collection of essays on multiliteracies, rightly pointing out that "there are at least two competing and contradictory ideas about writing, teaching writing, and our field at play here": one promoting "'rhetorical dexterity in responding to a variety of complex, changing rhetorical situations'" and the other emphasizing "'technology and multimodality for their own sake'" (Wardle 2014, 664). It is when she asks, "Which view will win out?" that we have to take seriously an option (or perhaps growing necessity) to entertain the idea that rhetoric and communication, discourse and power, might be uncoupled.

As one of the *Peer Review* authors noted, the traditional faculty model is likely to persist in elite places, which perhaps helps explain the rush to claim "premier research university status," the stuff of much academic marketing today, as well as the continued frenzy over national rankings; austerity policies benefit this top group across the professional board. The effort to separate theories of rhetoric and theorizing itself from the teaching of writing, as Wardle fears, also aligns well with this economic/academic class division. And yet the traditional study of writing flourishing in the "boutique humanities departments of the top research institutions" (Gunner 2012, 626), the teaching of writing in stripped-down and

increasingly virtual form flourishing in lower tier institutions and programs outside the conventional higher education structure, and post-
humanist theories of writing and theories emerging from digital media
studies all are forms of consent to a refiguring of the field.

CONSENT AND/AS DISRUPTION

Some forms of consent can also be forms of resistance, the effect of discontent with a perceived status quo. Consent can take a creatively disruptive form of complicity, and indirectly consenting to comply with an
austerity agenda might open up space for change. A critical part of such
disruption is a willingness to imagine a path that is less bound by ideological critique, an effort to displace critique from the center, a refram-
ing of the ideologies that have been the historical structure and stric-
tures of the field. Some familiar works and scholars can be used here to
illustrate; I discuss them briefly, and I offer one further example, drawn
from cultural studies, to add to a possibly growing list of seekers of "the
great outdoors" beyond hegemonic frames—but also to ask the extent
to which our field is willing to entertain such ideas.

Sid Dobrin's *Postcomposition* stands in the hybrid zone of complicity,
resistance, and disruption. His is the most explicit recent work to search
for and welcome the study of writing beyond the traditional discipline of
composition, decoupling writing from the teaching and administration
of writing and writing students. His stated motive for the book is telling:
"a desire for disruption, a sense of frustration with the conservatism of
composition studies . . . It is an occasion of change" (Dobrin 2011, 5).
In this and throughout the book, he suggests the need not only for new
narratives of the field, but for a way past ideological discourse, beyond
composition's familiar narratives and histories that "can no longer
account of new conditions of writing" to seek "the contingent frontiers
of writing studies" (191).

In the book as a whole and particularly in an extensive discussion of
systems theory as an essential piece of a reimagined ecocomposition,
which would allow the study of "writing qua writing" (123), Dobrin
seeks to "actively think about disruption" (154). One goal in this discussion is to establish "a basis for *why* and perhaps *how* we might begin to
elaborate a complex systems theory rhetoric in which to theorize the
function of writing independent of the hegemonic rhetorics that have
shaped composition theory thus far" (153). Even as this move treats the
teaching of writing as a kind of junk bond to be snapped up by for-profit
ventures—constituting consent to the austerity-motivated reduction of

writing instruction to a debased instrumentalist element in the valuing and production of credential over knowledge—it also promises innovative ways to reimagine the field. Dobrin's argument resets the course of rhetoric and composition as a pure research field, a project in tune with the research universities that likely will remain in traditional form even as austerity reworks the rest of the higher education landscape. It is an interesting and even brave move that claims space for the field in this quite possible future scenario. It also offers one way of addressing the frustrations and disappointment that the cultural and social turns of the field represent in relation to the material reality we now face.

Along with Dobrin, those working in digital media fields have been among the first to register internally subversive questions, such as those Jeff Rice poses in *The Rhetoric of Cool*: "Is writing still the dominance of alphabetic notation, or does writing include imagery as well? . . . Does a writer really need purpose or a sense of audience each time she sits down to write?" (Rice 2007, 157). Rice's argument that "media change us, and media change the nature of our work" (157) has met with much greater acceptance than Dobrin's argument, in part because, even as it disrupts the conventional notions of academic writing, it consents to this change as an amplification of what we do, whereas Dobrin's proposal radically narrows and specializes the field. The conservative consent implicit in Rice's argument (and I see this as a functional effect, not as Rice's intention) makes his specific critique of and departure from the Kitzhaber-engendered historical conception of composing much more palatable than Dobrin's jettisoning of writing instruction. Yet Rice's work is clearly a push for creative disruption as he calls on the members of the field to "reimagine our status quos . . . reimagine ourselves and our work entirely" (157). Drawing on Greg Ulmer's work, Rice brings in Plato's concept of *chora* and argues that digital writing needs a rhetoric other than the conventional Aristotelian model, a rhetoric that accounts for information-linking, pattern, and connectivity (33–35).

Dobrin and Rice do not directly address the material implications of their arguments, but their arguments align with the material needs of corporate workplaces, in that research in an austerity regime increasingly requires corporate support and so serves corporate interests, and the changes in rhetoric and pedagogy Rice calls for support development of a new literacy central to the managerial skill of controlling information flows. But their work is not co-extensive with these interests and would not be fully co-opted by them. I think the work of both Dobrin and Rice contributes to creating a different path of resistance outside the ideological. My point is not to endorse Dobrin and Rice but to say this is the kind of thinking that creatively disrupts even as it consents—evidence of a desire for new paths, if not *these* paths necessarily, ways to "dwell in the ruins of the University" by trying "to do what we can, while leaving space for what we cannot envisage to emerge" (Readings 1996, 176).

I'd say the same of another vanguard area of the field, object-oriented rhetoric. Again technology and again an upending of conventional disciplinary notions disrupt the status quo of composition, but this time very specifically its traditions of ideological critique. Alex Reid's discussion of object-oriented rhetoric opens up questions about rhetoric's ability to continue in the Aristotelian and Burkean veins. Reid and others writing on object-oriented rhetoric draw on the correlationism of theorists such as Bruno Latour and French Speculative Realist philosopher Quentin Meillassoux to dismantle a humanistic understanding of rhetoric. In "What is Object-Oriented Rhetoric?" Reid (2012b) outlines some of the foundation-shifting premises that object-oriented rhetoric presents: "Conventionally, we understand rhetoric to be the study of human symbolic action," but we can also "imagine rhetoric as something not necessarily human and not necessarily symbolic." If we see language as an object, even if invented by humans, and understand that "symbolic action is not ours [and] language is a non-human other, then we begin to see that the conventional notion of rhetoric as human symbolic action just doesn't work as a definition, that there is no there there." A Latour blurb for Meillassoux's *After Finitude* states that Meillassoux's efforts will "liberate us from discourse" (Thorne 2011). Reid emphasizes that his interest is driven by his work in digital rhetoric and the associated scientific fields such as distributed cognition. As with Dobrin's work, Reid's arguments imply dissatisfaction with, a sense of the insufficiency of, ideological framings of relations, and his work is part of the "general philosophical movement away from some widely-held postmodern and cultural studies theoretical positions that have focused on discourse, ideology, subjectivity, and representation" (Reid 2012a, 1).

These works all point to a growing disturbance in the matter-of-course connections of writing, rhetoric, and ideology to the discipline, its history, and its future. Theories of post-hegemony coming out of British cultural studies may in part be understood as the recognition of that subject cut loose from writing, from the concept of writing as the discipline of rhetoric and composition represents it; from discourse, as we have understood it ideologically. Post-hegemony theorists call into the question a necessary connection of ideology to and as the means of social organization. "Post" is not a matter of a chronological succession, a linear or pendular effect of a waning hegemonic age. Instead, post-hegemony can be understood as a recognition of emerging assemblages, shifting and asymmetric—the singularities of the multitude—and as an effect of the shift from discourse to affect as the means of social relation, affect being the technologically communicated/activated response to images and ideas shared by social media. Post-hegemony names a shift from the epistemologic to the ontologic; facticity and communications over normativity and representation; power-to instead of power-over (Lash 2007). It is a search for an "outside" to hegemony (Arditi 2007).

In a sense, post-hegemony theorists push for recognition of a "power *of* the people" no longer residing in a "proletariat-like mechanism with the brain on the outside" but instead with "the brain—or something like mind [Bateson 2000]—. . . immanent in the system itself," a kind of "collective brain" (Beasley-Murray 2003, 60). In this model, communication becomes "an operational problem dominated by the imperatives of channel rather than by a concern with signification, ethical truth, or rhetorical confrontation" (Terranova qtd. in Thoburn 2007, 83). Thus the centrality of affect: "One does not so much read the encoded information, as sense and embody the pattern of the pulsion . . . Affect is an experience of intensity . . . that changes the state of the body, that has concrete effects on individual and social practice" (Thoburn 2007, 84).

We can see this theoretical exploring as a parallel search for a new rhetoric: "Posthegemony signifies the shift from a rhetoric of persuasion to a regime in which what counts are the effects produced and orchestrated by affective investment in the social, if by affect we mean the order of bodies rather than the order of signification" (Beasley-Murray 2003, 120). We can see it as a creatively disrupted version of critical pedagogy where groups/assemblies "can participate and share resources on their own terms, quickly, visibly, and cost-effectively by setting up transient virtual communities of action that provide ad hoc modes of participation for people who are neither militants nor committed activists" (Arditi 2007, 223). We can also see this theoretical exploring as the attempt to account for the material potential of the virtual.

In *Networks of Outrage and Hope*, Manuel Castells (2012) argues that network culture "embodies material culture" and offers a space and mechanism for change "out of the system" (228). Castells's argument adds to the recognition of this technological shift the critical post-hegemonic element: "change can only take place out of the system by a transformation of power relations that starts in people's minds and develops in the form of the networks built by the projects of new actors constructing themselves as the subjects of the new history in the making. And the Internet that, like all technologies, embodies material culture, is a privileged platform for the social construction of autonomy" (228). Castells points to decentered social movements that are "horizontal," take "multiple forms," occupy a hybrid "third space" that is virtual and in the urban public; are "spontaneous" because affective, with the "source of the call . . . less relevant than the impact of the message on the multiple, unspecified receivers, whose emotions connect with the content and form of the message" (223–24), leading to a viral effect.

Speaking of activist anti-austerity student groups in the United Kingdom that embody Castells's descriptions, sociologists Andre Pusey and Leon Sealey-Huggins argue that these movements need to be seen not so much as "anti-cuts" actions but "an attempt to engender a wider critique of the academy as a site of exclusion, and experiment with radical pedagogical alternatives, based on participatory methods" (Pusey and Sealey-Huggins 2013, 447–448). They argue that "[w]ithin all of these projects . . . there appears the material manifestation of a desire to go from a position situated *within* the academy, which is simultaneously *against* the university in its current form and yet also, through the collective experimentation with alternative models, go *beyond* the existent, towards an affirmation of another form, or forms, of knowledge production and learning" (451). Logic, evidence, and persuasive ability have not gotten us "outside" a system that uses our resistant efforts to solidify the necessity of its own. Ideological critique is being decentered as a political means and supplemented by "autonomous" measures.

TRANSCRITIQUE?

What is non-ideological resistance, or resistance that operates beyond hegemony in a dispersed as opposed to discursively organized way? It tends to be capillary more than static in organization. It challenges through suffusion. It may have its apparently "guerrilla" elements, but rather than a unified movement, these might be the product of self-organized actions among social media users, including "rogue" faculty themselves. A recent *Chronicle of Higher Education* blog post, for instance, tells of a biology postdoc grown frustrated with the print journal publication process who "taught himself code" and created a website that collapses the publisher/editor/author/reader relationship into crowd-sourced authors and user-reviewers. This new system, the biologist claims, is "algorithmic reputation building. It's far better than three people in a room deciding whether or not they like your work . . . It's the sum of thousands and thousands of people saying your work is good or bad" (Wolfman-Arent 2014). The dwindling power of the critical austerity narrative may be overtaken by the rise of "new frontiers" of communication for similar reasons: it is slow, it seems inefficient, and the audience for it is increasingly rejecting the primacy of institution, disciplinary authority, and academic expertise.

The Edu-factory Collective's (2009) freely downloadable book, *Toward a Global Autonomous University*, among whose chapter authors are transnational collectives, collaborators, and individual scholars (including Eileen Schell and Marc Bousquet), is an excellent example of the work of a group that is not centered, not institutionalized, irrupts in protests as well as conferences, and provides outlets of an unscheduled order in varied media for a wide range of activist transnational scholars. In a report on the Collective's The University Is Ours! Conference in Toronto in 2012, Edu-factory participant Enda Brophy asks:

> How is it that we can build alternative spaces for a knowledge production that are other than oppositional and constituent? These institutions of the common, in which ideas circulate but money does not, point the way toward an independent relationship toward knowledge, outside of the confines of the neoliberal university. Struggles within the academy will need to link up with these experiments occurring beyond them. (Brophy 2012)

Along with ideological approaches such as hard-core neo-Marxist critiques, for example, the Edu-factory Collective supports the kind of effort Brophy makes to open a new and different door, using it to occupy the "within" and the "outside." Such efforts include and revise ideological critique, lessening the risk of inducing a kind of closed and unresolvable mirror stage, in which the oppressor we encounter leads us to construct ourselves as a totalized body of resistance. We can see one example of such recursive co-construction in Bousquet's "The Waste Product of Graduate Education" (Bousquet 2002): the PhD glut is a system that works effectively to its intended end of a cheap labor supply. The resulting position we occupy is thus being pitted against a system we seek to join. In the same way, the closed system of austerity crisis immerses students and workers (and institutions such as the university) into a competitive system of winners and losers (Watkins 2008), all the time activating the libertarian notion of the self, so that winning and losing come to be naturalized as determined by individual efforts, leading to a bonding and identification with the oppressor. Ideological critique is a critically necessary theoretical tool, and an often materially effective one, but we cannot expect or demand that it serve as the ur-text for the multitude.

We would benefit from adding tools to the activist toolkit that apply to more than an oppression/resistance structure, for which many have lost the energy, the opportunity, and the belief. Exploring new space is not a binary matter, and even consent can possibly lead to an outside. Forms of consent can operate as moves around hegemonic order, producing a not-organized emergence of assemblies operating within and without, offering one path toward "theories of agency that work beyond the traditions of ideology critique and without the old formulations of the enlightened and enlightening subject" (Hardin 2009, 142). Ideological critique, in sum, should supplement activism; it need not totalize it. "[I]t is possible to change the world without seizing power by multiplying and expanding the cracks/refusals that appear in the texture of domination" (Holloway qtd. in Arditi 2007, 217): sociologist John Holloway suggests that change in but also to a hegemonic power system can co-exist, that individuals—or the multitude, in Hardt and Negri's sense—operate as "singularities," moving through and beyond hegemony and master narratives. Willing participation/consent on the part of the multitude can produce "new modes of worker organizing [that] rely not on the states, nor on parties, nor on top down bureaucratic union structures, but rather are self-generative, autonomous, and developed horizontally through networks both technological and biological " (Thorburn 2012, 259). Post-hegemony theorists point to Giorgio Agamben's theory of the state of exception, in which what is presented as a crisis, a uniquely necessary, only-common-sense policy, becomes business as usual as a function of a hegemonic order. Austerity remains a crisis discourse, but it is clearly the new real, the usual our business has become. How we respond to it must be at once from within and outside, the consent accompanied by disruption.

Again, I am not intending endorsement of a particular view but emphasizing the many alternatives to ideological critique that are emerging and suggesting the motives and conditions of which they are the product. Ideology fatigue is the beginning of a search for a third way. Fatigue is not the same as despair or quietism. The austerity crisis has opened up space for projects that wish to push beyond, perhaps representing "cracks" in capitalism (Holloway qtd. in Pusey and Sealey-Huggins 2013, 453). In a powerful critique of the field, *Dangerous Writing*, Tony Scott (2009) asks, "Is there still a place in rhetoric and composition at which we are willing to risk a utopian impulse?" and argues that such places need to be sought in "the broad ecologies of writing education . . .

all of which are aligned according to ideological assumptions" (187). A utopian impulse—a believing game—can help free us from boundaries and enclosures, which form centers and margins. Bill Readings (1996) argued that the center is an ideologically necessary but empty and powerless place (114–116). With him, I argue for the open question and communities of dissensus, even dissent from the disciplinary hegemony of ideological critique itself.

References

Albertine, Susan. 2013. "Toward the Next Century of Leadership: A Future Faculty Model." *Peer Review : Emerging Trends and Key Debates in Undergraduate Education* 15 (3): 4–7.

Arditi, Benjamin. 2007. "Post-Hegemony: Politics Outside the Usual Post-Marxist Paradigm." *Contemporary Politics* 13 (3): 205–26. http://dx.doi.org/10.1080/13569770701467411.

Armstrong, Elizabeth A., and Laura T. Hamilton. 2013. *Paying for the Party: How College Maintains Inequality.* Cambridge, MA: Harvard University Press. http://dx.doi.org/10.4159/harvard.9780674073517.

Bainbridge Education Summit. 2014. http://bainbridgeeducationsummit.com/.

Bateson, Gregory. 2000. *Steps to an Ecology of Mind.* Chicago: University of Chicago Press.

Beasley-Murray, Jon. 2003. "On Posthegemony." *Bulletin of Latin American Research* 22 (1): 117–25. http://dx.doi.org/10.1111/1470-9856.00067.

Bousquet, Marc. 2002. "The Waste Product of Graduate Education: Toward a Dictatorship of the Flexible." *Social Text* 20 (1): 8–104.

Brophy, Enda. 2012. "Our University." http://toronto.mediacoop.ca/story/our-university-edufactory/10786.

Castells, Manuel. 2012. *Networks of Outrage and Hope.* Malden, MA: Polity Press.

Dobrin, Sidney I. 2011. *Postcomposition.* Carbondale: Southern Illinois University Press.

The Edu-factory Collective. 2009. *Toward a Global Autonomous University.* New York: Autonomedia. https://studentsnotcustomers.files.wordpress.com/2014/11/the-edu-factory-collection.pdf.

Elbow, Peter. 1998. *Writing without Teachers.* 2nd ed. New York: Oxford University Press.

Gunner, Jeanne. 2012. "Disciplinary Purification: The Writing Program as Institutional Brand." *JAC* 32 (3–4): 615–43.

Hardin, Joe Marshall. 2009. "The Writing Program Administrator and Enlightened False Consciousness: The Virtues of Becoming an Empty Signifier." In *The Writing Program Interrupted: Making Space for Critical Discourse,* ed. Donna Strickland and Jeanne Gunner, 137–46. Portsmouth, NH: Heinemann Boynton-Cook.

Lash, Scott. 2007. "Power after Hegemony: Cultural Studies in Mutation?" *Theory, Culture & Society* 24 (3): 55–78. http://dx.doi.org/10.1177/0263276407075956.

Paris, David. 2013. "The Last Artisans? Traditional and Future Faculty Roles." *Peer Review: Emerging Trends and Key Debates in Undergraduate Education* 15 (3): 17–20.

Pusey, Andre, and Leon Sealey-Huggins. 2013. "Transforming the University: Beyond Students and Cuts." *ACME: An International E-Journal for Critical Geographies* 12: 443–58. Accessed through Open Journal Systems. ojs.unbc.ca.

Readings, Bill. 1996. *The University in Ruins.* Cambridge, MA: Harvard University Press.

Reid, Alexander. 2012a. "Minimal Rhetoric." Presentation at the Conference on College Composition and Communication, St. Louis, MO, March. https://www.academia.edu/673441/Minimal_Rhetoric_Gamic_Flow_and_Unit_Operations.

Reid, Alexander. 2012b. "What is Object-Oriented Rhetoric?" *Itineration* Big Ideas. http://tundra.csd.sc.edu/itineration/node/11.

Rice, Jeff. 2007. *The Rhetoric of Cool.* Carbondale: Southern Illinois University Press.

Scott, Tony. 2009. *Dangerous Writing: Understanding the Political Economy of Composition.* Logan: Utah State University Press.

Thoburn, Nicholas. 2007. "Patterns of Production: Cultural Studies after Hegemony." *Theory, Culture & Society* 24 (3): 79–94. http://dx.doi.org/10.1177/0263276 407075959.

Thorburn, Elise Danielle. 2012. "A Common Assembly: Multitude, Assemblies, and a New Politics of the Common." *Interface* 4 (2): 254–79.

Thorne, Christian. 2011. "Outward Bound: On Quentin Meillassoux's *After Finitude.*" http://sites.williams.edu/cthorne/articles/outward-bound-on-quentin-meillassouxs -after-finitude/.

Wardle, Elizabeth. 2014. "Considering What It Means to Teach 'Composition' in the Twenty-First Century." *College Composition and Communication* 65 (4): 659–71.

Watkins, Evan. 2008. *Class Degrees.* New York: Fordham University Press.

White, Edward M. 2005. "The Misuse of Writing Assessment for Political Purposes." *The Journal of Writing Assessment* 2 (1): 21–36.

Winston, Hannah. 2013. "2 Texas Colleges Will Offer Competency-Based Hybrid Degree." *Chronicle of Higher Education,* September 5.

Wolfman-Arent, Avi. 2014. "Frustrated Scholar Creates New Way to Fund and Publish Academic Work." *Chronicle of Higher Education,* June 5.

11
COMPOSITION'S DEAD

Ann Larson

It's impossible to deny that, for increasing numbers of young people, a degree is more likely to lead to a lifetime of debt than to a middle-class job (Hechinger 2013). I've been thinking about the debt and jobs crisis in relation to the "I Quit Lit" genre recently popularized by MA and PhD holders, many of whom were forced out of the academy because they could not string together enough low-wage teaching jobs to support themselves (Powers 2013). The old idea of higher education as a publicly funded resource for students and a viable career path for teachers and researchers now seems quaint in our "era of neglect" (Fischer and Stripling 2014). In that context, there have been relatively few accounts of what the scholarly fields we hoped to join look like once reflections on personal experience become deeper ruminations on the connection between individual lives and global transformations.

This essay examines rhetoric and composition from such a distance. My thinking about the issues raised here has been informed by scholarship that illustrates how education at all levels is being restructured according to capitalism's drive to consolidate power and wealth in the hands of a minuscule percentage of the population at the expense of everyone else (Federici 2014). For those who identify as compositionists, a principled disengagement from the failed politics of respectability and reform may be the only morally defensible choice in the discipline's aftermath.

THE COLLEGE AS BUREAUCRATIC CORPORATION

As of 2009, 75 percent of instructors at all two- and four-year colleges in the United States were hired in term positions off the tenure track ("Portrait of Part-Time Faculty" 2012). Part-time adjuncts earn an average of $2,700 per course. Most have few benefits, no guarantee of continued employment, no voice in their respective departments, and—let's be

DOI: 10.7330/9781607324454.c011

honest—virtually no chance at regular, full-time employment anywhere. Unsurprisingly, African Americans and women are disproportionately represented in non-tenure track positions (Bahn 2013; Cottom 2014).

Academia's job market collapse is largely a result of federal and state disinvestment in public education at all levels and the corresponding rise in institutional and student indebtedness (Quinterno and Orozco 2012). Recent data shows that "annual published tuition at four-year public colleges has grown by $1,850, or 27 percent, since the 2007–08 school year, after adjusting for inflation" (Oliff et al. 2013). In California, which is leading the trend toward privatization, more than half of the financing for public colleges now comes from tuition dollars, not state funding (Kroll 2012). That means administrators are free to use student fees on anything they choose, including capital development projects that have little to do with teaching and learning (Meister 2009). As a result, public universities in that state are already paying $1 billion each year in interest alone to Wall Street (Eaton et al. 2014).

This restructuring is not a withdrawal of state support so much as it is an *active* program of turning higher education over to financiers and manager-elites. Almost two decades ago, in *The University in Ruins*, Bill Readings predicted that universities would become "bureaucratic corporations," not substantially different from any other profit-driven, commercial entity (Readings 1997, 21). He was right.

NO SILVER LINING

Compositionists have often operated under the assumption that our field is immune from the bureaucratization of the university. In fact, conventional wisdom says that composition and rhetoric specialists enjoy an advantage in the academic job market. Instead, I argue, composition does not defy our rotten economic system; it exemplifies it.

A 2011 special issue of *College English* directly addressed the question of composition exceptionalism. "[F]aculty teaching courses in composition," wrote Mike Palmquist and Susan Doe, "have been affected most by [higher education's] growing reliance on contingent faculty. Nearly 70 percent of all composition courses . . . are now taught by faculty in contingent positions" (Palmquist and Doe 2011, 353–54). There is no silver lining for composition in these statistics. Many first-year writing programs are largely—if not entirely—staffed by contingent faculty and graduate students who work cheaply and can usually be counted on not to complain under the assumption that their position is temporary, a necessary apprenticeship on the road to a professional career.

The truth is that adjunct teaching is rarely a road to anything other than more adjunct teaching. Over 80 percent of adjuncts have been at their jobs for more than three years, and most have been teaching part time for more than six years ("Portrait of Part-Time Faculty" 2012). For most MAs, and PhDs, the future looks bleak indeed. Tenure-track positions are being rapidly replaced by teaching-intensive lectureships with limited contracts, including visiting positions (Weinbaum and Page 2014). The American Association of University Professors' (AAUP) report on the trend identified "whole departments of full-time non-tenure-track English composition instructors" as a manifestation of the shift in institutional priorities. "Whether these [contingent] faculty members teach one class or five," the report stated, "the common characteristic among them is that their institutions make little or no long-term commitment to them or to their academic work" ("Contingent Appointments and the Academic Profession" 2003).

In addition to contract teachers, a growing number of institutions hire compositionists to run writing programs and perform other administrative duties in the bureaucratic university. This implies a troubling relationship between the material and the intellectual: statistically speaking, a compositionist is more likely to get a tenure-track job if she is willing to supervise low-paid, marginalized workers. No doubt, most composition specialists expect to do "admin" work at some point in their careers. But considering the grim prognosis for so many aspiring professors in general, perhaps we should all be less comfortable with the fact that, for compositionists in particular, "the future holds the very real prospect of . . . overseeing the labor of others" (Miller 1999, 98).

The neoliberal transformation of the university into a rigidly hierarchical bureaucracy largely staffed by an increasingly precarious class of workers leads us to Marc Bousquet's argument in *How The University Works* that composition has had a major role in processing under-employed degree holders, those he called the "actual shit of the system—being churned inexorably toward the outside" (Bousquet 2008, 27). Writing programs that employ low-wage teachers are often headed by directors with composition credentials. Compositionists in writing programs have been integral to designing curricula that are then deployed by part-time teachers in the classroom. Thus, as Bousquet wrote, composition's intellectual work has helped to legitimate "the practice of deploying a revolving labor force of graduate employees and other contingent teachers to teach writing" (166).

Bousquet's critique of composition inspired impassioned rebuttals from some who accused him of looking down on writing teachers and composition scholars from his perch as a cultural critic. Joseph Harris wrote that Bousquet, like most faculty in English departments, treated composition as the "instrumentalist Other of literature" (Harris 2002, 894). Peggy O'Neill argued that Bousquet was letting tenured faculty in literary studies off the hook for their "ongoing prejudices against Composition" and that he had failed to recognize that labor issues are "intimately connected to disciplinary concerns" (O'Neill 2002, 909). Compositionists have long struggled against intra-departmental hostility, or "prejudice." Later, I will discuss the broader implications of the field's obsession with earning respect in the academy. First, I will briefly trace the history of the idea that labor exploitation in English departments is attributable to disciplinary discrimination.

THE RISE OF THE PROFESSIONAL-MANAGERIAL CLASS

Composition's status as a discipline is inseparable from its history as a site of low-wage work. Since the field's inception there have been a few attempts to address the adjunctification of college teaching. The pioneering document known as the Wyoming Resolution is an important example. Drafted by part-time and full-time professors at a 1986 summer conference, it was approved by the College Composition and Communication Executive Committee the following year. The resolution called on the profession to develop standards for writing teachers' wages and working conditions. The Committee on Professional Standards promoted the resolution in *College Composition and Communication*: "All teachers of writing," they wrote,

> are entitled to design and implement the curricula they think most effective and to use whatever materials they find necessary to that end; all teachers of writing are entitled access to relatively private office space, telephones, and other lines of communication that are standard within the institution; all teachers of writing are eligible for and/or are entitled to compete for whatever sources of research support are available at their institutions; all teachers of writing are entitled to salaries that are commensurate with workload, rank and teaching experience; all teachers of writing are entitled to be eligible for promotion and tenure according to the prevailing standards of the institutions in which they work; all teachers of writing are entitled to achieve the job security that is necessary to preserve their academic freedom. (CCCC Committee on Professional Standards for Quality Education 1989, 61)

Importantly, the committee did not make a distinction between professionally trained compositionists and those with MAs or PhDs in literature who were assigned to teach "comp" each semester. To the proponents of Wyoming, "all teachers of writing" meant *all* teachers of writing.

It is obvious that these demands—from fair pay to academic freedom—could still be made today on institutions and departments no more willing to grant them. Not much has changed. From another point of view, a lot has changed. Composition has grown into a bona fide academic field led by a cadre of high-profile scholars teaching in well-regarded institutions from coast to coast. There are PhD programs, conferences, and journals devoted to writing theory and practice. How should we understand the field's rise to prominence in light of labor practices that endure thirty years after Wyoming?

One answer is that, in the field's early years, relatively privileged composition scholars transformed popular anger against labor exploitation into a campaign of non-discrimination that ultimately benefited themselves. In doing so, they diverted the field from the urgent task of building the kind of organization that could back up demands for justice (such as those in the Wyoming Resolution) with action that couldn't be ignored. I do not believe that compositionists made a purposeful decision to use the anger of the dispossessed to achieve their own professional goals. Instead, I am interested in how individual motives and actions are inseparable from their moment in history and in how past failures can inform current struggles.

THE "EROSION OF OPPOSITION" IN COMPOSITION

In 1988 John Trimbur and Barbara Cambridge supported the Wyoming Resolution in *Writing Program Administration* (*WPA*). They called for sweeping changes to institutional priorities and value systems in order to end "the blatant exploitation of part-time faculty." Yet, considering the authors were then full-time faculty, their advocacy for part timers is curiously inclusive. "We do not have to accept second-class status," they wrote, "because we are interested in the study and teaching of writing" (Trimbur and Cambridge 1988, 13). Trimbur and Cambridge's use of the pronoun "we" is extremely telling. It suggests how elite members of the emerging discipline interpreted the anger and bitterness of contingent faculty as their own. In the context of an academic culture that values scholarship above teaching, this view is understandable. But it does not follow that, as Trimbur and Cambridge wrote, "resist[ing] the unnecessary and unhelpful polarization of scholarship and pedagogy" is the key to winning composition's class struggle (16).

Of the many lessons to be learned from the aftermath of the Wyoming Resolution, one is surely that treating the "blatant exploitation" of workers as a *symptom* of an intra-disciplinary turf war has utterly failed as a strategy of reform. The problem of disciplinary discrimination may be real, but it is undoubtedly of less concern to those teaching in dead-end jobs for near-poverty wages than to an arriviste class focused on attaining professional legitimacy in hierarchical institutions.

The treatment of class inequality as merely symptomatic is not limited to academia. The political theorist Adolph Reed described how counter-hegemonic social movements in the 1960s collapsed into a "pluralistic politics" that "construe[d] political issues solely in terms of competition over goods and services within the bounds of fixed system priorities" (Reed 1986, 63). Composition came into its own as some professionals were promoted through the ranks of a fixed system. In response to an outcry from those teachers who were *actually* marginalized, a dominant discourse emerged: adjuncts' demands for fair pay and reasonably secure jobs in workplaces and elites' demands for legitimacy and recognition in academic departments were the same struggle. Composition as a discipline has never recovered from this category mistake.

I am not the first to point out the failures of the non-discrimination program that defined composition's early years. In 1991 James Sledd argued that composition's middle-class professionals were working at odds with those for whom they often claimed to speak. He asserted that the Wyoming Resolution would never be implemented because the "newly risen Compositionists and their freshly bedoctored students" benefit from a labor system in which other people (viz., adjuncts) do the work that they theorize about. "With that solution," Sledd continued, "the compositionists are apparently content, since it marks the literary establishment's acceptances of their claims to shared glory" (Sledd 1991, 275). Sledd's disdain for the intellectual work of composition may offend, but he was correct to point out that the rise of a small group of professional compositionists was made possible *due to* the existence of a class of exploited teachers that were sometimes scorned by a self-styled vanguard, including Maxine Hairston who wrote in the 1980s that "most composition teachers" did not share her interest in composition research and, thus, did "not know what they were doing" (Hairston 1986, 117).

Some composition scholars recognized the inherent conflict in advancing claims for disciplinary status when most writing teachers and students would never benefit from those gains. In 2000, Duke's writing program administrator, Joseph Harris, wrote: "Following [Jeanne]

Gunner and Sledd, I have come to believe that we have succumbed to a professional logic in which establishing composition as a research field is seen as the key to improving the teaching of writing to undergraduates" (Harris 2000, 56). Harris's proposed solution was to work within the boundaries of a system of apparently unchangeable inequities. We must "move beyond our seeming fixation on the Ph.D. and the availability (or not) of tenure-stream jobs," he advised, "and instead agitate at a local level for better working conditions for the people actually teaching writing" (2000, 56). Harris's position was commendable in that it rejected a distinction between professional scholars and "the people actually teaching writing." Yet, his argument was essentially that compositionists should give up the battle for a transformation of the academic labor system *qua* system. Ironically, it is only in the absence of a militant labor movement in composition (not to mention in higher education in general) that Harris's recommendation *not* to build one could be made. From the perspective of "the university in ruins," it is clear that what has unfolded in composition over the last thirty years—and in the academic labor system more generally—is what Reed in his eulogy of 1960s radicalism called an "erosion of oppositional content" (Reed 1986, 7).

COMPOSITION'S CRITIQUE OF COMPOSITION

Compositionists themselves identified the erosion of opposition early on. David Bartholomae discussed the connection between professionalization and remediation in his well-known essay "The Tidy House," which begins with the revealing sentence: "I found my career in basic writing." The field, he wrote, "is a reiteration of the liberal project . . . where in the name of sympathy and empowerment, we have once again . . . confirm[ed] existing patterns of power and authority [and] reproduc[ed] the hierarchies we had meant to question and overthrow" (Bartholomae 1993, 18). In other words, basic writing as a curricular program was a milquetoast commitment to "opportunity" and to "respect for difference" that posed no challenge to the exploitative system in which it was embedded. Bartholomae's solution was a mix of small-scale reforms based on advocating for students who entered the university under the remedial rubric. "The Tidy House" was published during an era when remedial programs were under attack by a conservative counterinsurgency against open admissions, which partly explains why Bartholomae made no mention of the underpaid, part-time instructors who staffed burgeoning basic writing programs. This erasure was a sign that composition was firmly in the grip of neoliberalism. By the 1990s, ignoring the labor conditions endured by basic writing teachers had become a virtual requirement for defending basic writing.

Other scholars deepened composition's critique of policies and discourses of access. At City University of New York (CUNY), Mary Soliday (2002, 48) wrote that segregating students into special literacy programs was actually a "crisis management tool" that allowed institutions to manage growth and maintain an aura of selectivity in a context of greater demand for college access. In 1996, Bruce Horner argued that basic writing's existence was a function of composition's push for legitimacy. Quoting Mina Shaughnessy, he noted that early basic writing scholars had described the field as "frontier territory." "Cast as frontier pioneers," Horner (1996, 210) explained, "Basic Writing teachers could be granted credibility as 'professionals.'" Scholars have long known that the professionalization of composition happened concurrently with the de-politicization of the academy. Literature professor Walter Benn Michaels described the problem with presuming that demanding entrance to exclusive spaces is effective political action. "It is not prejudice or discrimination that makes people rich or poor," he wrote. "It is capitalism, neoliberal capitalism in particular" (Michaels 2006).

Compositionists have also theorized the limitations of educational initiatives designed to provide access to hierarchical systems for underrepresented groups. In 2004 Donna Strickland wrote that

> the rise of composition studies brought with it the initiation of many new "basic writing" programs, which in turn led to the appointment of new directors to lead "writing labs" or "writing centers" that would offer tutorial services for these at-risk students. Thus, the discourse [of idealism] that set "democratization" in motion also set in motion various administrative structures . . . I recount the "myth" of composition's democratic agenda not to unveil it as "false" but as limited, limited precisely by the lack of attention to the administrative imperative within the profession. (Strickland 2004, 130)

Strickland's Foucauldian thesis that composition's "administrative imperative" is in conflict with its supposed "democratic agenda" was built on prior research about declining labor conditions for writing teachers, the feminization of composition teaching, and the circulation of management discourses in higher education. Indeed, in the twenty-first century, compositionists who seek professional status often have little choice but to assume the role of the scholar-manager who maintains "a permanently subordinate class of teacher-technicians" as Tony Scott (2004, 156), in *Tenured Bosses and Disposable Teachers*, described them.

A blistering critique of composition as "management science" (to use Bousquet's term) can be found in composition itself.

FROM ANTI-DISCRIMINATION TO ZOMBIE POLITICS

Class analysis by a generation of compositionists is threatening to the field's elites because it undermines the identity of the discipline as a democratic force in higher education. Composition's professional-managerial class is still focused on defending the field's claims to status on those grounds. In 2013, a dispute erupted between Rebecca Schuman, a blogger and *Slate* columnist, and New School professor Claire Potter, otherwise known as the "Tenured Radical." Schuman (2013) published an essay that was critical of Modern Language Association (MLA) conference interview procedures and the treatment of job candidates. She described search committees as "elitist and out of touch." Potter (2013) wrote a condescending response criticizing the "chronic rage" and "hissy fits" of those shut out of academic jobs.

Some composition faculty entered the ensuing debate to offer advice to unemployed PhDs and graduate students. Steven Krause insisted that the job market in composition is a "completely different animal" than the market in literature. When people "express 'rage' about the terribleness of the job market," he wrote on his blog, "I have to wonder what it was they thought they were getting themselves into when they started down the PhD in literature path . . . I think a lot of [unemployed academics'] anger . . . comes from this realization that they didn't beat the odds, that they fooled themselves (and/or allowed themselves to be fooled) into believing that they were somehow immune from the job market laws of supply and demand" (Krause 2013).

From an historical perspective, Krause's assessment is astonishing. Today the academic labor crisis is no longer assumed to have been caused by "prejudice" or by disciplinary "discrimination." Such liberal epithets might have served the field's proto-professionals well in Mina Shaughnessy's day, but they no longer apply now that composition positions are more plentiful. Instead, the *neoliberal* justification for academic labor practices goes like this: *there are no adjuncts.* There are only immutable economic principles such as "the law of supply and demand" to which none of us can expect to be "immune." In this Panglossian paradise, Krause asserts, underemployed PhDs are not victims of discrimination; they are fools who failed to take personal responsibility for whether or not they could find a job in a field they chose and whether that job paid a living wage. The metaphor of "immunity" invoked by

Krause conjures the figure of the zombie referenced by Tony Scott in this volume. In popular culture, people bitten by zombies sometimes have a moment of clarity, when they "understand their coming deaths," just before reanimation. In the case of composition, ideologies of merit and professionalism have blunted our power to see, to understand, and to offer a clear, bold response to our own dispossession in the moments before the end of all memory.

THE LAST DAYS OF COMPOSITION

Is composition a living discipline? On an organizational level, is there a body of scholarship powerful enough or a group of practitioners sufficiently organized to have much of an influence on how writing is taught (a fairly modest expectation) in US colleges in the face of the dismantling of public education and the growing desperation of indebted students and contract faculty? On an individual basis, does a clever digital humanist wielding a cutting edge "writing studies" syllabus stand a chance against the corporate-funded Massive Online Open Course (MOOC) onslaught? I think the answer to these questions is no.

We can understand why by studying how compositionists themselves have grappled with the questions. Chris Gallagher responded to Marc Bousquet's critique of composition's management imperatives by emphasizing the discipline's inability to engage the public. Composition has been "a self-referential, recognizably middle-class psychodrama," he wrote, arguing that faculty needed to "disrupt" the "corporatization of the academy" (Gallagher 2005, 75–6). I certainly agree that disruption was, at one time, a worthy goal. But it seems a willed insanity to continue under the delusion that privatizing institutions in the last days of an all-out assault by politicians and Wall Street are in any sense reclaimable.

However, I think we have to take Gallagher's diagnosis seriously and ask a more basic question: what has composition's obsession with status—its "middle-class psychodrama"—meant for the majority of writing teachers, whether they are PhDs, graduate students, or contract faculty? By most accounts, writing teachers' working conditions have stayed the same or deteriorated during the period that composition scholars fought for disciplinary recognition in the academy (and then lamented the internalized dramas that emerged from that pursuit). The problem is *not* that compositionists lost the battle against disciplinary discrimination; *the problem is that they won it.* That campaign has been successful within the framework of reform in which it was first articulated. To "the people who actually teach writing," to use Harris's phrasing, it has been meaningless at best and destructive at worst. We should admit that failure and learn from it. It is clear that the solution is *not* to continue down the same road and create alternative models of professionalism for a "New Progressive era," as Gallagher (2005, 86) ultimately argued. Instead, we must acknowledge the emptiness of "Progressivism" as a political category and come to terms with the fact that, as Nathan Brown explained, "the university is one situation among many in which we struggle against debt, exploitation, and austerity" (Brown 2011).

WELCOME TO THE EDUCATION FACTORY

Just as Readings advised us not to allow the university to become "the object of romantic nostalgia for a lost wholeness," we should not mourn the loss of composition (Readings 1997, 129). The field was never a beacon of democracy. Historically, its mystifications and ideologies reflected broader politics, from the liberal commitment to "access" to closed systems to the neoliberal worship of "efficiency" within open markets. We can still learn from the discipline's passing about what kind of political commitments are likely to lead out of the "university in ruins." We can acknowledge that expanding the political rights of marginalized groups within an already oppressive system is not liberatory. "What if the historical truth of capitalist class power," Adolph Reed wrote, "is that, without direct, explicit and relentless, zero-sum challenge to its foundations in a social order built on its priority and dominance in the social division of labor, we will never be able to win more than a shifting around of the material burdens of inequality, reallocating them and recalibrating their incidence among different populations?" (Reed 2013).

The task ahead is not to recalibrate and reclaim composition—or even education more generally—within the social division of labor that exists. As public education is dismantled around us, those who identify as compositionists should consider taking the radical step of focusing our scholarly and pedagogical energies outside the boundaries of academic departments, disciplinary systems, and the already-failed politics of access and reform. The operative questions now must be: in whose interests should our knowledges be deployed and in what yet unimagined contexts might they be made valuable again?

There are many paths ahead including collectively withholding our teaching and administrative labor, forging coalitions with low-wage workers outside academia, and creating and supporting alternative educational spaces informed by democratic values. Ultimately, the goal ought to be dispensing with the business of building a discipline and joining the struggle to build a movement.

There are signs of progress. In the spring of 2014, faculty at University of Illinois–Chicago (UIC) walked off the job. Two strike organizers, Lennard Davis and Walter Benn Michaels, referred to all UIC faculty as "workers." They explained that the term was a key feature of a new coalition strategy. "If you've done any work on the history of professionalization," they wrote, "you know that one of the original points of the whole concept of the professional—as it applied to ministers, doctors, lawyers and professors—was to distinguish them from workers. But what we've all begun to realize is that, whatever it meant in the late 19th and early 20th century, in the 21st century that distinction is pure ideology. Professionals are workers—and professors are workers" (Davis and Michaels 2014).

I do not propose "workers" as simply a new identity category to be uncritically embraced by scholars and teachers in the neoliberal university. Rather, naming our collective position as laborers in an undemocratic system is a tactical move that clarifies a material relationship to the institutions that don't employ us and to the financiers who profit from mass indebtedness and from the privatization of higher education. In composition, that relationship has long been obscured in the fog of disciplinary politics. Furthermore, it is notable that historical research on professionalism informed the UIC strike organizers' strategy. Developing collective power requires that we examine and discredit ruling class rhetorical tactics that erode solidarity. To begin, we should stop seeing colleges and universities and the labor practices therein as having a special status with regard to capitalist social relations. They don't. Composition in particular must stop perceiving itself as having a special, democratic role within the academy. It doesn't. As intellectuals, we ought to give up, at long last, the quest to advance our own disciplinary cause. As human beings, such a withdrawal of consent might allow us to mourn the only loss that really matters: a generation of teachers and scholars who have either left the academy or are working in the bottom ranks of the education factory that elite members of a moribund discipline hardly acknowledge exists. We can never bring them back from the dead.

References

"A Portrait of Part-Time Faculty Members: A Summary of Findings on Part-Time Faculty Respondents to the Coalition on the Academic Workforce Survey of Contingent Faculty Members and Instructors." 2012. Coalition of the Academic Workforce. http://www.academicworkforce.org/survey.html.

Bahn, Kate. 2013. "The Rise of the Lady Adjuncts." *Chronicle Vitae*. https://chronicle vitae.com/news/206-the-rise-of-the-lady-adjuncts.

Bartholomae, David. 1993. "The Tidy House: Basic Writing in the American Curriculum." *Journal of Basic Writing* 12 (1): 4–21.

Bousquet, Marc. 2008. *How the University Works: Higher Education and the Low-Wage Nation.* New York: New York University Press.

Brown, Nathan. 2011. "Five Theses on Privatization and the UC Struggle." *The Distribution of the Insensible.* http://distributioninsensible.tumblr.com/post/12867 650744/five-theses-on-privatization-and-the-uc-struggle.

CCCC Committee on Professional Standards for Quality Education. 1989. "CCCC Initiatives on the Wyoming Conference Resolution: A Draft Report." *College Composition and Communication* 40 (1): 61–72. http://dx.doi.org/10.2307/358181.

"Contingent Appointments and the Academic Profession." 2003. American Association of University Professors. http://www.aaup.org/report/contingent-appointments-and -academic-profession.

Cottom, Tressie McMillan. 2014. "The New Old Labor Crisis." *Slate.* http://www.slate .com/articles/life/counter_narrative/2014/01/adjunct_crisis_in_higher_ed_an_all_ too_familiar_story_for_black_faculty.html.

Davis, Lennard, and Walter Benn Michaels. 2014. "Faculty on Strike." *Jacobin.* https:// www.jacobinmag.com/2014/02/faculty-on-strike/.

Eaton, Charlie, Cyrus Dioun, Garcia Santibáñez Godoy Daniela, Adam Goldstein, Jacob Habinek, and Robert Osley-Thomas. 2014. "Borrowing against the Future: The Hidden Costs of Financing U.S. Higher Education." Debt and Society. http://debt andsociety.org/publication/borrowing_against_the_future/.

Federici, Silvia. 2014. "From Commoning to Debt: Microcredit, Student Debt and the Disinvestment in Reproduction." https://archive.org/details/SilviaFedericiTalkAtGold smithsUniversity-12November2012-CpAudio.

Fischer, Karin, and Jack Stripling. 2014. "An Era of Neglect." *Chronicle of Higher Education,* March 2.

Gallagher, Chris. 2005. "We Compositionists: Toward Engaged Professionalism." *JAC* 25 (1): 75–99.

Hairston, Maxine. 1986. "On Not Being a Composition Slave." In *Training the New Teacher of College Composition,* ed. Charles W. Bridges, 117–24. Urbana, IL: National Council of Teachers of English.

Harris, Joseph. 2000. "Meet the New Boss, Same as the Old Boss: Class Consciousness in Composition." *College Composition and Communication* 52 (1): 43–68. http://dx.doi.org /10.2307/358543.

Harris, Joseph. 2002. "Behind Blue Eyes: A Response to Marc Bousquet." *JAC* 22 (4): 891–9.

Hechinger, John. 2013. "Overdue Student Loans Reach Record as U.S. Graduates Seek Jobs." *Bloomberg News.* http://www.bloomberg.com/news/2013-05-23/overdue -student-loans-reach-record-as-u-s-graduates-seek-jobs.html.

Horner, Bruce. 1996. "Discoursing Basic Writing." *College Composition and Communication* 47 (2): 199–222. http://dx.doi.org/10.2307/358793.

Krause, Steven. 2013. "In Which I Needlessly Weigh in on Academic Searches and 'The Humanities.'" StevenDKrause.com. http://stevendkrause.com/2013/12/28/in-which -i-needlessly-weigh-in-on-academic-searches-and-the-humanities/.

Kroll, Andy. 2012. "The Slow Death of California's Higher Education." *Mother Jones.* http:// www.motherjones.com/politics/2012/10/california-public-university-higher-education.

Meister, Robert. 2009. "They Pledged Your Tuition to Wall Street." *Keep California's Promise.* http://keepcaliforniaspromise.org/383/they-pledged-your-tuition.

Michaels, Walter Benn. 2006. "The Trouble with Diversity: An Argument between Walter Benn Michaels and Katha Pollitt, moderated by Scott Stossel." NYPL.org. http://www

.nypl.org/events/program/2009/05/20/trouble-diversity-argument-between-walter
-benn-michaels-katha-pollitt-scot.

Miller, Richard. 1999. "'Let's Do the Numbers': Comp Droids and the Prophets of Doom." *Profession:* 96–105.

Oliff, Phil, Vincent Palacios, Ingrid Johnson, and Michael Leachman. 2013. *Recent Deep State Higher Education Cuts May Harm Students and the Economy for Years to Come.* Center for Budget and Policy Priorities.

O'Neill, Peggy. 2002. "Unpacking Assumptions, Providing Context: A Response to Marc Bousquet." *JAC* 22 (4): 906–17.

Palmquist, Mike, and Susan Doe. 2011. "Contingent Faculty: Introduction." *College English* 73 (4): 353–55.

Potter, Claire. 2013. "Job Market Rage Redux." *Chronicle of Higher Education,* December 23.

Powers, L. S. 2013. "Quit!" *The Adjunct Project.* http://adjunct.chronicle.com/quit/.

Quinterno, John, and Viany Orozco. 2012. "The Great Cost Shift: How Higher Education Cuts Undermine the Future Middle Class." Demos. http://www.demos.org /publication/great-cost-shift-how-higher-education-cuts-undermine-future-middle -class.

Readings, Bill. 1997. *The University in Ruins.* Boston: Harvard University Press.

Reed, Adolph. 1986. *Race, Politics, and Culture: Critical Essays on the Radicalism of the 1960s.* Ed. Adolph Reed. Westport, CT: Greenwood Press.

Reed, Adolph. 2013. "*Django Unchained,* or *The Help:* How 'Cultural Politics' Is Worse Than No Politics at All and Why." Nonsite.org. http://nonsite.org/feature/django -unchained-or-the-help-how-cultural-politics-is-worse-than-no-politics-at-all-and-why.

Schuman, Rebecca. 2013. "Naming and Shaming: UC-Riverside English Gives Candidates 5 Days' Notice" PanKissesKafka.com. http://pankisseskafka.com/2013/12/20 /naming-and-shaming-uc-riverside-english-gives-candidates-3-days-notice/.

Scott, Tony. 2004. "Managing Labor and Literacy in the Future." In *Tenured Bosses and Disposable Teachers: Writing Instruction in The Managed University,* ed. Marc Bousquet, Tony Scott, Leo Parascondola, and Randy Martin, 153–64. Carbondale: Southern Illinois University Press.

Sledd, James. 1991. "Why The Wyoming Resolution Had to Be Emasculated: A History and a Quixotism." *JAC* 11 (2): 269–81.

Soliday, Mary. 2002. *The Politics of Remediation: Institutional and Student Needs in Higher Education.* Pittsburgh: University of Pittsburgh Press.

Strickland, Donna. 2004. "Making the Managerial Conscious in Composition Studies." *American Academic* 1:125–38.

Trimbur, John, and Barbara Cambridge. 1988. "The Wyoming Conference Resolution: A Beginning." *WPA: Writing Program Administration* 12 (1–2).

Weinbaum, Eve S., and Max Page. 2014. "Solidarity: An Argument for Faculty Unity." *New Labor Forum* 23 (1): 14–6. http://dx.doi.org/10.1177/1095796013512797.

12
AUSTERITY, CONTINGENCY, AND ADMINISTRATIVE BLOAT
Writing Programs and Universities in an Age of Feast and Famine

Eileen E. Schell

In May of 2014, Drs. Kathy Cawsey, Renee Ward, Lucie Kocum, and Becca Fawn-Dew Babcock made headlines by applying for the $400,000 position of University President and Vice Chancellor at the University of Alberta (U of A). In their "tongue in cheek" application letter featured in an article by Scott Jaschik in *Inside Higher Ed*, they argued that their "collective experience in academic and administrative leadership totals over 30 years" and that their preparation for the position was impeccable with "12 postsecondary degrees [between them], including four PhDs, which we believe will surpass the 'exceptional intellectual calibre' of any of your other single applicants" (Jaschik 2014). The four applicants promised to "each take only a fair and reasonable salary, rather than one which is four or five times that of a tenured academic and at least ten times that of a sessional [adjunct], and that this willingness will prove to society our belief in 'the importance of higher education,' and encourage others in similar positions to follow suit." Their letter, which went viral on the Internet, succeeded in highlighting the disparity between the compensation of higher education administrators and that of contingent faculty members. The writers also questioned the "rhetoric of austerity" being used by university administrators. As Cawsey told *Inside Higher Ed*: "'I don't think it [the letter] in itself will change anything, but enough small actions like this might get people thinking about the role of university administrators and the disparity for many of them between their actions and their rhetoric of austerity. It's a serious question . . . Is one person really worth what four (or even eight, given the current U of A president's salary) tenured professors

DOI: 10.7330/9781607324454.c012

could contribute?'" (Jaschik 2014). The University of Alberta "4 for the Price of 1" application letter sparked a dialogue about the growth and compensation of college and university administrative positions, a phenomenon that has been referred to colloquially and unflatteringly as "administrative bloat."

In this chapter, I analyze the costs and consequences of "administrative bloat" at US colleges and universities and the accompanying rhetorics of austerity and entrepreneurialism. On the one hand, university administrators who command the higher education equivalent of CEO-size salaries often argue for austerity measures, including "belt-tightening" around faculty hiring and the slimming down of department and program operating budgets. In the same breath, they often proclaim the need for entrepreneurialism: finding and exploiting new revenue streams, promoting corporate partnerships, and monetizing faculty research. So even as we, as faculty members, face shrinking instructional budgets, an increasingly contingent and underpaid faculty, a decline in state funding for public higher education, and an increasingly competitive environment for external research funding, we are urged to be entrepreneurs, to find new streams of funding while our students face rising tuition, fee rates, and soaring loan debt.

As I address the challenges of rising administrative costs, increasing instability and underfunding of the faculty ranks, and the rise of student debt, I also analyze what this dual rhetoric of austerity and entrepreneurialism might mean for writing programs and writing program administrators (WPAs) who are responsible for providing and supervising the instruction of thousands of America's college students enrolled in writing courses. My goal is not to denigrate administrative positions or those who seek them, but to ask tough questions about how money spent on managing the university organization and university programs and funds allocated to "entrepreneurial" or extracurricular initiatives have to be balanced against monies spent on the instructional budget in the form of stable, well-paid positions (both tenure-track and non-tenured) with benefits and professional development opportunities. I also argue that WPAs, along with other writing program faculty, both off and on the tenure-track, have a vested interest in intervening in debates over the allocation of instructional budgets and the role of shared governance—the right of faculty members and, where appropriate, students to determine the curricular goals, outcomes, and future of their colleges and universities. After all, our programs, departments, and students are most affected when our university and college instructional budgets are defunded and when those responsible for actually educating students are the lowest paid, most precarious employees who cannot speak out about students' teaching and learning conditions.

I am not alone, of course, in calling for faculty to examine the rhetorics of austerity, administrative bloat, and entrepreneurialism. Other scholars (see Bousquet 2008; Nelson 2011; Newfield 2008) and organizations like the American Association of University Professors (AAUP) have called for faculty of all ranks to address administrative costs, budgetary transparency, and the need for faculty of all ranks to defend and advocate for shared academic governance. My chapter follows the economic trends in higher education, especially by analyzing the rise of administrative costs and the shifts in faculty ranks, and concludes with organizing strategies that faculty can use to make alliances with each other and with student activists to address the future of higher education and to preserve shared governance.

RHETORICS OF ADMINISTRATIVE BLOAT

Every year, hosts of administrators and staffers are added to college and university payrolls, even as schools claim to be battling budget crises that are forcing them to reduce the size of their full-time faculties. As a result, universities are now filled with armies of functionaries—vice presidents, associate vice presidents, assistant vice presidents, provosts, associate provosts, vice provosts, assistant provosts, deans, deanlets, and deanlings, all of whom command staffers and assistants—who, more and more, direct the operations of every school (Benjamin Ginsberg 2011). Over a thirty-year period, between 1975 and 2005, US colleges and universities tripled their expenditures, with higher education spending rising to $325 billion per year (Ginsberg 2011). Between 2000 and 2012 both the private and public workforce in non-profit higher education "grew by 28 percent, more than 50 percent faster than the previous decade" (Desrochers and Kirshstein 2014, 1). From periodic articles detailing rising college costs to articles decrying that colleges and universities are full of lazy, underworked, spoiled tenured and tenure-track faculty, one might assume that this increased college spending is largely due to the costs associated with hiring and supporting faculty members and rising health care costs. While these expenditures are a factor, if we examine the data on changes in staffing, we learn that our current time period in US higher education history saw little change in the faculty-to-student ratio, with the numbers staying "fairly constant, at approximately fifteen or sixteen students per instructor," (Ginsberg 2011) not factoring in whether or not that instructor is tenure-track or non-tenure-track/contingent/part-time, an issue I will address at a later point in this chapter. As political science professor Benjamin Ginsberg summarizes in his seminal *Washington Monthly* article "The Administrators Ate My Tuition," what really changed in this time period is the skyrocketing number of administrators and professional staff members who were hired: in "1975, colleges employed one administrator for every eighty-four students and one professional staffer—admissions officers, information technology specialists, and the like—for every fifty students"; by 2005, the administrator to student ratio went to "one administrator for every sixty-eight students" and one professional staffer "for every twenty-one students" (Ginsberg 2011).

This is a significant boost in the number of non-instructional staff in higher education, yet numbers vary based on institutional type. Drawing on two decades worth of data from the US Department of Education's Integrated Postsecondary Education database, Donna Desrochers and Rita Kirshstein, writing for the Delta Cost Project,[1] find that public institutions experienced slow growth in hiring in the first decade of 2000 compared to their hiring trends in the 1990s because the "recent expansion in new positions largely mirrored rising enrollments as the Millennial Generation entered college" (Desrochers and Kirshstein 2014, 1). Public research universities and community colleges saw decreases in the hiring of staff, with "16 fewer staff per 1,000 full-time equivalent (FTE) students compared with 2000, while the number of staff per student at public master's and bachelor's colleges remained unchanged" (1). Private colleges, however, were a different matter and experienced significant hiring increases: "Private institutions employed, on average, 15 to 26 additional workers per 1,000 FTE students between 2000 and 2012. And even during the Great Recession, many public and private colleges kept hiring in response to the uptick in new students" (3), even as they reduced or flat-lined instructional budgets (2).

As Desrochers and Kirshstein (2014) indicate, professional staff positions, such as business analysts, human resources personnel, and admissions staffers "grew twice as fast as executive and managerial positions at public non-research institutions between 2000 and 2012, and outpaced enrollment growth" (3). This trend, in particular, demonstrates that colleges and universities are directing their dollars toward "noninstructional student services, not just business support" (3). The report indicates that across all institutional types, the "wage and salary expenditures for student services (per FTE staff) were the fastest growing salary expense in many types of institutions between 2002 and 2012" (3). As these numbers rose, the faculty and staff per administrator ratio dropped "by roughly 40 percent in most types of four-year colleges and universities between 1990 and 2012, and now averages 2.5 or fewer faculty and staff per administrator" (3). Faculty salaries have largely stayed flat for almost a decade; however, "additional savings from shifting to part-time instructors have not been enough to offset the costs associated with continued hiring and rising benefits expenditures" (3). The report concludes that these changes "represent long-standing trends" and that the hiring and support of administrative positions have taken precedence over instructional positions, something that many of us have noted in our daily lives.

Explanations, however, abound for the rise of administrative positions beyond the obvious expansion and democratization of higher education itself. One reason articulated for such hiring is compliance with increased government reporting standards. A second reason is the need to handle more complex tasks associated with students and operations from managing computing to managing facilities to increased student services. A third is an increased focus on fundraising as state and federal funding for higher education has declined (Desrochers and Kirshstein 2014, 15). While the Delta report clearly points to an increase in administrative spending, Descrochers and Kirshstein are hesitant to assume that the growth of these positions constitutes "administrative bloat" as opposed to necessity (13). Others like Ginsberg (2011), however, are quick to argue that administrative bloat is exactly what these trends and patterns indicate, "as colleges and universities have had more money to spend, they have *not* chosen [emphasis mine] to spend it on expanding their instructional resources—that is, on paying faculty. They have chosen, instead, to enhance their administrative and staff resources."

Meanwhile the expanded costs of higher education have been passed on to the students and their families as "inflation-adjusted tuition at public universities has tripled" while "at private universities it has more than doubled" since the 1980s (Ginsberg 2011). Not surprisingly, student debt is at an all-time high. The Institute for College Access and Success[2] recent report "Student Debt and the Class of 2012" reveals that "[s]even in 10 College Seniors who graduated in 2012 had student loan debt, with an average of $29,400 for those with loans" (Reed and Cochrane 2012). With many students facing uncertain job prospects due to the economic recession, it is imperative that student loan terms and college costs be addressed. Tom Hayden, the former leader of Students for a Democratic Society, former California legislator, and sociology professor, points out the irony that in the United States higher education is so expensive when "[u]ndergraduate education is virtually free [also known as heavily subsidized by the state] at the Sorbonne or the National Autonomous

University of Mexico, and a year at Oxford costs no more than community colleges charge here" (Hayden 2010). Hayden argues that we have chosen, as a society, to privatize public higher education and spend "three trillion dollars, by some estimates, on the war in Iraq instead of on our public universities; to bail out billionaires on Wall Street while hitting students and their families with repeated tuition increases." Such choices, Hayden contends, have a great impact on students and their families, faculty, staff, and for the future of higher education.

Even as the explanations for the administrative trends and rising college costs may vary, many faculty—and even some administrators—agree that it is time to roll back the administrative growth trend. One major factor is galvanizing faculty and students to debate and organize to address this issue. However, first, we must ask about the impact these new trends are having on writing programs and academic departments in the form of challenges with instructional lines, support for academic units, control of curricular and pedagogical matters, and shared governance.

CONTINGENCY, ENTREPRENEURIALISM, AND THE STRUGGLE FOR SHARED GOVERNANCE

The past thirty years have seen significant cost cutting in the instructional budget through tenure-line positions being replaced by contingent positions. The American Association of University Professors Subcommittee of the Committee on Contingency in the Profession (2009) notes in a recent report that

> By 2007 . . . almost 70 percent of faculty members were employed off the tenure track. Many institutions use contingent faculty appointments throughout their programs; some retain a tenurable faculty in their traditional or flagship programs while staffing others—such as branch campuses, online offerings, and overseas campuses—almost entirely with contingent faculty. Faculty serving contingently generally work at significantly lower wages, often without health coverage and other benefits, and in positions that do not incorporate all aspects of university life or the full range of faculty rights and responsibilities. The tenure track has not vanished, but it has ceased to be the norm for faculty.

The changes in the composition and working conditions of the faculty in American higher education are part and parcel of larger changes in higher education. As higher education expanded its reach and opened its doors to many students in late 1960s and 1970s, many institutions experienced precipitous growth and hired contingent faculty as stopgap measures to cover the demand for teachers of lower-division courses (Abel 1984). Of course, there were "moonlighting" adjuncts as well who were hired to teach specialized courses—people in industry with high-paying jobs during the day who brought their real-world skills to teaching an occasional evening class or two. After awhile, though, what was a temporary stopgap measure to cover introductory level courses became a long-term management strategy. It was simply cheaper to hire contingent faculty members when higher education institutions were growing in other ways, as noted earlier in this chapter: growing their administrative and staff ranks, growing their research and development endeavors, growing their athletic programs, growing their reach into community engagement endeavors, even as federal and state funding waxed and waned.

The challenges that contingent faculty face in our field as well as others have been well documented by many in our field: low pay, lack of contractual stability, scant or non-existent office space to meet with students, juggling teaching on multiple campuses to make a living (see Schell 1997; Schell and Stock 2001). One has to wonder why the very people responsible for instructing the majority of students often lack the very conditions to guarantee decent working conditions that lead to quality learning conditions for students. Why is it that a staff member with a BA degree working in the Office of Student Life or other support area has a guaranteed yearly salary, health benefits, a retirement plan, and paid sick and vacation days whereas a contingent faculty member with a master's degree or a PhD instructing the very same students will receive a per course section rate, few or no benefits, and overcrowded or non-existent office space? I do not ask this question to begrudge the staff member a decent salary and benefits, but to ask why the instructional budget must be a primary source of cost cutting and economizing?

As the instructional budget takes a hit and teachers are paid less and offered teaching conditions that make it difficult for them to innovate or continue to develop professionally, the curriculum and quality of a college education offered to students diminishes. How well can writing curricula be updated and engaged when the teachers implementing such curricula teach at two or three campuses just to make a living and have little or no time or funding to pursue professional development opportunities? Meanwhile, external pressures to standardize and corporatize curricula and put them online are increasingly coming to bear upon college and university writing programs.

Those of us who have worked as WPAs are often asked to raise course caps to save money; engage external assessment measures; experiment with or adopt packaged, externally produced writing curricula or software that are linked to corporate entities; and implement Massive Online Open Courses (MOOCs). We may also be asked to try out other programmatic and pedagogical endeavors meant to standardize or teacher-proof curricula or eliminate the need for large numbers of personnel altogether, whether contingent faculty or TAs. These moves are all part of the standardization, privatization, and neoliberalization of higher education. At the same time as these elements come to bear, faculty and departments within this neoliberal university environment are urged to be more entrepreneurial and do what they can to attract wealthy alumni and corporations as potential donors, compete for grants to bring in external monies, and market more attractive, trendy, and money-drawing degree programs and certificates. Faculty members are encouraged to monetize their research, a trend that is nothing new in the science fields but is now encouraged more than ever and in all fields and disciplines. In our field, Richard Miller (1998) has argued for WPAs to adopt an "entrepreneurial" stance toward these challenges and to capitalize on these conditions, although this "entrepreneurial" stance has been critiqued in essay collections such as *Tenured Bosses and Disposable Teachers* (Bousquet, Scott, and Parascandola 2003).

Many of us as WPAs, though, resist or eschew the entrepreneurial stance and choose, instead, to be change-agents, activists (Adler-Kassner 2008, 4), and enactors of a critical discourse of WPA work (Strickland and Gunner 2009, xii). Whatever stance we take as writing program leaders and writing faculty members, however, we cannot assume that WPAs or writing program faculty members are a homogenous group operating under the same conditions or facing the same set of circumstances. WPAs represent different institutions, different program types, different generations, different training (some with rhetoric and composition degrees and others with literature or creative writing degrees), different ranks (tenured to contingent), and different levels of experience, from fresh out of graduate school to thirty or more years in the profession. Moreover, what counts as a writing program is also an important question to ask since a writing program can be an independent writing program unit that serves as a department (as is the case with the academic unit I work in), to a first-year composition program/sequence within an English Department, to a first-year writing intensive program to a Writing Across the Curriculum (WAC) program (Malenczyk 2013, 6).

With over twenty-five years of college teaching and administrative experience, including assistant WPA to WPA to department chair, I place myself in the camp of those who argue for critical rhetorics for WPAs and faculty members in our field. A critical rhetoric enables WPAs and writing faculty members to move from the savvy entrepreneurial rhetoric, on the one hand, and a "struggling and getting by" survivor rhetoric, on the other, to a position of critical intervention and public problem-posing about university priorities and budgets.

With a growing and increasingly powerful administrative class, a dents being squeezed financially, there has been an alarming erosion of faculty governance and academic freedom with administrators making more top-down decisions, especially as states continue to defund higher education. Among those recent top-down decisions are unilateral wage cuts, furloughs, lay-offs, program eliminations, and other cost-reducing measures that have a major impact on students' learning conditions, teaching conditions, and the quality in general of American higher education. Across the country, students have experienced fee hikes, shrinking class options, and a general reduction in the numbers of faculty they can work with and count on as advisors and mentors.

Given these conditions, a line I have found myself repeating in my varied leadership roles as a former department chair, former WPA, and current university senator is this: we are in a battle for the soul of shared governance. We are in a battle for faculty members of all ranks to have a voice and an influence in matters of shared governance and to steer the budgetary and intellectual future of our colleges and universities. We can no longer take it for granted in the neoliberal university that faculty members have the right to design and influence curricula, to exercise academic freedom, and to continue to guarantee access to higher education for students of all incomes and backgrounds. Many of us have learned the hard way that our university administrations are choosing to govern from the top-down and that we cannot take shared governance for granted.

While it is important to point to professional and disciplinary conversations, committees, and groups organizing to address instructional positions and budgets, it is equally important to take steps to address these issues on our own local campuses. Interdisciplinary coalitions working toward labor solidarity and action can be particularly helpful modes of organizing, especially on private university campuses or "right to work" states where tenure-line faculty do not have the ability to unionize. As an indication of what is possible at the local level, I describe a coalition we have formed at Syracuse University (a private research university) that is centered on "campus equity."

RALLYING TOWARD CAMPUS EQUITY

The concept of "campus equity" as an organizing concept and rhetorical strategy has been circulated for a decade and a half now through the Coalition on Contingent Academic Labor's biennial Campus Equity Week organizing. Campus Equity Week is a national week of action and education on contingent labor, usually held on college campuses in the fall semester to raise awareness, improve working conditions, and encourage organizing. On the Syracuse University (SU) campus, a number of us worked with the local chapter of the AAUP and contingent faculty to hold three different Campus Equity Week events in 2001, 2003, and 2005, the final one which helped to assist with conversations pointed toward the unionization of contingent faculty. More recently, the concept of Campus Equity has been extended to address equity for students as well as contingent faculty, academic freedom, and transparency in university budgets (see Nelson 2011). To address these concerns and to call for an increasing need to address equity across varied campus constituencies, a group of faculty, graduate students, and undergraduate students held a Campus Equity Rally at Syracuse University in April 2014 and a panel discussion on contingent labor in February 2015. The sponsoring organization was the Syracuse University Labor Studies Working Group, a group based out of the Maxwell's Program for the Advancement of Research on Conflict and Collaboration (PARCC). The Labor Studies Working Group is an interdisciplinary group of Syracuse University faculty members from the Departments/programs of African American Studies, Anthropology, Geography, Religion, Sociology, and Writing and Rhetoric. Convened by two Assistant Professors, one in the Department of Geography and the other in Sociology, the primary goal of the group is to "institutionalize Labor Studies at SU and to elevate labor as a topic of intellectual inquiry and social and political importance on campus" ("Labor Studies Working Group" 2014). The group sponsors frequent lectures and panels by labor scholars and labor activists and co-sponsors direct action events to advocate for labor justice. In March 2013, the Labor Studies Group organized a conference on the "Crisis of Academic Labor" featuring Cary Nelson and other public figures associated with contingent labor organizing. The group also has been organizing around equity and labor justice issues for workers and students in the Syracuse area, including undocumented workers, farmworkers in the region, and others.

In the Spring of 2014, partly responding to the United University Professions (UUP) "National Mobilization for Equity" day on May Day, the Labor Studies group planned a Rally for Campus Equity issues on

April 29, 2014 on the last day of spring semester classes. Groups featured at the rally included the AAUP, Adjuncts United (the part-time faculty union on campus), Graduate Students United (a nascent union organizing campaign), United Students Against Sweatshops, the ANSWER Coalition as well as other campus and community groups. The Rally featured speeches as well as songs, chants, and a food drive meant to call attention to the fact that many graduate students and contingent faculty members have a hard time making ends meet in the summer when teaching contracts and stipends run out.

The Campus Equity Rally addressed the working conditions for contingent faculty, graduate students, and the learning conditions of students. Speakers highlighted contingent labor, graduate student labor, student debt, rising tuition costs, access to higher education, the Dream Act, and academic governance issues. The message delivered at the rally was that the quality of a university education depends on being able to retain and support a group of dedicated instructors, graduate students, and faculty. At the same time, the rally emphasized that the quality of higher education is threatened by the fact that graduate students and contingent faculty receive compensation that falls below a living wage. Speakers highlighted the connection between teachers' working conditions and students' learning conditions as well as shared issues of concern such as the growing student debt crisis, loss of academic governance, and administrative bloat.

The Campus Equity Rally made the work of the Labor Studies Group visible as a stakeholder in conversations about labor issues. A number of us involved in the Labor Studies Group also became active supporters of a student group on campus called the General Body that emerged in 2014–2015. The General Body held several rallies, events, and an extended sit-in in the administrative building to call attention to a variety of issues connected to the corporatization of higher education and recent administrative changes to university programs—the closure of our Campus Advocacy Center that supported survivors of sexual assault and relationship violence and the cancellation of a series of scholarships that supported students of color among other issues (The General Body 2015). Many of us from the Labor Studies Group spoke at the General Body's rallies, wrote letters of support, visited students in the administrative building during the sit-in, and spoke to the press. Throughout the academic year of 2014–2015, we remained actively involved in the students' organizing and do so to this day, lending support as we can.

When National Adjunct Walk-out Day was called for on February 25, 2015, the Labor Studies group discussed ideas for participation. The

Adjuncts United union contract did not allow part-time faculty to walk out, so the Labor Studies group planned a panel discussion, led by Professors Matt Huber and Gretchen Purser, entitled "Mobilizing the Academic Precariat: The Contingent Faculty Labor Movement at SU and Beyond." The panel took place a week ahead of the national action, and offered attendees a comprehensive picture of the data available on campus and nationally about contingent labor. Speakers not only explored the issue of contingent labor (I offered remarks on gender and contingent labor), but also discussed organizing solutions at Syracuse University and beyond. The goal was to create resources and visibility around contingent labor and offer ideas for organizing informed by national organizations addressing academic labor rights.

As a writing faculty member with experience organizing direct action events, I was able to contribute thoughts about strategy, goals, purpose, and also help direct some of the work at some of the Labor Studies Group events. For the 2014 Rally, in particular, I was able to draft and send out a press release, which drew two local TV stations to the event. I also was able to draft and compile feedback on a letter signed by rally attendees and others to the chancellor to begin conversations about how to improve labor conditions and learning conditions for students. I continued to draft letters throughout the General Body sit-in and lend my voice as a speaker when needed. I highlight the contributions I made to these endeavors not to showcase my own work as heroic or particularly skilled, but to point out that WPAs and faculty who embrace a critical rhetoric are well positioned to engage in a struggle for the future of teaching and pedagogy in higher education. Our field is well suited to providing us with the theory and research to knowledgably address why college and literacy matters to our students and to the future of our nation. Our rhetorical training also means we have good ideas about how to address questions of audience, purpose, and communication as we debate the futures of our institutions. As many of our field call for public engagement and community literacy as sites of work and scholarship for our field, let us not forget how greatly our pedagogical and rhetorical skills are needed in our own academic communities as well.

CONCLUSION

While none who were involved can say that the Labor Studies Group caused immediate change, what the group has helped create is a cross-disciplinary, cross-rank, and cross-sectorial coalition. Such a coalition can begin to address the working conditions of our instructors and graduate students and the learning conditions of our students. On our campus, faculty of all ranks, graduate students, staff, and undergraduate students have been galvanized to work together to fight for the future of the university—a future we can all believe in even as we might have different visions for what that future might mean for us individually or for our varied disciplines.

Finally, what this work demonstrated to many of us on our campus is that we are at a crossroads in higher education. If we do not act now to preserve the instructional base of university education and the opportunity to voice our opinions and visions about the future of our institutions through the shared governance process, we miss the opportunity to preserve what most of believe in despite rank and position: the right of faculty of all ranks to shape higher education curricula and innovative pedagogies and research, the right for higher education instructors to be adequately compensated and fairly treated, and the right for our students to access an affordable, high quality education. Without these rights, there is no university as we know it.

Notes

1. The Delta Cost Project draws on data connected to employment changes and patterns, administrative costs, and the recession's impact on higher education staffing (Lenihan 2012, 1–2). They also address how these patterns affect "total compensation, institutional spending patterns, and ultimately tuitions" (1).

2. This project is part of the non-profit Institute for College Access and Success, which has tracked data on student debt for almost a decade.

References

Abel, Emily K. 1984. *Terminal Degrees: The Job Crisis in Higher Education.* New York: Praeger.

Adler-Kassner, Linda. 2008. *The Activist WPA: Changing Stories About Writing and Writers.* Logan: Utah State University Press.

American Association of University Professors Subcommittee of the Committee on Contingency in the Profession. 2009. "Tenure and Teaching Intensive Appointments." American Association of University Professors. Accessed September 21, 2014. http://www.aaup.org/report/tenure-and-teaching-intensive-appointments.

Bousquet, Marc. 2008. *How the University Works: Higher Education and the Low Wage Nation.* New York: New York University Press.

Bousquet, Marc, Tony Scott, and Leo Parascandola, eds. 2003. *Tenured Bosses and Disposable Teachers: Writing Instruction in the Managed University.* Carbondale: Southern Illinois University Press.

Desrochers, Donna, and Rita Kirshstein. 2014. "Labor Intensive or Labor Expensive? Changing Staffing and Compensation Patterns in Higher Education." *Delta Cost Project at American Institutes for Research* (February): 1–34. Accessed September 21, 2014. http://www.deltacostproject.org/sites/default/files/products/DeltaCostAIR_Staffing_Brief_2_3_14.pdf.

The General Body. 2015. "About." Accessed 5 May 2015. http://thegeneralbody.org
/about/

Ginsberg, Benjamin. 2011 "Administrators Ate My Tuition." *Washington Monthly*,
September/October. Accessed September 21, 2014. http://www.washington-
monthly.com/magazine/septemberoctober_2011/features/administrators_ate_my_
tuition031641.php?page=all.

Hayden, Tom. 2010. "We Can't Afford to Be Quiet about the Rising Costs of College."
Chronicle of Higher Education, March 28. Accessed September 21, 2014. http://
chronicle.com/article/Rising-Cost-of-College-We/64813/.

Jaschik, Scott. 2014. "4 for the Price of 1." *Inside Higher Ed*, June 9. https://www.inside
highered.com/news/2014/06/09/four-faculty-members-offer-job-share-presidents
-duties-and-salary.

"Labor Studies Working Group." 2014. Program for the Advancement of Research on
Conflict and Collaboration (PARCC), Maxwell School for Citizenship, Syracuse
University. http://www.maxwell.syr.edu/parcc/Research/advocacy/Labor_Studies_
Working_Group/.

Lenihan, Colleen. 2012. "IPEDS Analytics: Delta Cost Project Database 1987–2010."
National Center for Education Statistics. https://nces.ed.gov/pubs2012/2012823.pdf.

Malenczyk, Rita. 2013. "Introduction, with Some Rhetorical Terms." In *A Rhetoric for
Writing Program Administrators*, ed. Rita Malenczyk and S. Anderson, 3–8. Anderson,
SC: Parlor Press.

Miller, Richard E. 1998. *As if Learning Mattered: Reforming Higher Education.* Ithaca, NY:
Cornell University Press.

Nelson, Cary. 2011. *No University Is an Island: Saving Academic Freedom.* New York: New
York University Press.

Newfield, Christopher. 2008. *Unmaking the Public University: The Forty Year Assault on the
Middle Class.* Cambridge, MA: Harvard University Press.

Reed, Matthew, and Debbie Cochrane. 2012. "Student Debt and the Class of 2012." *The
Institute for College Access and Success*, 1–23. http://projectonstudentdebt.org/files
/pub/classof2012.pdf.

Schell, Eileen E. 1997. *Gypsy Academics and Mother-teachers: Gender, Contingent Labor, and
Writing Instruction.* Portsmouth, NH: Heinemann, Boynton-Cook.

Schell, Eileen E., and Patricia Lambert Stock, eds. 2001. *Moving a Mountain: Transforming
the Role of Contingent Faculty in Composition Studies and Higher Education.* Urbana, IL:
National Council of Teachers of English.

Strickland, Donna, and Jeanne Gunner. 2009. "Introduction: Opening Up: Toward
A Critical Discourse for Writing Program Administration." In *The Writing Program
Interrupted: Making Space for Critical Discourse*, ed. Donna Strickland and Jeanne
Gunner, xi–xiv. Portsmouth, NH: Boynton/Cook Heinemann.

13
BEYOND MARKETABILITY
Locating Teacher Agency in the Neoliberal University

Shari Stenberg

In my interactions with TAs teaching in our writing program, I'm aware of a pervasive, almost tangible, anxiety that seems to increase as job prospects in English decline. There is fear about current job security—in this case, a teaching assistantship; there is angst about the inevitable "messiness" of pedagogy, especially as it relates to their evaluations (by students and administrators). TAs know that their doctoral degrees will not guarantee tenure-line employment, an uncertainty that heightens the pressure to view every seminar, every course taught, every award or grant applied for, as a test of future success. They know they must compete and win in a game that may not be winnable. Indeed, with the decline of state and federal aid to public universities and the growing replacement of tenure-line faculty with contingent labor, the economic consequences of austerity measures in university life are undeniable.

But there are other, less visible, ideological effects of these measures, which shape what Aimee Carrillo Rowe calls "conditions of belonging," a set of relations, values, and assumptions that determine one's inclusion, sense of value, and agency within a particular context (Rowe 2005, 20). In this age of austerity, the value of higher education, instructional activity, and instructors, themselves, face intense scrutiny. Austerity's ideological consequences determine who and what is deemed valuable, who and what counts as a "good investment" (Amsler 2014; Davies and O'Callaghan 2014).

This pressure to perform the self as a "good investment" inevitably narrows choices about self-representation in (and beyond) the classroom. Within increasingly privatized universities, argue Michelle Comstock, Mary Ann Cain, and Lil Brannon, the available space for "representing who we are and what we do" is "constrained in ways that make it difficult for teachers to re-present their identities, and thus their fullest range of

DOI: 10.7330/9781607324454.c013

perspectives" (Comstock, Cain, and Brannon 2010, 6). This narrowing of available "appropriate" identities is gendered and value-laden, marking anything other than "neutral" as a detriment. Within the context of austerity and neoliberalism, a "good investment" is equated with a "neutral," competitive, masculine subject who can acclimate, compete, and win within established power structures. On the other hand, Sarah Amsler observes, "certain forms of femininity and non-hegemonic masculinity are suppressed or treated as professional problems and *investment risks*" (Amsler 2014; my emphasis). This is reflected in the concerns I hear from TAs, who express fear that they will be read as too political, too female, too queer, etc., with "too" marking an excessive subjectivity in need of discipline.

Indeed, feminist scholars Miriam David and Sue Clegg observe that neoliberal values replace embodied actors with "individualized, decontextualized, competitive neoliberal subjects" (David and Clegg 2008, 488). This decontextualized individual is assumed to compete on a level playing field, which occludes attention to particular embodied subjects and the complex contexts in which they work—not to mention the student subjects whom they teach. And the notion that anybody can compete and win reifies an "ungendered but masculinist" culture—one that covers its masculinist values with neutrality (494). Consequently, the gendered effects of austerity and neoliberalism are at once experienced as constraining and yet inevitable: "just the way things are." And if the ideological effects of neoliberalism and austerity are not examined as systemic, social and economic, it is all too easy for the teacher to deny, or be pressured to deny, aspects of the self as a mere "personal problem."

In this chapter I focus on how we might support teacher development and agency even as belonging is increasingly constrained by austerity and neoliberalism. To offer an alternative to neoliberal values and effects, I draw upon feminist scholarship that views marginalized locations and practices as rich and vital resources for knowing and being. I then forward a concept of *located* agency, a practice that includes examining, valuing, and taking responsibility for our locations. Because enacting authority is such an important, and often fraught, part of teacher learning, I focus in particular on highlighting located agency with new teachers of composition. My aim is to counter neoliberalism's coercive and repressive effects on teaching subjectivities by helping new TAs discover the possibilities that emerge from the nexus of their subjectivities, locations, and relations.

BELONGING AND LOCATING AGENCY IN AN AGE OF AUSTERITY

At a time when, as Amsler describes it, "institutionalized criteria for achievement, recognition and human worth are not only rigged against one's own conditions of possibility, but actively negate them" (Amsler 2014), it is vital to reflect on how others have found ways to enact agency and belonging within similarly repressive conditions. From a wide span of disciplinary perspectives, feminist scholars including Patricia Hill Collins (1986), Adrienne Rich (1986), and bell hooks (1990) argue that the margins offer a keener view of dominant structures and that articulating located, embodied knowledge is both a channel to illuminate epistemological possibilities and to take responsibility for the partiality of one's perspective.

Whereas neoliberal agency presumably allows one to *possess* authority and exert control over oneself and others, these feminist perspectives forward a mode of *enacting* agency that insists upon illuminating traits covered over by neoliberalism and austerity measures: embodiment, location, and responsibility to and connection with one another. Feminist agency, Keya Maitra argues, enables one to "formulate choices" rather than to unreflexively accept existing options. Formulating choices involves a conscious consideration of "not just things are but of how they *could* be" (Maitra 2013, 361).

hooks, for instance, argues that there is a difference between marginality that is "imposed by oppressive structures" and marginality that one "chooses as a site of resistance—as a location of radical openness and possibility" (hooks 1990, 153). This is a choice she deems necessary as she learns, as a black girl in a small Kentucky town, what it means to cross the railroad tracks into a white world, where she can enter as an observer but may not live. From here, she writes, "We looked both from the outside in and from the inside out. We focused our attention on the center as well as on the margin. We understood both" (149). This view allowed hooks to develop a way of seeing, unknown to her oppressors, that "sustained us, aided us in our struggle to transcend poverty and despair, strengthened our sense of self and solidarity" (149). This is the marginality she chooses, one that serves as a site of creativity, imagination, and resistance. This choice of marginality elucidates Maitra's notion of a "formulated" choice. It is the result of careful attention to social contexts and histories (how things are), with a keen eye on new possibilities (how things could be) (Maitra 2013, 361).

When hooks later enters a predominantly white university, her mother warns, "You can take what the white people have to offer, but you do not have to love them" (hooks 1990, 150). Her mother knew, hooks explains, that she would be "tried," or made to feel that the only way to "make it" was to buy fully into dominant culture. But that wasn't the only available path. Hooks writes, "She was reminding me of the necessity of opposition and simultaneously encouraging me not to lose that radical perspective shaped and formed by marginality" (150). Here, knowledge created on the margins is viewed as a resource for counter-hegemonic insight, creativity, and possibility. But valuing the margin as a resource does not mean one must remain on the margins; rather, it means enacting alternative modes of belonging and creating alternative spaces, which allow one to both claim knowledge, practices, and locations that are devalued by dominant structures and to simultaneously seek new knowledge and experience (148).

Just as hooks's mother advises that she work within and against white university culture, Rowe argues for a practice of "differential belonging" that highlights, and creates possibilities for, alternative enactments of belonging. Drawing from Chela Sandoval's (2000) notion of "differential resistance," Rowe outlines four conditions of belonging, or ways of organizing social relations for marginalized subjects: *assimilationist*, which involves deemphasizing difference in order to be recognized as equals by those in power; *revolutionary*, where difference is used as a vehicle for critique of the current social structure; *supremacist*, where a group's differences are regarded as a better way of knowing or relating than are dominant modes, and are thus potentially transformative; and *separatist*, a mode of belonging which offers "an important site to dream, to create visions and try them on with others who begin with similar assumptions, politics and experiences" (Rowe 2005, 34). Differential belonging recognizes fluidity among these modes, and each may be necessary depending on the moment, situation, and dynamics at play. But *agency*, as Rowe sees it, emerges in the movement among them. "Becoming stuck in any mode or seeing modes as mutually exclusive can be counterproductive. It is precisely the movement across these modes that allows us to be politically productive" (34). Enacting one mode of belonging can fuel, or provide insight into, or critique of, another; drawing from multiple modes can offer possibilities that a single mode would occlude.

Together, these feminist scholars make a case for location as both embodied and enacted. That is, a located agency takes seriously both the limitations and possibilities that emerge from our material, embodied locations and knowledges, attending to how our geographic and institutional locations shape what is doable at any given moment. So unlike neoliberal agency, which is accessible to only those who can belong, compete, and win within a rigid set of rules (which are nevertheless framed as universal), a located agency provides a more expansive set of choices about how to navigate those dynamics, such that possibility can be drawn from the margins as well as the center, and from movement among different modes of belonging. This is where the importance of enactment emerges.

Rowe argues, for instance, that "politics of location" approaches may inadvertently fix identities or group belongings in a way that "erases the choices that we make around our belongings which are constitutive of our identities" (Rowe 2005, 32). That is, if we think of our locations as made up of fixed identities (e.g., I am a woman; I am a Midwesterner; I am white), we lose an opportunity to reflect on how the choices we make to enact our belonging may exclude and oppress, as well as to consider how we might act in new ways that disrupt habitual modes. This is particularly pertinent to privileged locations, like whiteness, which become both invisible and compulsory, such that both white people and people of color are expected to fall inside its norms. "[I]nvisibility," Rowe contends, "undermines agency; we cannot alter that which we cannot see" (30). Indeed, once these modes of belonging are made visible, we can imagine ways to disrupt and challenge them and to enact more expansive modes of belonging.

While heeding Rowe's warning about the risk of fixing locations, however, I hold that in a time when neoliberal discourses fetishize standardization and deny local contexts, it is crucial that we emphasize location, which I understand to encompass a dynamic interplay among embodiment, social spaces (institutional and cultural), and the relations that animate them. If we do not pay adequate attention to location, both material, embodied location and the specific contexts that simultaneously enable and prohibit our enactments, it is too easy to slip back into neoliberal assumptions of level playing fields and individual autonomy, which are deepened by austerity measures. I am drawn, for instance, to the metaphor Sandoval and Rowe employ, where differential belonging and resistance function like a clutch in a manual transmission automobile that allows the driver to decide in each moment how to deploy the engine's power. But it's also necessary to observe the road, the conditions both internal and external to the car, the speed limit—and the relationship of the driver to those conditions. Is the driver a person of color in Arizona, at risk of being read as an illegal immigrant? A white woman in a Lexus or minivan driving down a suburban street? An African American male driving down that same suburban street? One's deployment of the engine is always dependent on locations—embodied, geographic, and geopolitical. Enacting a located agency, then, takes into account differential belonging, and pays close attention to the subject as always in relation to other subjects and to the specific contexts in which she lives and works. Ultimately, as I'll show, located agency serves not only the actor, but extends outward to deepen and extend ways of knowing, knowledge practices, and connections among subjects.

TEACHER LEARNING AND LOCATED AGENCY

As I work with new writing instructors, who often see acclimation as the only path to agency, I strive to make alternatives visible by illuminating how embodied, situated knowledge may be a resource for, not a detriment to, agency. One way I begin such conversations is by illuminating assumptions that arise in our readings and conversations that demonstrate expectations of the neoliberal subject in the classroom—the modes of belonging deemed necessary to "fit in" as university instructors and future professors, particularly during moments of austerity. But I also point TAs to scholarly examples that depict *located agency*. Here, teachers assess their own subjectivities in relation to local contexts and then discern possibilities for illuminating embodied knowledge as a resource—while also acknowledging the risks that accompany this work.[1]

Brenda Jo Brueggemann and Debra Moddelmog's essay "Coming Out Pedagogy: Risking Identity in Language and Literature Classrooms" offers one such example. The authors explore the relationships "both oppressive and enabling, between what has been *named* (a position of identity as an absolute) and what has been *claimed* (a position of identity as contingent)" (Brueggemann and Moddelmog 2003, 213; my emphasis). Here, claimed identity functions as a mode of differential belonging, allowing one to carefully formulate choices regarding how to engage difference within a particular context. For instance, on the first day of class Brueggemann identifies herself as deaf. It is a move that helps her create effective classroom communication and address any necessary classroom modifications, but it also begins to challenge normative conceptions of deaf individuals (her named identity). She explains what she can and cannot hear (that it is not a simple matter of silence versus sound) and how she navigates communication practices with technology, lip-reading, reliance on context-clues, and body language. She then moves from identifying what she calls "functional reasons" for naming her disability to "ethically *claiming* a disability identity" (214; my emphasis). Here, she replaces deaf with "hard-of-hearing," which not only more accurately defines her experience but also "represents a hyphenated existence," challenging solid categories of belonging. She writes, "I am not (that) old; I do use (some) sign language, although not here in the Ohio State University English classroom; I clearly am speaking (and don't deaf people have trouble speaking?); I look (pretty) normal; and I am, after all, the teacher (the voice and body of authority), am I not?" (214–15).

The parenthetical phrases break the repetition of normative roles, and, she notes, they spark questions on the part of her students, as they begin to think differently about what it means to be disabled or able-bodied, and how these are temporary and fluid states, existing in relationship to other social locations. Brueggemann, for instance, explains that had she not been white and middle class, which allowed her belonging within dominant categories, she may not have been mainstreamed in school and allowed the academic path she pursued. At the same time, the practice of claiming her marginalized identity—what could easily be characterized as a detriment—allows her to both draw agency from her location and to help her students consider how the institutions (e.g., family, medicine, religion, education, etc.) and normalizing discourses shape our identities and boundaries of belonging (229).

For the students in my composition theory and practice seminar, texts like Brueggemann and Moddelmog's serve to highlight the possibilities—for cultural critique, for expanding notions of agency, for relating to others—that emerge from valuing our embodied locations as integral to teaching and learning and, in so doing, disrupt normative conceptions of belonging.

POSSIBILITIES FOR TEACHER AGENCY

In addition to engaging others' navigation of agency, TAs also need room to consider their own locations as a valid option for intellectual work, especially at a time when choices about self-representation are constrained. While this is never something I require, several students each semester—typically those for whom navigating their embodied or marked identity has felt fraught—choose to examine issues of location and agency in their "Pedagogical Insights" essay. I model this essay after those included in the reader *Relations, Locations, Positions: Composition Theory for Writing Teachers* (2006), where teachers describe how the composition theories they engage animate their work in the classroom with students, and they show how teaching is also theory-making. For the examples to which I now turn, the teachers come to see that these insights emerge as a result of articulating their locations, and discovering how location may serve as a site of agency.

As does Brueggemann, my students often describe the navigation of teacher authority as beginning on the first day of class, when the teacher enters the classroom and wonders whether she or he will be recognized as such. Here, Monica Rentfrow describes her own navigation—literally and figuratively:

> The sound of a small motor carries down the old basement hallway, passing like a shadow into every classroom. Students sitting in desks of their first college semester hear the hum, unsure of what it is until it rolls through the doorframe. They might think the occupant is a fellow student as they pull desks to clear a path for her. She crosses the room, parking behind a table at the front, under the wall-to-wall white board. Jaws do not drop. When the time is right, she introduces herself—her name, her year and focus of study in the Master's program in the department. She passes around an introductory writing course syllabus. Nothing about height or motors is mentioned.

While Monica notes that she had no choice but to "come out" to her students on the first day—"being a little person half dependent upon her scooter, there was no opting to 'hide' my 'disability'"—it wasn't until later in the semester when she explicitly acknowledged dwarfism as part of her identity. She did so by modeling her public writing assignment with a pamphlet she designed to raise awareness about the national organization Little People of America, Inc. In her essay, she gives two reasons for her moment of "claiming" her identity as disabled. First, she wants to provide students a "tangible example" of how we can make arguments from our commitments, passions and locations. But second, she writes that to ignore her dwarfism feels false, especially as she reflects on how her family taught her to "be strong and humble enough to find ways of working with the world." For Monica, this means both showing her students how her embodied location could be used as a "tool for learning in the classroom" as well as acknowledging that it sometimes meant she had to ask her students for assistance. She jokes, "I do not ever pretend as if I can go-go-Gadget my arm up to pull down the projection screen."

Monica also describes wrestling with the question of whether acknowledging her disability might undermine her students' sense of her as a traditional authority. In the end, though, Monica determines that "there are many ways to establish authority dynamics within the classroom." For her—at least that particular semester, with those particular students—it meant making her politics of location as a creative writer, an MA student, *and* a disabled person a complex text that might facilitate students' re-visionary thinking about authority, disability, and agency. It might, that is, disrupt ideas about what it means to belong in a university setting—for both teachers and students.

Another student in my course, Dae-Joon (D. J.) Kim, grapples with politics of location and pedagogy as determined by his location in a Korean versus US classroom. As a first-time teacher in Korea, D. J. describes the unquestioned authority he received from students due to the easy match between his subjectivity and cultural expectations—there was little need to assimilate in order to belong.

When he changed geographic locations, moving to teach university composition in Lincoln, Nebraska, as a non-native speaker, he no longer fit expectations of an authority. He describes experiencing a mix of both "hospitality and hostility" from the students as they "read" his identity on the first day of class. "Most of them did not recognize me as a teacher; rather, they thought of me as an international student who came in the wrong room," he writes. He goes on to consider his transnational identity: "On a geopolitical level, I represented a borderland between American and Asia across the Pacific. On a linguistic level, my articulation with accented English and minor grammatical mistakes undermined my authority as an English teacher."

Ultimately, D. J. decided to make this liminal position as a teacher of English and learner of English visible to his students, by addressing the multiplicity of his position: Asian, non-native speaker, graduate student of contemporary American fiction, and a "visa-holding non-immigrant who can easily be misunderstood as illegal yellow peril." By highlighting these locations, D. J. shows students how our modes of belonging are multiple, contradictory, and fluid. He is both an English language learner and an advanced graduate student in American fiction; he is both an authority in English (as indicated by his position as instructor) and someone who speaks English with an Asian accent and makes occasional grammatical mistakes (as do most of us, native speakers or not).

These (seeming) contradictions break the repetition of what counts as expertise in English, an authoritative teacher, a member of the campus community, and in so doing, they allow us to consider what Rowe (2005, 28) calls "the often overlooked conditions of belonging." D. J. describes his choice as also opening conversation with his students, as they asked questions about his life and experience in Korea and conflicts between North and South Korea. As he wrote, "marking my 'situatedness' . . . thawed out frozen borderlands between the students and me" and, in turn, helped him complicate the notion that any teacher holds a finished expertise, including, he jokes, the seemingly "know-it-all native speaker teacher." Interestingly, new TAs, native speaking or not, often articulate a dread of their students' discovery that they are not know-it-all experts; it is also challenging this idea that often allows for connection, and dialogue, to occur.

RECLAIMING AMBIGUITY TO CHALLENGE UNIVERSALISMS

As Michelle Gibson, Martha Marinara, and Deborah Meem observe in "Bi, Butch, and Bar Dyke: Pedagogical Performances of Class, Gender, and Sexuality," scholars interested in challenging cultural norms and essential identities often view the sharing of particular experiences and locations as a crucial means to disrupt prohibitive "universalisms." But the particulars, they write, "have their own universalisms" (Gibson, Marinara, and Meem 2000, 468). That is, if an instructor comes out as a lesbian, students may believe they already know the story of that identity, which is based largely on what it is not—straight, "neutral," normative. For this reason, the authors advocate a move away from viewing locations as grounded, which "negates the possibility for inter-reference between any two [or more] landscapes" (469). Instead, they call for highlighting the fluid ways we enact our identities depending on the ever-shifting relationships we negotiate.

One of my students, Sindu Sathiyaseelan (2011), navigates this very territory in her essay, "Negotiating the bi-nary: Strategic Ambiguity and the Non-nameable Identity in the Classroom." As a bisexual female— one who wears "shoulder-length hair" and has as an "affinity for pencil skirts"—she is cognizant that her students are likely to read her as straight (3). Her concern is both with remaining "in the closet" in the classroom and with foreclosing an opportunity for her students—especially those who identify as LGBTQ—to work with an "out" teacher. She is also aware of the tensions between enacting her identity as a campus activist for LGBTQ issues and as a classroom instructor in a red state: what are her roles and responsibilities in each site? And yet, she understands that the narrative of "coming out" often boxes subjects in to identity categories that are based on "hegemonic ideals of normative behavior" (2). As someone who is "not gay or lesbian but rather something beyond the binary itself," coming out is not as simple as identifying herself as belonging to one side of dualism.

Sindu draws from Marinara, who, in the aforementioned article, describes performing her identity as bisexual in the classroom, moving in and out of positions of straight and lesbian. Bisexuality, Marinara argues, cannot be easily pinned down as a knowable social category, and consequently, it is an "identity without visible rules, almost without referent" (Gibson, Marinara, and Meem 2000, 479). This allows Marinara to strategically deploy her locations in a way that "poses hard questions about the nature and definitions of political subject positions" (471). She also observes the alliance with, and responsibility to, queer students that results from her named location. When she and her students encounter a text with a gender ambiguous narrator who describes a physically intimate relation with a man, her first instinct is to dodge questions of sexuality. The weight of stares from three lesbian students, however, nudges her to examine same-sex affection as part of their collective reading.

Marinara's enactment of an identity that is multiple and fluid allows Sindu to enact a located agency not by verbally claiming her identities, but by performing ambiguity. Sindu writes, "However important my coming out may be to me, it is perhaps reinforcing binaries to label myself in any way in the classroom. Instead, I seek to complicate my students' understandings of gender and sexuality by performing a nonnameable ambiguity" (4). While she considers that this choice may reinforce notions of neutrality, she differentiates it from a neutrality that functions in opposition to a "politicized" identity. Rather, it involves "stepping in and out of my queerness" in a way that demonstrates a "constantly shifting identity that resists categorization and dichotomization" (4). Sindu holds that this allows her a "strategic positionality" which facilitates an ability to question students' resistance to (or easy embracing of) particular texts without it being read as her personal response; at the same time, it also allows her to ally herself, when called for, with queer students. In this way, Sindu repurposes ideas of neutrality or ambiguity, showing how these locations can be engaged to challenge, rather than affirm, fixed identity categories.

At the same time, this complication of dualistic, fixed categories of identity also serves as a useful reminder about how we read students. As the teachers I work with consider their own social locations in relation to their students, they are often surprised at the complexity of their students' positions and locations. They learn that teaching in a "red state," working with a group of rural students, or even with a particular learning community, does not mean a uniformity of positions, assumptions, or locations. Located agency should, ideally, make room for both teachers and students to approach identity more expansively and as in process—and, as I argue in the next section, to allow for connections among subjects to be made.

AGENCY AS ALLIANCE

Henry Giroux observes that austerity measures "purposely accentuate
the shark cage relations emphasized by the economic Darwinism of
neoliberalism and in doing so emphasize a world of competitive hyper-
individualism in which asking for help or receiving it is viewed as a
pathology" (Giroux 2015). Within this logic, the necessity and value of
connection and collaboration are undermined in favor of the subject
who acts alone. This makes advancing located agency, which ultimately
involves a turn toward others, all the more crucial. Rowe contends that
this shift involves a rewriting of "I-dentity" to a sense of "self" that is
"radically inclined toward others, toward the communities to which we
belong, with whom we long to be, and to whom we feel accountable"
(Rowe 2005, 18). This move reconceptualizes agency from "power over"
to "power with." We see examples of enacting "power with" in the narratives above, as well. For instance, when Sindu finds ways to illuminate
her queer identity so that she can serve as an ally to GLBTQ students,
she exercises "power with." When Monica acknowledges to her students
that she will sometimes need to ask for help reaching the screen, she
demonstrates an authority that also requires relationship with, and reliance on, others. This parallels the way we hope our students will find
ways to write with agency in their writing, at the same time they will come
to understand writing as a collaborative process that is aided by the
input of others. When D. J. presents himself as a language learner, he
disrupts the idea that the teacher is a finished product, and that learning
language is ever complete. He and his students are learners together.

Of course, as is true of all pedagogical practices, there is no guaranteed outcome; there is no promise that students will embrace or learn
from a "power with" approach. Some students will inevitably crave a
traditional classroom dynamic, or a teacher who performs agency in
ways that are expected and familiar. Brueggemann describes receiving
a paper from a student who wrote, "My mother doesn't think it's right
that my English teacher is deaf" on it (Brueggemann and Moddelmog
2003, 214). And yet, comments like this only underscore the need to disrupt the cultural repetition of assumptions and stereotypes; they make
the work of challenging norms of able-ism and modes of belonging all
the more crucial.

Enacting a located agency requires a different kind of risk than does
abiding by normative expectations. Students may become uncomfortable or hostile; the teacher may become uncomfortable, or fear (or experience) a lack of belonging in the classroom. And yet, as Brueggemann
and Moddelmog (2003, 216) argue, the "risk of discomfort" can co-exist

with the "concurrent possibility of discovery," and, I would add, the concurrent possibility of alliance and connection, which challenges neoliberal hyper-individualism and competition. I have noticed that when TAs talk about enacting different modes of agency and belonging in their classes, it creates opportunities for others to do the same. They develop connections among themselves and find ways to support each other through the risk-taking. Indeed, as part of such conversations, a white, straight, male TA reflected on the fact that his students could not see the background of poverty in which he grew up or the fact that his family had, for a time, been homeless. But what if they could, he asked? How would knowing I didn't come from the middle class change my students' assumptions about a college instructor? And in fact, he does now regularly share this information with students, and in so doing, helps them think in new ways about it means to be "belong" in an academic culture—as well as to surface issues of socio-economic class, which are covered by neoliberalism.

As we learn from each other's locations and belongings, we can begin to cross lines of separation that "deaden and wound" (Rowe 2005, 38). Indeed, part of working with new students—whether they are first year writers or graduate students—is acknowledging the complexity of belonging and fostering opportunities to facilitate practices that support inclusivity and connection. A located agency, then, is a process that aims to value knowledge produced from our embodied locations and to insist on education as relational, at a time when our connections with and responsibilities to others are too often denied.

Notes

1. The collection *The Teacher's Body: Embodiment, Authority, and Identity in the Academy* (2003), for instance, traces teachers' navigation of disability, pregnancy, race, sexual orientation, size, age, and linguistic difference in the classroom.

References

Amsler, Sarah. 2014. "For Feminist Consciousness in the Academy." *Politics and Culture*, March 9. Accessed April 16, 2015. http://politicsandculture.org/2014/03/09/for -feminist-consciousness-in-the-academy/.

Brueggemann, Brenda Jo, and Debra A. Moddelmog. 2003. "Coming Out Pedagogy: Risking Identity in Language and Literature Classrooms." In *The Teacher's Body: Embodiment, Authority, and Identity in the Academy*, ed. Diane P. Freedman and Martha Stoddard Holmes, 209–34. Albany: State University of New York Press.

Comstock, Michelle, Mary Ann Cain, and Lil Brannon. 2010. *Composing Public Space: Teaching Writing in the Face of Private Interests*. Portsmouth, NH: Heinemann.

Collins, Patricia Hill. 1986. "Learning from the Outsider Within: The Sociological Significance of Black Feminist Thought." *Social Problems* 33 (6): S14–32. http://dx.doi.org/10.2307/800672.

David, Miriam, and Sue Clegg. 2008. "Power, Pedagogy and Personalization in Global Higher Education: The Occlusion of Second-Wave Feminism?" *Discourse (Abingdon)* 29 (4): 483–98. http://dx.doi.org/10.1080/01596300802410201.

Davies, Helen, and Claire O'Callaghan. 2014. "All in this Together? Feminisms, Academia, Austerity." *Journal of Gender Studies* 23 (3): 227–32. http://dx.doi.org/10.10 80/09589236.2014.913824.

Freedman, Diane P., and Martha Stoddard Holmes (Eds.). 2003. *The Teacher's Body: Embodiment, Authority, and Identity in the Academy.* Albany, NY: State University of New York Press.

Gibson, Michelle, Martha Marinara, and Deborah Meem. 2000. "Bi, Butch, and Bar Dyke: Pedagogical Performance of Class, Gender, and Sexuality." *College Composition and Communication* 52 (1): 69–95. http://dx.doi.org/10.2307/358545.

Giroux, Henry. 2015. "Authoritarianism, Class Warfare, and the Advance of Neoliberal Austerity Policies." *Truthout,* January 5. Accessed April 16, 2015. http://www.truth-out .org/news/item/28338-the-shadow-of-fascism-and-the-poison-of-neoliberal-austerity -policies.

hooks, bell. 1990. *Yearning: Race, Gender, and Cultural Politics.* Boston: South End Press.

Maitra, Keya. 2013. "The Question of Identity and Agency in Feminism without Borders: A Mindful Response." *Hypatia* 28 (2): 360–76. http://dx.doi.org/10.1111/hypa .12017.

Rich, Adrienne. 1986. "Notes toward a Politics of Location." In *Blood, Bread, and Poetry: Selected Prose,* 210–31. New York: W. W. Norton.

Rowe, Aimee Carrillo. 2005. "Be Longing: Toward a Feminist Politics of Relation." *NWSA Journal* 17 (2): 15–46. http://dx.doi.org/10.2979/NWS.2005.17.2.15.

Sandoval, Chela. 2000. *Methodology of the Oppressed.* Minneapolis: University of Minnesota Press.

Sathiyaseelan, Sinduja. 2011. "Negotiating the Bi-nary: Strategic Ambiguity and the Non-nameable Identity in the Classroom." Unpublished MS.

Vandenberg, Peter, Sue Hum and Jennifer Clary-Lemon. 2006. *Relations, Locations, Positions: Composition Theory for Writing Teachers.* Urbana, IL: National Council of Teachers of English.

14
ANIMATED BY THE ENTREPRENEURIAL SPIRIT
Austerity, Dispossession, and Composition's Last Living Act

Tony Scott

It is all very well (and sometimes insightful) to delineate the horrors of "the split self"—the human subject that projects unpalatable aspects of its self onto despised others. But it is something else again to analyze the horrors of a split society. Yet it is precisely here that crucial aspects of modern horror originate, in the painful and traumatic processes through which non-capitalistic social bonds are dissolved, individuals subjected to market forces, and impersonal relationships created between the dominated and the dominant.

David McNally (2009, 12)

If you work in higher education and you aren't sure what entrepreneur-ialism is, there is good reason to spend some time figuring it out. Over the past twenty years and with increasing momentum, higher educa-tion has seen a blossoming of academic programs in entrepreneurial-ism, and it is now not only commonplace for faculty to be encouraged to be entrepreneurial at our institutions but also within the academic discourse and sites of practice of composition. Entrepreneurial rhetoric has become such a common means of framing challenges, goals, and new initiatives that the ideological assumptions from which it derives can be all but invisible. It is now the default idiom of higher education.

As I drafted this chapter, the chancellor at my institution published an open letter as part of a series published at the university website that draws many of its elements from the topos of entrepreneurial rhetoric: alignment with a reform initiative or brand; an emphasis on innovation, risk-taking, and adaptability; an appeal to a vaguely defined but seem-ingly united public; and a presumption of a need for urgency. About "Fast-Forward Syracuse" (a brand with urgency), the chancellor writes:

DOI: 10.7330/9781607324454.c014

"[I believe that] to get better, we need to take risks, we need to embrace the entrepreneurial spirit that animates so many parts of this campus and we need to move nimbly. In that spirit, given the opportunities and challenges before us, I believe we must get started soon, and be nimble and agile every step of the way" (Syverud 2014). The letter does not acknowledge differences in status, authority, opinion, and commitments among the public it addressees as the "Orange Friends." It does, however, differentiate those who have been "animated" by an "entrepreneurial spirit" and those who haven't but *need* to be—a public of animated and not-yet-animated parts. So this call to entrepreneurialism might be read as a call to transformation with a presumed, urgent need for nimble action, but the action seems valuable for its own sake, with no explicitly articulated origins or aims.

As I drafted this chapter, I also received the call for papers for the 2015 Conference on College Composition and Communication (CCCC). That call, by conference chair Joyce Locke Carter, draws from the same entrepreneurial topos as the "Dear Orange Friends" letter. The conference theme, "Risk and Reward," similarly presumes an undefined urgency as it promotes entrepreneurialism, innovation, and risk-taking and as it appeals to a broad "we": "We celebrate our innovative teachers, innovative programs, innovative research, and innovative writing" (Carter 2014). However, with celebration also comes reproach and the suggestion of lassitude: "it's easy to forget that innovation is a product of risk-taking with no guarantee of reward and the very real possibility of failure" (Carter). The call moves from celebrating a single "us" to creating a dividing line between the entrepreneur and its others, who are invited or chided to "reimagine the concept of 'risk' not as something to be mitigated or feared, but rather as something to be sought out." As with the chancellor's letter, the dividing line within the "we" seems to center on innovation and risk-taking as stand alone values that are divorced from histories, agendas, and ideologies. Carter exhorts: "At a time when our organization and our membership has demanded more engagement with our governments, the press, and our broader society, we need to risk getting out of our own comfort zones." But who is "demanding" engagement, and toward what ends? What is different about this conference call to action and past calls?

A review of conference themes since CCCC began to have specific themes (1971) reveals that public engagement has arguably been the most common theme of the conference: "Serving Our Students, Our Public, and our Profession" (1982); "The Uses of Literacy: A Writer's Work in and out of the Academy" (1987); "Strengthening Community through Diversity" (1992); "Composing Community" (2001); "Connecting Community through the Street" (2002); "Making Composition Matter: Students, Citizens, Institutions, Advocacy" (2004); "Composition in the Center Spaces: Building Community, Culture, Coalitions" (2006); "The Public Work of Composition" (2013). New in the 2015 call is not its focus on public engagement, but the unmistakably neoliberal forms of engagement that it hails. The call emphasizes forms of engagement that foster marketization of scholarly and pedagogical work, cross or dissolve boundaries between higher education and industry, and facilitate efficiency imperatives in writing programs. The 2015 CCCC could therefore be an important marker for composition, if only because it more explicitly channels latent trends that have already been shaping composition work for years in a more explicitly entrepreneurial, and neoliberal, direction.

In its emphasis on transformation, animation, and immediacy, and with the construction of its others as fearful and unresponsive, entrepreneurial rhetoric evokes the tropes of vampire and zombie stories. In *Monsters of the Market: Zombies, Vampires and Global Capitalism*, political scientist David McNally (2012) relates the contemporary fascination with vampires and zombies to the political economic order of globalization. He argues that zombie and vampire stories are a metaphorical expression of the processes of dis- and re-possession that characterize neoliberalization. The technologized and granular incorporation of labor, resources, and consumption within global algorithms of exchange and accumulation of symbolic capital, and a corresponding upheaval in people's senses of place, identity, and relationships with others are among the dissonances caused by the marketization of every aspect of people's lives. With this dissonance, McNally argues, comes a deep sense of loss of human kinship, creative agency, and purpose—a feeling of being-for-capital that finds public expression in macabre "walking dead" metaphors.

From McNally, my argument is that entrepreneurialism in composition is facilitating "decomposition": the field's dissolution and full absorption into the "free" market. Within this process, professional compositionists are compelled to reanimate into what Wendy Brown (2005, 40) has called *homo œconomicus*, the subject produced by a marketized political economy in which "all human and institutional action [becomes] rational entrepreneurial action, conducted according to a calculus of utility, benefit, or satisfaction against a microeconomic grid of scarcity, supply and demand, and moral value-neutrality." The extent to which composition work is, and should be, entrepreneurial is therefore existential in that it brings the field's distinction, historical memory, and fundamental identity into question. Neoliberalism's reordering of social relations and production and a diffused sense of common purpose is potentially leading to the fragmentation and dissolution of composition as a professional culture and field of scholarly praxis.

THE ACADEMIC CAPITALIST KNOWLEDGE/LEARNING REGIME

First, I will offer some framing of academic entrepreneurialism within the political economy of neoliberalism and relate the emergent subject of the academic *homo œconomicus* to the conditions of austerity. Entrepreneurialism has become such a pervasive part of perceptions and rhetorics of higher education that "the entrepreneurial turn" in academia is now its own field of research. A 2007 study found that in the years between 2000 and 2005 alone, 127 articles were published that researched some aspect of academic entrepreneurialism (Rothaermel, Agung, and Jiang 2007, 695).[1]

The rise of academic entrepreneurialism is no historical accident, though: it is a reaction to, and creation of, austerity; it responds both to the way that the resources of public institutions have been channeled toward private industries and to the need for new efficiencies and revenue generation created by steady cuts in direct government funding. While we certainly sometimes hear the term associated with doing public good, it is rare to hear of work in higher education referred to as "entrepreneurial" that doesn't involve some aspect of marketization or isn't cost-cutting or at least cost-neutral. The academic entrepreneur may be someone who creates a partnership with a private company, gaining some funding as the company uses university talent and infrastructure for research and development, or someone who has launched a new distance-learning initiative that purports to efficiently deliver more undergraduate FTE with reduced labor costs, greater accountability, and/or a more scalable curriculum. Someone who brings initiative and creativity to push for reducing the exploitation of part-time teaching labor or who argues that an institution responsibly fund its writing program isn't likely to be called entrepreneurial. This is an important point. We shouldn't let entrepreneurialism assume a non-ideological, or non-historical hue. There are no socialist entrepreneurs, the term is an obvious oxymoron: entrepreneurialism in higher education is a singularly capitalist response to a normative crisis created by decades of austerity capitalism.

The academic entrepreneur fits within a changing vision for higher education which higher education scholars Slaughter and Rhoades (2004) describe as an historic move from a public good knowledge/learning regime to an academic capitalist knowledge-learning regime. The public good/knowledge regime became codified as the professional norm in the second half of the twentieth century when what came to be called "Mertonian norms" in academia and went by the acronym CUDOS (communalism, universality, disinterestedness and organized skepticism) became aspirational values throughout higher education.[2] The public good regime valued the independence of academic research and the freedom of scholars to pursue the research that they saw as valuable for the public, regardless of its possible potentials for commercial application. At least in terms of aspirations and ideals, the public good regime created knowledge for the benefit of the public, largely without proprietary, commercial claims over its use. It valued the necessity of maintaining apparatuses and professional cultures that enable the sharing of ideas and findings as openly accessible, public property. The public good regime also maintained a strong conceptual and organizational separation between public and private research and functions. This distinction between research, education, and capitalist activity was fundamental to academic culture and also to a broader philosophy of public/civic life in liberal democracy. Of course, the public good knowledge/learning regime was never uniform or pure in practice. Industry has never been hygienically cordoned from higher education, and higher education has never operated outside of political economy.[3] But there has been a general and consequential perception of distinct roles and responsibilities.

As government expenditures for direct instruction have been cut and institutions have been expected to generate more of their own funding, the emergent academic capitalist knowledge regime has aimed to blur or erase even perceptual boundaries between academic and capitalist functions and professional cultures. Faculty inquiry is channeled more toward commercial ends and faculty discoveries and knowledge often become the property of the institution or of private entities with which the institutions or faculty have partnered. Students are recast as consumers who become targets of advertising and profit upon admission to and during their time at institutions—so tuition is only the beginning of entrepreneurial opportunities for textbook companies, curricular technologies, food service contractors, sports apparel companies, and university schemes like expensive premium residence halls and extra fees for access to services like health clubs that were formerly covered by tuition.

The academic capitalist regime is an extension of a neoliberal political economic philosophy that makes no distinction between serving the public good and serving private industry. As an emerging professional

ethos within the academic capitalist regime, entrepreneurialism therefore troubles the role of faculty and the purposes of higher education
itself. Within the merging worlds of education, research, and capitalist
enterprise, faculty are faced with intractable contradictions between private and public interests and missions. Accompanying these contradictions are challenges to the status, expertise, and authority of faculty, and
changes in what sorts of scholarship and teaching are to be discouraged
and promoted.[4]

While elements of the public good knowledge-learning regime certainly still exist, they exist alongside of the academic/capitalist knowledge-
learning regime. One sees plenty of evidence of this tense juxtaposition
in the 2015 CCCC conference call as it awkwardly zigzags between disciplinary and commercial discourses, with many of the forms of risk-taking
it names promoting efficiency imperatives and various forms of marketization. An unwillingness to name austerity as the urgent exigency for
innovation and risk-taking creates lacuna within its rhetoric, giving it
the uneasy feel of a non-sequitor. In other words, the call appeals to the
sense of crisis that many CCCC members feel as a result of austerity measures and the marketization of literacy work, but then tacitly supports
the facilitation of marketization as the response.

For example, in the list of questions intended to inspire sessions
at the conference, the call offers "Profession: Is tenure worth it?" as a
potential question for a session topic. The question might have been
framed in a way that invites discussion of how retrenchment is affecting
curriculums, research, or the institutional structures needed to maintain the viability of composition as a field of research and *praxis*. The
unelaborated question instead makes it seem as though enough tenure-
line jobs are still there, with tenure a matter of private choice rather
than a collective, public issue facing the profession. The call likewise
frames curricular decisions with deep implications and extensive histories of research, theorization and debate into a set of flattened free market choices: "Pedagogy: expressive, current-traditional, postmodern?
Focusing on grammar? Style? Working in service-learning? Trying new
assignment formats (multi-modal, electronic), encouraging new topics?"
Here, choosing from among pedagogical movements with remarkably
different assumptions about literacy and learning is reduced to a matter of individual preferences: in a market (rather than an academic profession), we make choices from among a hodge-podge of options, like
choosing the color and style of jacket from a store rack. Shoulder pads,
purple, and current traditionalism look to be good sellers in this market—the 80s are back!

Terms like innovation, risk-taking, current traditionalism, and public engagement are changed when they are displaced from a history of disciplinary dialectic or the particular material consequences of enactment. The fundamental, ongoing concerns of composition—from program assessment, online education, and the nature and maintenance of expertise in writing, to adjunctification and the methods and justifications for granting writing credit—might evoke deep questions about agency and power, purpose and what constitutes responsible teaching and labor practices. Instead, entrepreneurial rhetoric flattens scholarship and praxis into unfettered choices and pushes the history of disciplinary expertise, dialectic, and contention that surround terms like "expressive" and "current-traditional" to the margins. Foregrounded are agile choice-making and the "risks" in program administration that involve branding, marketing, and competition. But how risky are these moves in today's institutions where upper administrations pressure and even offer financial incentives to instructors and writing program administrators (WPAs) to create or expand distance education programs and where state and federal governments push Massive Open Online Courses (MOOCs) and Competency-Based Education as cost-cutting efficiency measures (primarily through cutting and deprofessionalizing jobs at the level of direct instruction)? These "risks" seem far more likely to come with rewards for individual entrepreneurs than asking questions about the qualitative differences between online and face-to-face writing courses, or inquiring into the long-term implications of how online instruction models might reorder, further diminish, and discipline composition labor. Opportunistic, and accepting of austerity as rational and inevitable, *homo œconomicus* is best positioned for reward when innovating within, rather than challenging, the constraints of "a microeconomic grid of scarcity, supply and demand" (Brown 2005, 40).

ENTREPRENEURIALISM, BRANDING AND DECOMPOSITION

Taking entrepreneurial "risks" can be a means of pushing composition's scholarly inquiry, debate, and disciplinary expertise further to the margins—for instance through creating direct relationships with vendors who supply market-friendly curriculums, offer technologies that enable ongoing surveillance of students' work and teachers' performance, and manage networks that connect cheap teaching labor from anywhere to paying students from anywhere. In an article in *Writing Program Administration*, Keith Rhodes argues that instructors are now compelled to engage in what he calls "post-academic teaching": teaching in a market-driven

scene in which "customers" (students) buy a "product" (writing education) delivered by teachers (Rhodes 2010, 62). Calling on the field to
accept political economic realities in the present, Rhodes argues that
writing programs must now expect to compete for resources in a system
driven by efficiencies and competition. He reasons that because composition professionals don't control the scene of writing education and
composition is not highly regarded in institutions of higher learning, it
follows that writing programs need a more sophisticated marketing strategy for our product: "There is no short-term hope to rescue the reputation of all writing instruction, because on the whole it is an unbranded
'commodity,' offered in many forms entirely beyond the control of fully
informed, fully supported composition professionals. Composition professionals could, however, establish a strong 'brand' of well-informed
composition. Such a brand would establish an independent and higher
public profile, and it could become a 'market leader' that would improve
the quality and reputation of all writing instruction" (58).

Rhodes positions his branding strategy within a political economic
milieu in which actors are in a struggle for agency and resources. As
he makes his case, he also draws parallels between his branding strategy and the model Linda Adler-Kassner outlines in *The Activist WPA:
Changing Stories about Writing and Writers,* which won the 2010 Council of
Writing Program Administrators Best Book Award. In her response, also
published in *Writing Program Administration,* Adler-Kassner (2010) seeks
to distance her activist model from the branding strategy advocated by
Rhodes. She argues that *The Activist WPA* encourages active consensus
building with others, which is different from developing a brand and
finding a means of persuading potentially receptive audiences.[5] Adler-
Kassner's response is clarifying in terms of the intent of the book, but it
is worthwhile to explore why Rhodes assumed a commonality of purpose
and function between his entrepreneurial WPA and Adler-Kassner's
activist WPA; Rhodes's and Adler-Kassner's exchange is another illustration of the broader ideological dissonance within which composition
is now being enacted. Because Adler-Kassner relies heavily on the individual beliefs of WPAs and others designated as stakeholders in college
writing and does not position WPA activism in relation to the economics
and ideological struggles of higher education and academic labor, her
activist WPA is easily read as sharing many of the attributes of the entrepreneurial WPA, subject to being animated by the same ideology of production, competition, and market promotion.

For instance, much of the penultimate chapter of *The Activist WPA,*
"Taking Action to Change Stories," details tactics of message development,

which are very similar to the marketing strategy described by Rhodes in their emphasis on creating successful messages for a diverse audience of stakeholders and their bracketing of disciplinary expertise and dialectic. Adler-Kassner makes it clear that the activist WPA is an agile negotiator, and not a public intellectual, at least not in stance, locating the unique expertise of the activist WPA in her ability to relate to audiences, create a successful messaging/narrative strategy, and foster alliances. Adler-Kassner draws a sharp contrast between the activist and the public intellectual who, she claims, adopts a stance that "stems from an analysis of audience that is neither nuanced, flattering, nor accurate" in a "one-way process of communication (expert > audience)" that inhibits the "base development and alliance building . . . essential to changing stories about writing and writers with audiences outside of the field" (Adler-Kassner 2008, 136). The approach she advances is "that of an activist, but not public intellectual, because the activist role facilitates the kind of dialogue through which bases are built and alliances developed" (136).

Articulating a strategy that is heavily discursive, Adler-Kassner imagines a WPA who uses rhetorical acumen, understanding, and energy to build coalitions and change "the story of writing and writers" through strategic coalition building among interested actors within a public sphere that appears largely devoid of competing political economic imperatives and ideologies of labor. *The Activist WPA* does not take an explicit position in relation to the political economics of higher education or the broader material imperatives or narratives of academic capitalism and austerity. Centering on finding means of alliance building, *The Activist WPA* also doesn't necessarily hold any non-negotiable disciplinary stances or explicit positions on teaching labor or pedagogical philosophy. Rather, Adler-Kassner grounds perceptions of "the good" and the principles of her organizing primarily in her own individual religious beliefs, described in the book, and in the individually formed and held beliefs of others who are positioned as relevant stakeholders. To be clear, I think *The Activist WPA* is valuable, and I also don't question Adler-Kassner's disciplinary knowledge or commitments, but if the compositionist is not asserting disciplinary, intellectual expertise in writing, what is the foundation of her authority and stance beyond an administrative post that might also be occupied by someone with equal or greater organizational skills, but no scholarly or experiential background in composition? Given the clear trends in higher education and without an articulated position on academic labor and composition, WPA activism imagined outside of political economy seems adaptable as a transposable set of management techniques that serve the ends of marketization.

Though they are articulated in different ways, both Rhodes's branding approach and Adler-Kassner's alliance building and message development are carefully crafted, earnest attempts to locate some agency in a situation of crisis. In this crisis, the fragmentation of the academic field of composition studies into independent actors, programs, and commercial ventures coincides with the diminishment of an institutional/ cultural apparatus that is capable of supporting a viable relationship between research and practice. This "decomposition" results not only from efficiency imperatives imposed by state governments and institutions where even part-time teachers in brick and mortar classrooms are now made to appear too expensive, but also from an academic field that seems to be shaping its theory in ways that facilitate its long-term dissolution for the sake of short-term survival—if in a radically altered form.

The question is existential. What is composition studies without institutional structures that recognize the expertise of composition specialists in writing and maintain a relationship between scholarship and writing education as material practice? Jeanne Gunner points out that a writing program need not have any necessary affiliation with "the field" of composition. A program can have "a changeable disciplinary provenance and its objectives and effectiveness may be purely contextual matters, since its professional claims may be mobilized as much by institutional needs as disciplinary affiliations" (Gunner 2012, 615). Gunner calls writing programs an "organizational schema . . . a malleable form within a changing institutional structure itself shaped by market forces" (615). A program may be informed by, or in conversation with, the research and theory of the scholarly field, or it may have no real connection to the field at all. As a malleable form, a writing program can be "a brand of activity" rather than a site of disciplinary inquiry or practice. Gunner speculates that the future of composition could be managed by marketing professionals and organized around the promotion of collective representations, as the shrinking scholarly realms of the field retreat further into our own pacified hermetic conversations. With branding, "the disciplinary knowledge of the field gives way to its marketable form. With fewer faculty to manage, with a more dispersed and posthuman notion of teaching in play, and with a commodified and portable writing curriculum, the writing program brand is freed from the romantic teacher icon, the managerial demand is reduced, disciplinary content is purified to the brand, and this flattened brand increasingly becomes the material context of writing program work" (638). This vision of the future of the field—though perhaps, as Gunner puts it, "grim"—seems a real possibility without critical understanding and response to the forces that are shaping our work. As the transformation of what constitutes a session at the Conference on College Composition and Communication further blurs the lines between scholarly conference and industry tradeshow, we must ask what is "composition"? Is it an academic discipline that serves the public good through fostering sustained inquiry into best practices in postsecondary literacy education? Is it a more purely intellectual pursuit performed by tenure-line PhDs that retreats from the circumstances and responsibility of writing education as large-scale material practice in order to inhabit a shrinking space of cloistered scholarly exchange? Is it a new frontier for entrepreneurial opportunity that has no necessary connection to scholarship, the public good, or a distinct professional culture? As the chapters in this collection make clear, it can't continue to be these things at the same time—the center is not holding.

ACCUMULATION BY DISPOSSESSION

"Accumulation by dispossession" has long been identified by political economists as a fundamental strategy of crisis capitalism. Through the International Monetary Fund, for instance, countries have been put into the category of "debtor nations" and then compelled to enact austerity measures that include the elimination of public safety nets and the opening up of protected markets and natural resources to external entrepreneurs. Fundamental changes couched as neutral necessities are actually ideological transformations of political economies. The marketization of public services, commons, indigenous lands, natural resources, education, and even control over monetary policy is described as "dispossession."[6]

   Composition is now undergoing an intensified phase of dispossession as industry and academic partners, with the encouragement and cooperation of governmental reform initiatives, seek out opportunities for profit through the promise of greater access and efficiencies. Of course, not nearly as much profit potential exists in writing education as in some other fields. We don't develop new pharmaceuticals, alloys, or financial analysis software: if campuses were Monopoly boards, composition would be dark purple. What composition primarily has to offer to the market is access to millions of student-consumers taking required courses each year and the institutional surpluses created by making already low-cost teaching even cheaper—largely through the sale and maintenance of curricular technologies and assessments that serve to scale pedagogy, decrease the numbers of already exploited teachers, and certify literacies without conducting actual courses. The hidden cost is teachers' professional status, students' agency and literate possibilities, and the diminishment of a scholarly apparatus able to inquire into and support best practices in writing education.

This is not inevitable though. There are contradictions within the current political economic regime that, especially in the wake of the 2008–2009 market crash, are becoming obvious. The rhetoric claiming benefits for all in neoliberalism clashes with the reality of increasing wealth for a few and increasing economic precariousness and loss of agency for the many. In addition to strong political movements in regions as distinct as Brazil, Greece, and India, that have galvanized around explicitly anti-neoliberal agendas, there is a wider-spread if still less politicized understanding that the current "'[e]pidemic' of depression, anxiety, obesity and addictive behavior register[s] as an indictment on societies that have made calculated self-interest and competitiveness tacitly constitutional principles" (Davies 2014, 3) Compositionists can appeal to values that are shared among faculty, students, and parents who, by and large, value personal relationships and face-to-face interactions between students and faculty, and curriculums that are open-ended and responsive enough to provide opportunity for unanticipated discovery and creative innovations. Composition studies might stay clear of the dead-end of scholarship for its own sake, renew its commitment to teaching and scholarship for the benefits of writing education in a just society, and devote itself to radical, creative possibilities at its material sites of production. Tenured compositionists have a responsibility to our field, our students, and the contingent teachers who do most composition work. We should not use tenure as a secure platform for entrepreneurial profitmaking—our terms of work are sustained by others: none of us works in a vacuum. Entrepreneurial subjectivity is inextricably tied to the correlative, neoliberal notions of economics, education, society, and labor that sustain and valorize it; rejecting it, we still have the power to say no, be vocal, informed critics, and maintain critical, creative spaces in which alternative futures beyond austerity can be imagined and pursued.

CONCLUSION: THE SPLIT SELF OR WHO ANIMATES WHOM?

McNally theorizes that vampire and zombie stories arose in the West in the nineteenth century as a means for people to come to grips with the trauma and social crises wrought by industrialization. In the classic story, the vampire, an aristocrat, sucks the blood from his victims, leaving them transformed into malleable servants of the same creature who has stolen their life-essences. McNally links Frankenstein's creature to the market for body parts of the deceased indigent that flourished in London during Mary Shelly's time: the pieces of bodies shattered by industrial work are pieced together and re-animated by a member of the ruling class. Shelly's Frankenstein might be read as the story of a bricolaged proletarian who gains agency and refuses his prescribed role. In the twenty-first century, we are once again surrounded by stories of vampires and zombies, not just in popular culture in the West, but in regions like sub-Saharan Africa, where people are coming to grips with a transformation of social relations wrought by new forms of integration into the global capitalist system. These stories of death and reanimation into servitude are a way to project and understand a condition in which laboring bodies are voided of creative and intellectual agency and transformed into a diminished form of life: "Like Victor Frankenstein and his Creature, the vampire and the zombie are doubles, linked poles of the split society. If vampires are the dreaded beings who might possess us and turn us into their docile servants, zombies represent our haunted self-image, warning us that we might already be lifeless, disempowered agents of alien powers" (McNally 2009, 253).

There is a recurring moment in contemporary stories in the now very established genre of zombie apocalypse in which characters, bitten by a zombie, understand their coming deaths and the ghostly resurrection of their bodies and minds that will follow. They often make some last "human," statement or act before they die, and then they come back to a new type of "life" driven by reaction, ceaseless movement, and the urgent, itchy desire to pursue and consume with no memory or distinguishing identity. If composition is to be more fully animated by entrepreneurialism, we are already seeing its last living acts.

Notes

1. See also Etzkowitz 2003, Mars 2007, Slaughter and Rhoades 2004, Agrawal and Henderson 2002, and Bercovitz et al. 2001.
2. Robert Merton outlined his highly influential "institutional norms" in "The Normative Structure of Science," first published 1942. Slaughter and Rhoades (2004) point out that Mertonian values in higher education are closely associated with the Vannevar Bush model (28).
3. For the second half of the twentieth century, partnerships between universities and contractors like General Electric and Westinghouse were instrumental in the development of the nuclear power industry (Slaughter and Rhoades 2004, 29).
4. In spite of its seeming inevitability, "the entrepreneurial turn" is causing responses that range from enthusiasm to concern to critique and organized resistance. The

academic capitalist regime has fissures and faces widespread skepticism within academia. A study of dispositions toward various aspects of entrepreneurialism among faculty at seventy-one research universities, for instance, found substantial differences and nuances in faculty attitudes by discipline. Perhaps not surprisingly, faculty in the Humanities showed much more disapproval of commercialization than faculty in the sciences, engineering, and the social sciences (Goldstein 2010, 4–5). However, the study found that faculty across all disciplines "disapprove of commercialization activities that either (1) restrict access to what is produced within the university or (2) pose conflicts between the faculty member's interests and responsibilities as a member of a scholarly community and as working for a for-profit company" (6). More generally, while the survey did not indicate that faculty see technology development for industry as necessarily "a violation of normal science," it also showed "widespread opposition within the academy to the commercialization of knowledge" (6).

5.   Drawing on the language of Martin Buber, Adler-Kassner describes an administrative activism grounded in processes of negotiation that involve "some degree of sacrifice of one's hard-held values in order to engage with another" (Buber qtd. in Adler-Kassner 2010, 144).

6.   See, for instance Davies 2014, 2; Harvey 2006, 91–93; Klein 2007; and McNally 2009, 38–40.

References

Adler-Kassner, Linda. 2008. *The Activist WPA: Changing Stories about Writing and Writers.* Logan: Utah State University Press.

Adler-Kassner, Linda. 2010. "Response to Keith Rhodes' 'You Are What You Sell: Branding the Way to Composition's Better Future'." *WPA: Writing Program Administration* 34 (1): 141–5.

Agrawal, A., and R. Henderson. 2002. "Putting Patents in Context: Exploring Knowledge Transfer From MIT." *Management Science* 48 (1): 44–60. http://dx.doi.org/10.1287 /mnsc.48.1.44.14279.

Bercovitz, J., M. Feldman, I. Feller, and R. Burton. 2001. "Organizational Structure as a Determinant of Academic Patent and Licensing Behavior: An Exploratory Study of Duke, Johns Hopkins, and Pennsylvania State Universities." *Journal of Technology Transfer* 26 (1/2): 21–35. http://dx.doi.org/10.1023/A:1007828026904.

Brown, Wendy. 2005. *Edgework: Critical Essays on Knowledge and Politics.* Princeton, NJ: Princeton University Press.

Carter, Joyce Locke. 2014. "Call for Program Proposals: Risk and Reward." Call for Proposals for the 2015 Annual Convention of the Conference on College Composition and Communication. http://www.ncte.org/library/NCTEFiles/Groups /CCCC/Convention/2015/2015_4C_CFP.pdf.

Davies, William. 2014. *The Limits of Neoliberalism: Authority, Sovereignty and the Logic of Competition.* Los Angeles: Sage.

Etzkowitz, H. 2003. "Research Groups as 'Quasi-Firms': The Invention of the Entrepreneurial University." *Research Policy* 32 (1): 109–21. http://dx.doi.org /10.1016/S0048-7333(02)00009-4.

Goldstein, Harvey A. 2010. "To What Extent is Academic Entrepreneurship Taken for Granted Within Research Universities?" *Higher Education Policy* 23 (1): 1–15. http:// dx.doi.org/10.1057/hep.2009.16.

Gunner, Jeanne. 2012. "Disciplinary Purification: The Writing Program as Institutional Brand." *JAC* 32 (3–4): 615–43.

Harvey, David. 2006. *Spaces of Global Capitalism: Towards a Theory of Uneven Development.* New York: Verso.

Klein, Naomi. 2007. *The Shock Doctrine: The Rise of Disaster Capitalism.* Toronto: Alfred A. Knopf.

Mars, M. M. 2007. "The Diverse Agendas of Faculty Within an Institutionalized Model of Entrepreneurship Education." *Journal of Entrepreneurship Education* 10:43–61.

McNally, David. 2009. "From Financial Crisis to World Slump: Accumulation, Financialization, and the Global Slowdown." *Historical Materialism* 17 (2): 35–83. http://dx.doi.org/10.1163/156920609X436117.

McNally, David. 2012. *Monsters of the Market: Zombies, Vampires and Global Capitalism.* Chicago: Haymarket.

Rhodes, Keith. 2010. "You Are What You Sell: Branding Your Way to Composition's Better Future." *WPA: Writing Program Administration* 33 (3): 58–77.

Rothaermel, Frank T., Shati D. Agung, and Lin Jiang. 2007. "University Entrepreneurship: A Taxonomy of the Literature." *Industrial and Corporate Change* 16 (4): 691–791. http://dx.doi.org/10.1093/icc/dtm023.

Syverud, Kent. 2014. Letter published online, June 24. http://chancellor.syr.edu /messages/m/fast-forward-syracuse.html.

Slaughter, Sheila, and Gary Rhoades. 2004. *Academic Capitalism and the New Economy.* Baltimore: Johns Hopkins University Press.

Afterword
HACKING THE BODY POLITIC

Lil Brannon

It's early June 2011. In a coffee shop I meet with my colleague Lacy
about the Writing Project work she is doing in the Charlotte city schools.
She has been leading workshops in writing/new media and building a
technology alliance. We are talking about how just as teachers are using
digital media as composing technologies, the district has made a counter-
move: in these schools with a high percentage of children in poverty, the
district is mandating that all forty-five minutes of English/language arts
time be given over to Achieve 3000—also known as Teen Biz 3000 and
Kids Biz 3000, touted as the leader in differentiated instruction.

We are worrying about how the deeply human engagement of teaching is getting lost, that children's writing is being "read" only by machines, when in the noisy coffee shop my cell phone vibrates the text:
Peter Gorman, Superintendent of Charlotte Schools resigns.

Resigned?

On the iPad I toggle from Kindle to Safari: got to figure out what's going on. Lacy opens her laptop.

The headline: "Gorman in a surprise announcement today resigned
his position as Superintendent to join News Corp as Senior Vice-
President."

News Corp?

Google News Corp. Rupert Murdoch's News Corp. Rupert Murdoch
who also owns The Wall Street Journal and Fox Broadcasting.

I try Bloomberg News: "Peter Gorman, 47, the superintendent of
schools . . . [will focus] on building the division's business inside public-
school districts."

Business? Inside public-school districts?

DOI: 10.7330/9781607324454.c015

Big business, according to Bloomberg News: "News Corp's education division is focused on 'individualized, technology-based' content and tools for students and teachers."

There's more: "In November [News Corp] hired Joel Klein, 64, the former New York City schools chancellor, to help build an education business. Two weeks later, News Corp. agreed to buy 90 percent of education-technology provider Wireless Generation for $360 million."

But still not enough: "In a speech last month in Paris, Rupert Murdoch owner of News Corp called education 'the last holdout from the digital revolution' . . . The key to improving education, Murdoch said . . . 'is the software that will engage students and help teach them concepts and to learn to think for themselves'" (Pulley 2011).

From pre-kindergarten to the university, neoliberal policies and austerity measures pervade, serving to open new markets for large private corporations. In areas like writing instruction where social constructivist views of literacy underpin the professional literature and thus make the work not easily commodified, companies like Achieve 3000—instituted by Gorman in the Charlotte-Mecklenburg schools before he left to help Murdoch build in-roads into the education market—tap into "common sense" functionalist (basic-skills and building-block) notions of literacy, making their digital workbooks seem more efficient and accountable than human teachers. Achieve 3000, in partnership with MetaMetrics (the company that markets Lexile reading levels) and Teach for America (the temporary teacher agency), made $23 million in sales in 2009—and reported a further 93 percent sales increase in 2011 (Achieve 3000 2014). How do they do it? By using tropes like "individual learning," "equity," and "ongoing formative assessment" to wrap their products in the language of education fairness. By advancing claims of "scientific" measures that bring into schools the corporate management rhetoric and pressures of continuous improvement.

All the while students are sorted and isolated from each other, interacting primarily with a keyboard. (An Achieve 3000 motto is "The Power of One.") In Achieve 3000 programs, students receive a topic rewritten from the news at their "scientifically determined" MetaMetrics Lexile reading level—a reading level that is monitored *daily* as they "progress" toward reading and writing "proficiency," as measured on their post-tests. They learn to write by filling in information into boxes to demonstrate that they can read informational texts, a requirement of the federal Common Core State Standards. The corporation confidently states that its students practice "higher order" thinking—by having students check "Agree" or "Disagree" about the text they read. The Achieve 3000 program also calculates daily Lexile score "growth," so there is no need for a teacher, only a low-wage monitor to maintain discipline. The assessments, which purport to accurately measure student learning, serve to make these digital workbooks seem accountable. Hence the difficult-to-commodify work of literacy instruction becomes commodified. Social constructivist understandings of literacy are supplanted with the restoration of functionalism.

The logic of functional literacy—the belief in technological rationalism, in writing as a set of technical skills or tools that once acquired (like a hammer or ax in a different economy) promises success—became federal policy in the early 1980s with *A Nation at Risk* (United States Department of Education, National Commission on Excellence in Education 1983). It has enjoyed bi-partisan support ever since. In fact, the Common Core State Standards are the latest manifestation of the national standards movement, which The National Governors Association began promoting in 1986, when Arkansas Governor (later President) Bill Clinton was chair. Clinton was preceded in the position by Lamar Alexander—then governor of, now senator from, Tennessee—who became George H. W. Bush's Secretary of Education and who began federal funding for the development of standards. From Bush I to Clinton to Bush II to Obama, the standards movement progressed. The National Council of Teachers of English got into the game, seeking federal resources to develop its own standards—which Barack Obama's Secretary of Education Arnie Duncan then set aside in favor of new "more rigorous" standards developed by a beltway think-tank funded by the National Governors Association, the Council of Chief State School Offices, and several corporate foundations, including the Bill and Melinda Gates Foundation.[1]

Running parallel with this standards and accountability movement has been the increasingly vicious and manufactured attack on teachers, blamed for the supposed "failure" of public education proclaimed by the authors of *A Nation at Risk*. Stepping in to save schools from teachers is technology: low-wage dispensable teachers can serve as monitors while machines take over their teaching, including their responding to and evaluation of student writing. The deeply uncertain work of teaching and learning is thus plowed under, all differences erased, as children and adults are required to submit their work to standardizing agents that track and monitor their progress. In this way, then, the technologizing of education and the restoration of functionalist notions of literacy have proceeded hand in hand—with robo-objective assessments now creeping onto college campuses through systems like Accuplacer (computerized placement tests that slot students into beginning courses) and Turnitin.com (which, combined with its new rubber-stamp comment program GradeMark is slithering into writing programs across the curriculum). As Noam Chomsky (2006) explains, functionalism both seeks the "rapid and efficient inculcation of skilled behavior" and relies on "objective tests" that are in fact self-serving, self-reinforcing, and designed to "demonstrate the effectiveness" of functionalist methods themselves (89).

This encroachment on teaching, of course, fits with a patriarchal capitalist culture as it impacts most directly the bodies of women—women K–12 teachers and women writing teachers—under pressure to produce the very same student widgets (the same student-generated ideas, with the same reasons to be for capital punishment or against gun control). Meanwhile the nonlinear, inexact, and social nature of teaching and learning gets suppressed for linear, sequential, prepackaged workbooks in glitzy digital form. This encroachment on, and casualization of, teaching is also happening through what Alan Greenspan (1997) in testimony before the US Congress lauded as the *success* of the US economy in imposing greater worker *insecurity* to ensure that workers perform better (Greenspan 1997). With more insecurity, so the logic goes, workers no longer request better wages or unionize or even lay claim to their own bodies and minds.

It's 2014: multitasking in a Writing Project workshop at Discovery Place (a science museum in Charlotte), I am toggling between a Skype backchannel convo and my email when I see the post: the essay I wrote with Tony Scott on first-year writing assessment has won *College Composition and Communication*'s Braddock Award.

Wow. The essay that banished me from working in the first-year writing program.

In that essay Tony and I examined how the Southern Association of Colleges and Schools (SACS) assessment papered over the labor conditions in our first-year writing program: more than 60 percent of faculty, mostly women, teaching part-time while the previous assessment claimed all was just fine. For being a campus activist, I've been banished from the first-year writing program.

My new assignment: teach English methods to secondary teachers.

At noon I have to leave Discovery Place to attend training on the newly required North Carolina teacher licensure system: edTPA—a nationally normed, high-stakes, teacher licensure exam. A Pearson product, edTPA requires pre-service teachers to video-tape themselves teaching real children and submit that video with their lesson plans to objective, calibrated unknown distant readers. Using fifteen rubrics, those readers will score and ostensibly measure potential teacher effectiveness.

Because the austerity narrative feels so persuasive and overpowering, it seems there is little, if anything we can do to stop the commodification of labor in public education and the narrowing of literacy to a set of behaviors desired by the marketplace. Yet the essays in this volume suggest ways forward through reclaiming attention to bodies, locations, belonging, and collectivity. It joins other work that is likewise trying to theorize the body and restore the importance of materiality, history, and place:

- In her introduction to *Composing (media) = Composing (embodiment)* (Arola and Wysocki 2012), Anne Wysocki focuses on the tension between our assumptions about bodies and media. One set of assumptions has to do with feelings of embodiment, about how we experience the world in and through our bodies (like being in a coffee shop and feeling our phones vibrating on the table) and how without the sensing capacities of our bodies, we do not have a world. The other has to do with how language, and through language, culture and institutions, (like schooling and assessments and media conglomerates) constitute the body, how bodies are composed through these social enactments. *Composing (media) = Composing (embodiment)* shows the importance of keeping this tension in balance, of not erasing bodies when self-constructions happen only from institutions, and of the importance of teachers and students producing new media texts and reflecting on how those productions re-inscribe or re-mediate ourselves and our worlds, creating communities as we are constituted by them.
- Teachers College's Lesley Bartlett (2007) likewise offers possibilities for agency and action when institutions overwhelm us. Bartlett reclaims literacy from the ways schools have commodified it by seeing it as "something one actively does [continually ongoing] in concert with other humans (who may or may not be physically present) and the material, social, and symbolic world (53). Bartlett, drawing on the work of Mollie V. Blackburn, understands literacy and its teaching as "performing," where "people 'read and write words and worlds such that any one performance is among innumerable other performances, each of which is both similar to and different from all of the others, both confirming and disrupting one another'" (Blackburn, qtd. in Bartlett 2007, 55).

• In *Queer Phenomenology*, Sara Ahmed (2006) reminds us that "disorientation" happens to us in our everyday encounters; "disorientation" unsettles us, shifts the terms of our location. Disorientation can also be dis/organization, "the failure of organizations to hold things in place" (158). What matters in times of dis/organization is the potential to reorient ourselves in new ways: "If orientations point us to the future, to what we are moving toward, then they also keep open the possibility of changing directions and of finding other paths, perhaps those that do not clear a common ground, where we can respond with joy to what goes astray" (178).

The orientation of education today toward measurable, commodifiable behaviors, can be shifted, disoriented, if we learn to see what goes astray. Reclaiming our embodied locations, orienting ourselves differently in relation to neoliberal austerity measures and building coalitions with others in our communities can give us new ways of working.

It's 2014. Monday morning. At 5:30 AM preachers, teachers, old and young board the bus for the weekly Moral Monday ride to Raleigh. The Moral Monday group protest a range of policy initiatives enacted by Governor Pat McCrory and a conservative state legislature. The air is crisp. The energy of the group ignites as newcomers joining us introduce themselves. Each Monday the group gets larger. Our bus will be joined by others from all over the state. We join our voices to say "no more" to stagnant teacher pay, to the demolition of public health, to austerity measures which eliminate unemployment benefits and food for the poor. We make signs. Some sing. Others pray. We come together as a community embracing our differences. We see we are not alone.

An email, obviously a mass mailing, circulates among colleagues across institutions as I write this. From the Nielsen company, it begins: "As a faculty member, you are at the forefront of education, and you should have a voice in how educational technology is developed" (Nielsen Book Team 2014). It goes on to solicit participation in a survey that the email claims will assess faculty perceptions of the pace of technological change in education. The generous return for filling out the survey will be a "free executive overview" of the survey results, and entry into a drawing for a $100 gift certificate. There is no direct link to the Nielsen company from the email, which offers no description of the company, but the company website reveals an organization with a variety of ventures that center around measurement and technology. As the state Board of Governors exerts steady pressure and provides short-term incentives to create online courses and programs, a marketing firm, in its efforts to gain market information about higher education, offers faculty "a voice" in the future of education. A similar survey was distributed by "Impatient Optimists," a part of the Bill and Melinda Gates Foundation, earlier in the semester. The Bill and Melinda Gates Foundation is also willing to recognize that faculty are "on the front lines of higher education" and therefore "have insightful first-hand information about the successes and struggles that are part of student learning" (Greenstein, 2014). What is remarkable about the rhetoric is how it displaces educators from the center of education: faculty are on the forefront, not at the center, and we are *being granted* the opportunity for a voice by a corporation and philanthropic foundations.

Austerity is the looming threat of displacement. Among the themes that tie the chapters in this volume together is their steady emphasis on agency, materiality, bodies, and labor. Objectivism in education relies on the obfuscation of laboring bodies through the magic of capitalization. Assessment is a means of converting the labor of teachers and students into abstract values, shifting emphasis away from the professional skills and generative possibilities of teachers and students, and toward the efficient achievement of quantified indicators. As Chris Gallagher suggests, the field played along "like good citizens" when mandates for outcomes and assessments started to emerge, but we were "bamboozled." A focus on outcomes is a turning away from embodied labor and actual existing social relations, and by "aligning ourselves with an institutional practice and logic in which 'outputs' are all that matter, we opened the door to those who argue that where and how and under what circumstances one learns are irrelevant. As we turned to outcomes assessment, we failed to insist that we were offering particular kinds of *experiences* that could not be attained elsewhere" (Gallagher, this volume). Deborah Mutnick similarly describes how outcomes assessment, a tool for the marketization of composition, "squeezes the life out of education, fetishizing data through a discourse of assessment that reifies and obscures the dynamic, messy, material labor of teaching and learning" (Mutnick, this volume).

Increasingly robbed of agency over our own labor and opportunities to enact our hard-earned professional judgment, we seek alternative spaces to do our work. Chapters by Marcelle Haddix and Brandi Nicole Williams and by Mary Ann Cain describe spaces outside of institutions where people are able to develop as writers and thinkers in ways not determined by outcomes-determined curriculums. Haddix and Williams juxtapose their work in *Writing Our Lives*, a community literacy project, against school curriculums that are shaped by the Common Core State

Standards (CCSS). Providing developing writers with the opportunity to write in a variety of genres and for a variety of contexts outside of school, *Writing Our Lives* supplements CCSS, which focuses more narrowly on a standard set of functionalist genres practiced as preparation for state assessments. Cain provides other examples of literacy education that flourish in "third places" or "the gaps within privatized corporate spaces" (Cain, this volume). This work in non-school spaces is often done for free. While Nancy Welch reminds us that we must be wary of the history of "women's work"—the domestication of teaching labor (still mostly performed by women) as a means of undervaluing it—these "off the (official) grid" initiatives can be spaces of galvanization, agency, and the imagining of alternatives (Welch, this volume).

We are living and working in a time of crisis that results from austerity, but it is only a "crisis" because we refuse the terms, refuse to allow the dispossession of our labor to stabilize as the norm. As I join others on the bus in collective response to the austerity politics of a state government that is determined to neoliberalize education in North Carolina, I am aware of our bodies, our labor, and the struggle for the right to our creative and professional agency. We are "on the frontline" of education, but that is the source of our power. The chapters in this volume are a welcome reminder that the teachers and students on the frontline of writing education *are* writing education, not the quantified indicators of outcomes, and not the private corporations and predatory philanthropists who are seeking to control it.

Notes

1. Though this has been lived history for some of us, many scholars have documented the development of standards and the Common Core State Standards including general news pieces like Bidwell (2014) and Ravitch (2013) as well as scholarly articles and editions (Zancanella and Moore 2014; and Larson 2013).

References

Achieve 3000. 2014. http://www.achieve3000.com/.

Ahmed, Sara. 2006. *Queer Phenomenology: Orientations, Objects, and Others*. Durham: Duke University Press. http://dx.doi.org/10.1215/9780822388074.

Arola, Kristin L., and Anne Wysocki. 2012. *Composing (media) = Composing (embodiment)*. Logan: Utah State University Press.

Bartlett, Lesley. 2007. "To Seem and To Feel: Situated Identities and Literacy Practices." *Teachers College Record* 109 (1): 51–69.

Bidwell, Allie. 2014. "A Guide to the Common Core." *U.S. News & World Report*, February 27.

Chomsky, Noam. 2006. *Language and Mind*. New York: Cambridge University Press. http://dx.doi.org/10.1017/CBO9780511791222.

Greenspan, Alan. 1997. "The Federal Reserve's Semiannual Monetary Policy Report Before the Committee on Banking, Housing, and Urban Affairs, U.S. Senate." February 26. http://www.federalreserve.gov/boarddocs/hh/1997/february/testimony.htm.

Greenstein, Daniel. 2014. "Turning Our Ears Toward Faculty." October 10. http://www.impatientoptimists.org/Posts/2014/10/Turning-Our-Ears-Toward-Faculty.

Larson, Joanne. 2013. "Foreword: Operationalizing the Neoliberal Common Good." In *Closer Reading of the Common Core*, ed. Patrick Shannon, ix–xvi. Portsmouth, NH: Heinemann.

Nielsen Book Team. 2014. Commercial mailing received November 11.

Pulley, Brett. 2011. "Murdoch Hires Two Public-School Managers to Run News Corp. Education Unit." *Bloomberg News*, June 8 June. http://www.bloomberg.com/news/2011-06-08/news-corp-hires-kristen-kane-peter-gorman-to-help-run-education-division.html.

Ravitch, Diane. 2013. "Why I Oppose the Common Core Standards." *The Washington Post*, February 16.

United States Department of Education, National Commission on Excellence in Education. 1983. *A Nation at Risk: The Imperative for Educational Reform.* Washington, DC: Government Printing Offices.

Zancanella, Donald, and M. Moore. 2014. "Research and Policy: The Origins of the Common Core: Untold Stories." *Language Arts* 91 (4): 273–79.

ABOUT THE AUTHORS

NANCY WELCH is Professor of English at the University of Vermont where she helped lead the drive to unionize faculty and where she is active in regional labor solidarity. She is author of *Getting Restless: Rethinking Revision in Writing Instruction* (Boynton Cook 1997), *The Road from Prosperity: Stories* (Southern Methodist UP 2005), and *Living Room: Teaching Public Writing in a Privatized World* (Boynton Cook 2008) as well as co-editor of *The Dissertation and Discipline: Reinventing Composition Studies* (Boynton Cook 2002). Her articles have appeared in *College English, College Composition and Communication, JAC,* and *Pedagogy,* and her short stories have appeared in such journals as *Ploughshares* and *Prairie Schooner.* In 2010 she received *College English*'s Richard Ohmann Award for "'We're Here and We're Not Going Anywhere': Why Working-Class Rhetorical Practices *Still* Matter."

TONY SCOTT is Associate Professor in the Writing Program at Syracuse University, where he is also Director of Undergraduate Studies. His scholarship includes *Dangerous Writing: Understanding the Political Economy of Composition* (Utah State UP 2009) and the collection he coedited with Marc Bousquet and Leo Parascondola, *Tenured Bosses and Disposable Teachers: Writing Instruction in the Managed University* (Southern Illinois UP 2004). In 2014, Tony and co-author Lil Brannon won the Richard Braddock award for "Democracy, Struggle, and the Praxis of Assessment."

SUSAN NAOMI BERNSTEIN's most recent book is *Teaching Developmental Writing, 4e* (Bedford/St. Martin's). She also writes the blog "Beyond the Basics" for *Bedford's Bits: Ideas for Teaching Composition.* She has published in *Journal of Basic Writing, Modern Language Studies,* and elsewhere, and her essay on lessons from Hurricane Sandy appears in *Reflections: A Journal of Public Rhetoric, Writing, and Service Learning.* Susan currently is a lecturer at Arizona State University in Tempe and co-coordinates the Stretch Program

LIL BRANNON is Professor of English at the University of North Carolina Charlotte (UNC Charlotte), where she directs the UNC Charlotte Writing Project, a site of the National Writing Project. Her latest book, with Michelle Comstock and Mary Ann Cain, is *Composing Public Space: Teaching Writing in the Face of Private Interests.* With Tony Scott she received *College Composition and Communication*'s Richard Braddock Award for "Democracy, Struggle, and the Praxis of Assessment."

MARY ANN CAIN is Professor of English and affiliated faculty of Women's Studies at Indiana University Purdue University Fort Wayne. She has published two books of scholarship, most recently *Composing Public Space: Teaching Writing in the Face of Private Interests* (Heinemann-Boynton/Cook 2010), along with articles in journals such as *College Composition and Communication* and *College English* as well as book chapters in several collections. Her literary work includes a novel, *Down From Moonshine* (13th Moon Press 2009) and dozens of short stories and essays in literary journals such as *The North American Review, The Denver Quarterly,* and *Bitter Oleander.* Her latest nonfiction book focuses on the legacy of artist-teacher-activist Dr. Margaret Burroughs, co-founder of the South Side Community Arts Center and the DuSable Museum of African American History in Chicago.

ELYSE EIDMAN-AADAHL is Executive Director of the National Writing Project (NWP). Co-author of *Because Digital Writing Matters* and *Writing for a Change: Boosting Literacy and Learning through Social Action* (Jossey-Bass 2010 and 2008), she is also co-founder of NWP's *Digital Is* project and community (supported by the John D. and Catherine T. MacArthur Foundation's Digital Media and Learning Initiative) and founder of the DML's Youth and Participatory Politics research network. As a founding member of the Connected Learning Alliance, she helped establish the YOUmedia Learning Labs network, the Make to Learn Initiative, and Educating for Democracy in a Digital Age.

TOM FOX is Professor of English at California State University, Chico (CSU, Chico) and Associate Director, Site Development for National Writing Project. At the National Writing Project he and his colleagues have led programs on diversity and equity. Currently, he is co-leader of a program serving high-need secondary schools in rural areas. At CSU, Chico, Fox teaches undergraduate and graduate courses in rhetoric and composition, and has administered a variety of writing programs. He is the author of *The Social Uses of Writing* (Ablex 1990) and *Defending Access* (Heinemann 1999) and co-editor of *Writing With* (SUNY 1994). He has written articles and book chapters on race, the politics of writing instruction, institutional change, and other related topics.

CHRIS W. GALLAGHER is Associate Dean of Teaching, Learning, and Experiential Education and Professor of English at Northeastern University. His books include *Radical Departures: Composition and Progressive Pedagogy* (NCTE 2002), *Reclaiming Assessment: A Better Alternative to the Accountability Agenda* (Heinemann 2007), *Teaching Writing that Matters* (with Amy Lee, Scholastic 2008), and *Our Better Judgment: Teacher Leadership for Writing Assessment* (with Eric Turley, NCTE 2012). His articles on writing pedagogy, writing assessment, and educational reform have appeared in a variety of journals in rhetoric and composition as well as education.

JEANNE GUNNER is Vice Chancellor for Undergraduate Education and Professor of English and Comparative Literature at Chapman University in Orange, California. She has published on writing program administrator–related issues and theory and has been active in CWPA, NCTE, and CCCC, including serving as *College English* editor. Her recent publications include *The Writing Program Interrupted,* co-edited with Donna Strickland, and a *JAC* article on the branding of writing programs and the loss of disciplinarity.

MARCELLE M. HADDIX is Dean's Associate Professor and Director of English Education programs in the Reading and Language Arts Center in the School of Education at Syracuse University. Her research, addressing the persistent literacy gap for children of color and the need for racial and linguistic diversity in literacy teacher education, is featured in such journals as *Research in the Teaching of English* and *English Education*. She also directs the *Writing Our Lives* project, supporting the writing practices of urban youth within and beyond school contexts.

EMILY J. Isaacs is Associate Professor of English at Montclair State University. Her research projects are primarily empirical and address such issues as writing assessment, placement, and trends in writing instruction at universities and colleges across the nation. Recent articles have appeared in *College English, Journal of Teaching Writing,* and *WPA,* and in book collections from Hampton Press, Lexington Press, Parlor Press, and Utah State UP. She is co-author of the forthcoming *Intersections* (Bedford/St. Martins).

TOBI JACOBI is Associate Professor of English at Colorado State University where she teaches courses on writing and literacy theory with a specialization in the work of incarcerated women writers. She directs the CSU Community Literacy Center and trains student and community volunteers to facilitate writing workshops with incarcerated adults and at-risk youth in Northern Colorado. She has published on community literacy and prison writing in book collections and journals such as *Community Literacy Journal, Corrections Today, Feminist Formations*, and the *Journal of Correctional Education*. Her edited collection (with Dr. Ann Folwell Stanford), *Women, Writing, and Prison: Activists, Scholars, and Writers Speak Out* (Rowman and Littlefield), was published in 2014. She is currently working on an archival project on the Hudson Training School for Girls with the Prison Public Memory Project in Hudson, New York.

ANN LARSON holds a PhD in English from the City University of New York Graduate Center where she researched first-generation college students and basic writers in a non-selective college. Her writing on labor, education, and debt has appeared in *Al Jazeera America, Dissent, Jacobin, New Labor Forum*, and *South Atlantic Quarterly*, among other publications. She is a co-founder of the Rolling Jubilee debt cancellation initiative and co-director of the Debt Collective, a platform for collective action by debtors. She has taught as an adjunct instructor at many colleges in New York City. She is also the author of the blog Education, Class, Politics where an early version of "Composition's Dead" first appeared.

DEBORAH MUTNICK is Professor of English at Long Island University's Brooklyn (LIU Brooklyn) campus, where she is also an assessment fellow and co-director of LIU Brooklyn Learning Communities. She is author of *Writing in an Alien World: Basic Writing and the Struggle for Equality in Higher Education* (1996). Her work has appeared in *College English, College Composition and Communication, Rhetoric Review, WPA: Writing Program Administration, Journal of Basic Writing, Basic Writing e-Journal*, and *Community Literacy Journal*. She recently completed an NEH Digital Humanities Startup Grant for the Pathways to Freedom Digital Narrative Project documenting civil rights history in Brooklyn, New York, and is continuing to develop the Brooklyn Civil Rights Oral History collection.

EILEEN E. SCHELL is Associate Professor of Writing and Rhetoric and Faculty Affiliate in Women's and Gender Studies at Syracuse University where she teaches undergraduate and graduate courses in academic writing, creative nonfiction, rhetorical studies, and feminist theory. She is the author of *Gypsy Academics and Mother-teachers: Gender, Contingent Labor, and Writing Instruction* (Heinemann 1997) and co-author with Kim Donehower and Charlotte Hogg of *Rural Literacies* (Southern Illinois UP 2007). She is also co-editor of three edited collections: *Moving a Mountain: Transforming the Role of Contingent Faculty in Composition Studies and Higher Education* (NCTE 2001); *Rhetorica in Motion: Feminist Rhetorical Methods and Methodologies* (U of Pittsburgh P 2010); and *Reclaiming the Rural: Essays on Literacy, Rhetoric, and Pedagogy* (Southern Illinois UP 2012).

SHARI STENBERG is Associate Professor of English and Composition Program Director at the University of Nebraska-Lincoln, where she teaches courses in writing, rhetoric, and pedagogy. She is the author of *Professing and Pedagogy: Learning the Teaching of English* and *Composition Studies Through a Feminist Lens*. Her articles on socially conscious and feminist pedagogies appear in *College English, College Composition and Communication, Pedagogy*, and *Composition Studies*. Her new book *Repurposing Composition: Feminist Interventions for a Neoliberal Age* is forthcoming from Utah State UP (2015).

BRANDI WILLIAMS is a doctoral student in the Literacy Education Program in Syracuse University's Reading and Language Arts Center. Her scholarship promotes developing literacy and critical thinking skills for all children through the use of social justice and ethnically diverse authors and critiques standardization and privatization in education while exploring holistic forms of assessment.

INDEX

able-ism, 202
academic capitalism: accumulation by
  dispossession, 44, 215; adjunctification,
  5, 13, 166, 211; branding/rebranding,
  43, 136, 211–12, 214, 218–19; casualization, 6, 28, 141, 151, 223; contingent
  faculty, 6, 44, 137, 164, 165, 167, 174,
  177, 178, 182–84, 186–88, 191; continuous improvement, 221; higher education restructuring, 5, 6–7, 9–10, 134,
  136, 138, 163, 164; managerialism, 8,
  152; privatization, 7, 9, 15, 35–36, 37,
  40, 115, 121–22, 129, 136, 142, 152,
  164, 174, 184; retrenchment, 9, 210;
  standardization, 31, 184, 195. *See also*
  marketization
academic freedom, 166–67, 185–86
academic labor rights, 188
activism: ANSWER Coalition, 187; Campus
  Equity Week, 186; coalition/alliance
  building, 16, 22, 46, 173–74, 179, 185,
  188, 213–14, 220, 225; Coalition on
  Contingent Academic Labor, 186;
  community-based partnerships, 115;
  Moral Mondays movement, 225;
  Occupy Movement, 14, 46, 92–93,
  95–97, 100, 103–4; Occupy Sandy, 14,
  96, 103; organizing, 95, 126, 160, 179,
  185–88, 194, 213; Parent Revolution,
  32; Poor People's March, 95; Quebec
  student strikes, 12; United Opt-Out,
  12, 46, 48, 49; United Students Against
  Sweatshops, 187
adjunct faculty, 4, 43, 52–53, 58
administration, 116–17, 131–35, 167; and
  bloat, 159–60, 161, 163; and spending,
  114–15, 118, 119, 123–24, 125; and salaries, 161–62. *See also* writing program
  administration and administrators.
American Association of University
  Professors, 165, 179, 182, 189
American Council on Education, 32
American Recovery and Reinvestment Act,
  9, 40
assessment: accountability, 3, 5, 10, 13,
  21, 26, 29, 36–37, 39, 41, 47, 84, 81,

85–86, 123, 135, 140, 142, 208, 222;
  assessment of prior learning, 25, 27,
  29–30, 32, 33; edTPA, 224; Educational
  Testing Service (ETS), 26; evidence-
  based education, 86; inquiry-based
  assessment, 47; machine grading,
  56, 220, 222; National Center for
  Academic Transformation (NCAT),
  52; outcomes assessment, 12–13, 21,
  23–25, 31, 35–42, 46–47, 124, 226;
  push assessment, 52. *See also* business of
  literacy education; education reform
Association of American Colleges and
  Universities, 152
austerity: and 111th Congress, 77; and
  Bill and Melinda Gates Foundation,
  26, 32, 222, 226; and corporatization/
  marketization, 4, 6, 24, 42, 132, 136,
  140, 172, 187, 207, 208, 210, 214, 215;
  and crisis, 141–42, 209; definition of,
  71, 82, 84; and displacement, 208; and
  entrepreneurialism, 178–79; and innovation, 89; narrative of, 150, 151; and
  precarity, 141; and Race to the Top, 11,
  140; and resistance, 15, 89, 193, 195;
  response to, 7, 9, 37, 46, 56, 60, 62, 66,
  80, 83–84, 88, 109, 116, 157, 168, 172,
  180, 208, 215, 218, 227; rhetorics of, 4,
  139, 178–79, 208; and Shock Doctrine/
  therapy, 6, 8–9

Basic Writing, 14, 42–43, 92–93, 95,
  97–104, 106, 136, 169–70
business of literary education: Accuplacer,
  223; Achieve 3000, 220–22, 227;
  Bedford/St. Martin, 55; Coursera,
  52; GradeMark, 223; Lexile (reading
  levels), 221–22; McKinsey Company,
  41, 48; MetaMetrics, 221; *MySkillsLab*,
  56–57; Nielsen (company), 225;
  Pearson, 32, 41, 48, 56–57, 151, 224;
  Pearson-Texas A&M-Commerce-South-
  Texas College Collaboration, 151;
  SMARTHINKING, 58; StraighterLine,
  32; Turnitin.com, 223; Udacity, 52. *See
  also* marketization